DRIVING IN THE
MIDDLE LANE

Pat Schuch

DRIVING
IN THE
MIDDLE
LANE

Business and Life Lessons
From the Auto Industry

PAT SCHUCH

Integra Resources LLC
Brighton, Michigan 48116

DRIVING IN THE MIDDLE LANE

Library of Congress Cataloging-in-Publication Data

Schuch, Pat.
Driving in the middle lane: business and life lessons from the auto industry / Pat Schuch.
1. Business. 2. Self-help. 3. Inspiration. 4. Leadership.
5. Automobile Industry. 6. Business Women.
7. Christian Life. 8. Work-Life Balance. 9. Manufacturing.

1st Edition
ISBN-13: 978-1-511866-50-7 (paperback)

Cover Design by Jean Schuch Rennich
Front Cover Photo by Jon Schuch
Back Cover Photo by Patrick Rennich
Interior Formatting by Jean Schuch Rennich

Published by:
Integra Resources LLC
Brighton, MI 48116

Printed in the United States of America
by CreateSpace.com

For additional copies of this book, go to:
createspace.com/5382421 or **integraresources.org**

DEDICATION

This book is appreciatively dedicated to all of the hard-working employees of the auto industry.

SPECIAL THANKS

I want to express my thanks to those who were with me on this 30-year journey:

God—my heavenly Father, His Son Jesus Christ, and the Holy Spirit; and my immediate family—Jon, Joe, and Jean.

My heartfelt gratitude also goes out to those special friends who helped improve this book. May God bless you abundantly for generously donating your time and talent to support this project.

"Do not follow where the path may lead.
Go instead where there is no path and leave a trail."

- Ralph Waldo Emerson

"I am the Lord your God, who teaches you what is best
for you, who directs you in the way you should go."

- Isaiah 48:17

"Your word is a lamp unto my feet,
and a light unto my path."

- Psalms 119:105

"I can do all things through Christ
who strengthens me."

- Philippians 4:13

CONTENTS

INTRODUCTION

I was nearly 27 years old in 1977, when I started my 30-year career in the automotive industry. While there were a few women already employed in the business, I frequently had the privilege and the challenge of being the first woman in the production, quality, and engineering departments at various automotive facilities where I worked.

Most books about automobile companies have been ghostwritten from the point of view of a well-known corporate leader. While I had high hopes of one day becoming an auto industry executive, I actually spent most of my career in middle management. For this reason, I felt moved personally to write a different kind of book, portraying the more common view of someone who—like so many other unknown people—worked in the *middle* of a large automotive organization. This is the story of the adventures I had, the prejudices I encountered, and the successes and disappointments I experienced. Together they provided memorable business and life lessons during my career.

Aside from my immediate family members, the names of the people involved in these stories have all been changed. Let me be clear, however, that I am grateful to all of the individuals—both the helpful and the hurtful—who touched my life and are anonymously referenced in this book. They each contributed to the body of wisdom which for me has been a most satisfying learning adventure through the many facets of the auto industry—including component parts quality, vehicle assembly, metal fabrication, reliability and test, product engineering, vehicle development, strategic planning, and research and development.

While the stories in this book generally have automotive specifics, the lessons learned apply to many occupations and industries. My goal is that each reader will find at least one idea or insight personally useful.

My general advice is simple, but not easy: have courage, keep your sense of humor, keep moving forward toward the dream in your heart, and enjoy the adventures of the journey. Believe that with God's help, all things are possible.

And when bad stuff happens, just remember this: often the best stories of your life are those describing how you recovered from the bad stuff.

Pat Schuch
October 11, 2015

Note: The stories in this book have been told as I remember them. There are probably at least a few inaccuracies and I welcome any comments from my former colleagues to set the record straight for future editions.

1978: Pat discussing heavy-duty truck damage
that occurred during transport

PART I

REVVING UP A CAREER

(1975-1983)

In Line for an Opportunity

A life-changing opportunity was presented to me when I was 25 years old, the busy stay-at-home mother of two children: Joe, who was two and a half, and Jean, who was nineteen months old. I was waiting in a Ponderosa Steak House buffet line in southwest Ohio with my husband, Jon—each of us holding a squirming child. A man's voice from behind us exclaimed, "Pat Suszek—it's been years since I've seen you!" Standing in line was a physics professor, who had been my boss five years earlier when I worked as a research assistant in college.

Freeing up my right arm to shake hands, I laughed. "Now it's Pat Schuch—pronounced 'shoe,' just like what you wear on your foot." Then I introduced him to Jon. In response to his prompting, I provided a brief update on my activities since working for him—teaching high school physics and junior high physical science, doing community volunteer work, and currently finishing a master's degree.

The professor explained that several years earlier he was named the Head of the Physics Department. He then surprised me by saying, "You know, running into you like this may provide the solution to a problem that I have. One of the university's physics professors needs to increase his research time and decrease his teaching load next semester. I've been trying to find someone to teach his four-credit freshman physics class. You were always a natural teacher and you would be perfect for the job! How would you like to be working in the university's Physics Department again, this time as a part-time faculty member?"

Holding onto my wiggling daughter as the buffet line slowly inched forward, I stood there, stunned. I had intended to have a career in industry or education once the children were in school. My plan was not to work for several more years, believing it was important for me to be a stay-at-home mom.

The professor pointed out that the physics course he wanted me to teach was the standard freshman level, 90-student, tiered lecture hall class running from 1:00 to 1:50 p.m. Monday through Thursday. He then explained the per diem pay for teaching the one semester course.

"You can get a babysitter, put the kids down for their naps, and be home by the time they wake up. The same amount of time you spend working on your master's degree and volunteer work, can now go into making some money and having fun teaching part time at the university."

I reminded him that, while my master's degree coursework was complete and my thesis was in the final approval stage, I was still a few months away from officially graduating with my master's degree.

"No problem, especially since you would be considered a part-time faculty member, not a permanent hire," he said. "Remember, I'm now the Head of the Department and can bring in whomever I want. Who knows? After one semester you may enjoy it so much you'll want to do it again. Right now I only need you to commit to teach from the beginning of January through the end of April. If it is too hard on your family, you can just stop working after that."

I looked over at Jon, who had been silently listening to the whole exchange. His expression looked neutral, but supportive. We needed to have a long discussion, especially about the issue of childcare. I asked the professor for a few days to consider his proposal. He shook my hand and gave me his card. Flashing a big smile, he said how good it would be to see me back in the halls of the university's Physics Department. He looked forward to my call.

By this time, Jon had made our food selections, and was ready to pay the cashier and take our trays to our table. My heart was racing as this new possibility ran through my head. Looking down at my everyday clothes and shoulder bag full of toys, finger food, and child paraphernalia, I wondered if anyone else had ever had an impromptu interview and a professional job offer while holding a toddler in the buffet line of a Ponderosa restaurant.

I took the job.

Pearls from Pat

1. Be aware that life-changing opportunities can present themselves at any time, in any place.

2. Do excellent work, even during part-time student employment. You never know where the people you interact with will be in the future and what kind of great job they may be in a position to offer you.

Part-Time Work

Teaching at the university was a wonderful experience. I repeatedly told the college students that my name was *Mrs.* Schuch, but they kept calling me Dr. Schuch anyway. Deep down inside, I liked it and wondered if some day I would return to school and earn that title for real.

I was passionate about teaching physics and enjoyed the challenges of helping kids gain confidence and prepare for the working world. However, despite the job satisfaction of the classroom, I longed to know whether I could succeed in a career outside of academia.

~~~~~

After the semester ended, a local township office employee approached me with a job offer. Previously having served on a volunteer citizens' study group that analyzed an adjacent city's annexation proposal, I had interfaced with many of the local government employees. Knowing of my house design experience and ability to read blueprints, the Township Zoning Inspector called me because she needed a part-time assistant. She offered me a job that included reviewing plans for new commercial buildings, shopping centers, and subdivisions to assure all building ordinances were met. Other responsibilities included issuing necessary permits and facilitating requests for variances to be reviewed by the Township Planning Commission.

The pay was better than my teaching job at the university, and there was the promise of a raise after the first year. Another township office worker even suggested a terrific woman who already provided childcare in her home for a few children, and could probably take care of Joe and Jean four afternoons a week.

I took the job.

The Zoning Inspector, who was an experienced woman in her mid-fifties, was a wonderful teacher and mentor. Before long, I had mastered the office routine and could easily handle my boss's responsibilities when she was gone. Rather than being pleased with my skill, however, my boss seemed agitated when people told her how well things had gone in her absence. When a year had passed and the time came for my raise, my boss said she had decided that my current pay was sufficient. Despite the promise made to me, there would be no increase this year.

I had planned to work part time for the township until both children were in school full time. This unfulfilled promise of a raise prompted me to see that there was not much chance for continued growth in such a small office. I began to wonder, "What do I really want?"

~~~~~

My next goal was to do engineering work part time for 2½ years for a big company with long-term career growth potential. When I shared my aspirations with Jon, who worked for a "Big Three" auto company, he responded, "No big corporation I know of has part-time employees, especially engineers." Undeterred, I set out to arrange interviews with the six major automotive facilities that were within 30 miles of our home.

When I met with people from the personnel departments at each of the various automotive facilities, I used a similar approach. First I said that I was very interested in working as an engineer in the auto industry. Then I gave them time to digest my resume and ask questions.

When I saw a flash of interest in the interviewer's expression, I went into my sales pitch: "As you can see from my resume, I have a bachelor's degree in physics and a master's degree in educational administration, and also passed the state's Professional Engineer-in-Training exam in Mechanical Engineering. I am very interested in working as an engineer for a progressive company three days a week for several years, until my children are in school. Then I will be able to start working full time."

Usually, the interviewer replied that the company had no part-time workers and that their personnel and payroll systems were not designed to accommodate anything but full-time employees.

Then I responded, "I know your company has engineering co-op students, who alternate going to school for a few months and then working for a few months over the course of five years. By the time they are ready to graduate and work full time, they are knowledgeable about the company and are considered real assets. I know I could wait 2½ years until my children are in school and then apply here for a full-time job. However, I would be much more valuable to you by starting now, working three days a week learning the ins and outs of the company."

When the interviewer looked like he was pausing to at least consider this outlandish idea, I hit him with my clincher. "Although this arrangement would benefit both your company and me, it could be difficult for even a progressive organization to commit to my proposal, not knowing the potential impact it might have on others in the workplace. Perhaps you could offer me a three-day-a-week engineering job for a six-month trial period, and then evaluate the effectiveness of the part-time arrangement. If you are not pleased with my performance, or if any problems arise, you can give me the choice to either work full time or quit."

Male-dominated companies were being urged to hire women, and women engineers were very rare in 1977. In spite of this, two of the six companies I interviewed with said, "Look, Pat, you either want to work, or you don't want to work. There's no in-between here." Two other companies turned me down, albeit much more politely. More encouraging, one facility said they would offer me a part-time job, if they could find someone else to job share with me, to cover the days when I was not working.

Finally, the last company gave me just what I requested—a three-days-a-week engineering job with no job sharing. I would be a low-level reliability engineer-in-training in a factory that made compressors and other components for automotive air conditioning systems. Job duties would include doing statistical studies on the torque variation of all automatic equipment used to tighten critical fasteners, as well as warranty analyses on all product lines.

The downside to this offer was that it came from the same division where my husband worked as a process engineer.

Jon and I discussed the two viable offers I had received. I really wanted to accept the job with Jon's division, but knew my position would be controversial. I didn't want him adversely impacted. We both felt I had been blessed with this opportunity and agreed it was a promising career move. Jon assured me that he didn't work with anyone from the Quality Department, so we probably would have very little contact with each other.

I was a bit concerned that, as a woman with a master's degree, I was starting two levels lower than the men being hired full time with bachelor's degrees. However, I was getting the job I wanted, on the terms I wanted, at a pay rate higher than that of the Township.

I took the job.

This was the start of my 30-year career in the automotive industry.

1. Realize that sometimes disappointments or broken promises can be just the incentive you need to break free from the familiar.

2. Figure out what you want. Then pursue it with a passion, even if people tell you it has never been done.

3. Emphasize during your job interview what the company will gain by hiring you. Suggest a trial period when proposing a special arrangement.

What You Can Do With Degrees

I was excited to start my first day on the new job in the automotive components factory. Dress requirements included wearing slacks, a conservative shirt, and closed-toed, flat-heeled, rubber-soled shoes. Personnel processed my entry paperwork and provided an employee ID badge, safety glasses, and earplugs. Then I was escorted out to the middle of the plant to an enclosed mezzanine office overlooking several noisy component assembly lines. The Quality Superintendent, who was now my boss, was about 10 years my senior. He had a firm handshake and a direct-eye-contact manner of speaking that I immediately liked and trusted.

I said, "It's a pleasure to meet a man courageous enough to do something out of the ordinary, and agree to let a woman join his department on a part-time basis. I appreciate the opportunity you're giving me. I know you will not regret your decision." He went over some preliminary information with me, introduced me to a few other people who were there in the office, and then called on his two-way radio to summon Al, the General Foreman.

When Al arrived in the office, the Quality Superintendent said, "This is Pat Schuch. She'll be starting work today in our department as a reliability engineer. I'd like you to take her on your scooter right now and give her a tour of the plant."

Al glared at me and then said to his boss, "You've got to be kidding! I've got a hell of a lot more important things to do than drive a broad around the plant!" The superintendent calmly reaffirmed to Al that he should take me along on his scooter and do whatever he had to do; in the end, he had to show me around the factory.

With a growl, Al led the way down the stairs to his parked scooter. I hopped on the back seat and held on tightly with my feet facing rearward. I turned my head sideways in order to hear whatever Al might have to say as we rode back-to-back through the noisy factory.

"Are you married?" he asked, while driving between the lines of conveyor belts and operators.

"Yes, I'm married," I replied.

"In my opinion, women—especially married women—shouldn't work. You're taking a job away from a man. Why are you here?"

"Well," I responded, "I really like this kind of work. I've been technically trained and I'm very excited about this job."

He said, "Do you have kids?"

"Yes, I have a son and a daughter."

"Well, that's *really* bad. Your kids are going to get totally messed up with you working." After a short pause he continued, "You know something? I'll bet you you're one of those smart-ass college kids. How many degrees do you have?"

"I have two."

Al immediately retorted, "Well, I'll tell you something, little lady. A thermometer has degrees, too, and you know where you can shove one of those!"

I was shocked. Saying nothing, I tried to seem unaffected by his comment. This was my very first day working at the largest auto company in town. It was clear that interfacing with the men in the plant was going to be a lot more challenging than the technical aspect of the job.

~~~~~

Whenever I sensed someone on the factory floor talking or joking about me behind my back, I would turn around, go right up to the employee, look him in the eye, and say, "Hi, I don't think we've met yet. My name is Pat Schuch. What's your name?" It was easy for a man to make comments or jokes about a woman who was just a faraway object. However, once that object became an actual person talking with him one-on-one, it was a little harder to continue with the snide remarks.

Over time, Al and the other workers adjusted to having me around. The initial catcalls I received walking by the assembly lines were replaced with a wave, or "Hi, Pat!" Treating each person with dignity became my operating mode, even if some of them did not initially show me respect.

There was one memorable incident that happened while I was speaking with a maintenance man. Another employee came up behind me and gave me a quick kiss on the back of my neck. I didn't want to overreact, but I didn't want to let it pass, either. I waited a second, and then swatted the back of my neck. The employee came around to the front of me smiling and said, "Anything wrong, Pat?"

"No," I replied innocently. "It was just an annoying bug or pest of some sort."

The employee's face fell, and the maintenance man—who witnessed the whole interaction—did his best to hold back a smirk.

Nothing like that ever happened to me again. I was slowly breaking down prejudices and changing attitudes, while doing my job well. In short, I was making progress.

1. Convey appreciation to bosses and other people who support you. They may be experiencing more hassles for helping you than you realize.

2. Try to appear unabashed when you are the first to do something and people express resentment.

*3. Resist the urge to avoid individuals who do not seem to respect you. Instead, spend **more** time with them, enabling those people to come to know you, as you come to learn about them.*

The Uncontrollable Wife

One day I was asked to check the torque variation on a new piece of expensive equipment that had been installed in the plant. This was the first of several identical pieces the Plant Engineering Department purchased to replace some older machinery. The equipment supplier claimed that this machine would install bolts with a very small variation in torque (the amount of turning force used to tighten the bolt). However, the data I collected indicated that the expensive, new equipment had more variation in torque values than the old equipment and, in some cases, had values outside the specified range. The new equipment was unacceptable.

I wrote up a report and personally explained the situation to the Quality Superintendent, who had requested the study on the new equipment. With my report in hand, he promptly went to see the Manufacturing Engineering Director, who happened to be my husband's boss's boss.

A reasonable person might expect the Manufacturing Engineering Director to be grateful to find out, prior to production runs being made, that new equipment was not operating to specification. Well, this didn't happen.

Instead, the Manufacturing Engineering Director became furious because someone dared to question the new equipment he had approved. Seeing the torque variation report from the old equipment attached and referenced for comparison made him even angrier.

Noting my name on the report, he confronted Jon after a meeting later in the day. Angrily explaining the nature of the report he had in his hand, the Director went on to say, "That &^$$%# wife of yours is causing me nothing but trouble! I want you to have a talk with her and get her under control."

Jon slowly replied, "I'm afraid I've never been able to control my wife, so I don't think I'll be able to now. Besides, if the data shows the equipment can't meet the specification, shouldn't the information be given to the supplier to resolve before shipping the rest of the machines?"

The Manufacturing Engineering Director went off in a huff, mumbling under his breath.

Things eventually calmed down. The plant later installed other new equipment, which consistently held torques within the specified range, and everything ended well. However, I realized then that it would be better for Jon and me to work at different divisions in the future.

1. Be aware that just by doing your job, you can sometimes inadvertently make other people look bad.

2. Understand that when a couple works at the same location, some issues may arise that cause discomfort.

Ignoring Logic

Things were going very well with my reliability engineering job, and most people did not realize I was in the plant only three days a week. There were no negative consequences; so, after six months, management decided to have me continue working part time for another two years.

Joe and Jean attended a Montessori program on the days I was on the job, and they were thriving in that preschool environment. Jon and I were working well as a team completing various home improvement projects on the ranch-style home we had designed and built three years earlier. Things were going smoothly—and then it happened: Jon was offered a job in the corporate energy group, which would require a move to Michigan.

Both of us were initially thrilled at his promotional offer. However, we began to have second thoughts about leaving our home and disrupting the children's preschool routine. I was uncertain about finding another division of my company in Michigan willing to let me work part time for another sixteen months. Financially we would be going backwards because the cost of living was higher and Jon's current job paid overtime whereas the new job would not. True to his logical engineering background, Jon did a written analysis—rating, weighing, and totaling all the pros and cons of both alternatives. The results were not even close. The logical decision was to remain in Ohio.

Jon turned down the job.

For the next week, Jon seemed quieter than usual. "What's up?" I said. "You act like something's bothering you."

"I keep thinking about the job offer I turned down. It didn't make sense to take it, but somehow I keep wondering what great things I might have been able to accomplish in the new job."

I responded, "Listen, Jon, don't worry about what your logical analysis says. Pray about it, and if, deep inside, you think you should take the job, just do it. I will support you all the way."

"What if you can't find part-time work like you have now?"

"Don't worry," I replied. "I talked one division into hiring me part time. Now that I have a good track record, it should be easier for me to convince another division to hire me under the same conditions."

Then Jon said, "I turned down the job last week. I can't call the energy executive back and say I changed my mind. What if he has given the job to someone else?"

I replied, "The energy director came to you out of the blue and offered you the promotion because you are uniquely qualified with your outstanding accomplishments and leadership during the recent national energy crisis. If I were in his position, and you called me back and said you reconsidered and now wanted the job, I would be thrilled. Call him."

Jon called the energy executive, who was indeed thrilled that Jon had changed his mind. He said the job was still open and was Jon's if he wanted it.

Jon took the job.

Pearls from Pat

1. Go through a logical analysis of pros and cons when making important decisions. In the end, however, go with the answer that comes from deep inside.

2. Don't be afraid or too proud to reverse what later feels like a bad decision.

The Women's Restroom

After several days of house hunting in the new city, we found a subdivision that we really liked. We decided once again to design and construct a new home—this one, a Spanish-style two-story. With our new house location chosen, I began to research my company's divisions that were located closest to our future home, this time excluding the division where my husband would be working.

While Jon waited in the car, I walked into the Personnel Office of the Truck Division to drop off my resume. I explained that my husband was being transferred to the area and I was looking for a job as well. As the Personnel Manager glanced over my resume, her face lit up.

"We really need engineers—especially women engineers."

I replied, "I should explain that I have been working three days a week and want to continue doing this for another sixteen months, until my children are both in school all day."

The Personnel Manager replied, "We've never done anything like this before. However, if another division has set up an arrangement for you, we should be able to just copy what they did procedurally. Stay here for just a minute, while I see if the man in charge of the Quality Department happens to be in his office right now. I know he would want to meet you."

Soon I was in the office of the Executive Director of Quality, answering his questions about my education and work experience. Twenty minutes later, he extended his hand and said, "We'd love to have you join our organization. We can offer you a promotion to the next level, which comes with a 10 percent raise. We can have you work three days a week for sixteen months with the understanding that you would then work full time. How's that sound to you?"

"It sounds great! Please have Personnel get me the offer in writing. I'll discuss it with my husband and get back to you early next week."

I left the office in a daze. Originally stopping by the Personnel office just to drop off my resume, I never expected an interview, let alone a job offer. Jon was still in the car waiting for me. As I got in, he immediately said, "You were gone longer than I expected. What happened in there?"

"You won't believe it. I not only got another three-day-a-week reliability engineering job, but they're also giving me a promotion!"

~~~~~

One month later we moved into a two-bedroom townhouse apartment, which would be our temporary home while we planned and monitored construction of our new house. After one week, Jon was settled in his new job, Joe and Jean adjusted to their new school, and the boxes were all unpacked. I called the Personnel Department at the Truck Division, explained how I had gotten my family settled sooner than expected, and asked if I could start work the following week. Their enthusiastic answer was, "Yes, the sooner, the better."

My new job was located in Building 45, where quality audits and some repair procedures were conducted on completed trucks. My new boss, Vlad, and my engineering colleagues were smart young men, whom I liked immediately. My previous job had focused only on air conditioning system components. Now to be working with entire vehicles—heavy-duty trucks—was very exciting and complex. There was, however, one small issue: Building 45 had no women's restroom.

I had been the first woman in an area before, surviving and succeeding because of my personal unwritten rules:

- Never complain.
- No matter how bad things get, do not expect special treatment because you are a woman.
- Accept the fact that you have to work twice as hard as any man just to be thought half as good.

Keeping my personal rules in mind and using my normal problem-solving mode of thinking, several options came to mind to address the issue of no women's restroom.

- Refrain from drinking anything all day.
- Try to program my body to need a break only at lunchtime. Then I could walk ten minutes to the main administration building where there was a cafeteria and the nearest women's restroom.
- When nature called, ask a colleague to go with me to stand guard outside the men's restroom, while I quickly used it.
- Go to the men's restroom alone, hanging a temporary "WOMEN'S RESTROOM" sign on the door while I was in there.
- Ask Vlad to have the Facilities group construct a women's restroom in Building 45. This could be viewed as violating my second unwritten rule, and certainly would not help in the short term. However, I figured it was likely that there would be more women working in or visiting this building sometime in the future. If so,

at least a small women's restroom seemed like a good idea for more than just my own convenience.

When I spoke with Vlad about the lack of a women's restroom, I asked, "Do you have any suggestions on what I should do?" He replied, "Well, I wouldn't drink much coffee in the morning." Then after a pause, he said, "You know it's up to you to figure out what to do. I'll also think about it and see if any good ideas come to mind."

The next day I spotted something strange under my desk. It was a molded plastic potty chair used to toilet train two-year-old children. The label taped to its base read, "Building 45 Women's Restroom." Seeing the surprised expression on my face, Vlad laughed and said, "Just keep that under your desk, ready to use whenever you need it."

The message was clear: "If you are a woman working here, you're going to have to adjust, adapt, and figure out how to meet the challenge. Your problem is not my problem."

I used all five options to address the restroom issue at one time or another. After lots of practice, I trained myself to go for long periods between comfort breaks, and to get in and out faster than most men. Several years later a women's restroom was installed in Building 45. By the time it happened, I was working in a larger building in the truck plant complex—one that already had women's restrooms.

1. Do not complain. Remain upbeat regardless of your situation.

2. Think creatively, adapt quickly, and make do in the short term, whenever you are confronted with an issue. Work on a long-term fix that will benefit others, as well as yourself.

The Still, Small Voice

Throughout my life, I have periodically been gently guided by a still, small inner voice to do or say things that turned out to be very helpful. One such incident occurred a few months after Jon and I started our new jobs in Michigan.

We were both pleased with our new assignments and our new home construction was well underway. Unfortunately, progress on the building was slower than expected, and the four members of the Schuch family were going to be temporarily living in the two-bedroom townhouse apartment for longer than we had planned. Our unit #810 was in a long row of look-alike structures two blocks from a busy main street and three blocks from a city park with a duck pond.

While my work kept me in town, Jon's job required him to travel to various plants across the country, establishing energy conservation programs for the corporation. In the beginning, Jon was very conscientious about leaving me his itinerary and the phone numbers where he could be reached. After a while, however, this practice became rather hit or miss. I never pressed Jon to leave me his contact information mainly because he called every night when he was away. There was usually no problem handling whatever came up while he was gone.

On one particular autumn night, while Jon was out of state, I was awakened around midnight by a voice in my head that kept repeating with progressively increasing volume, "Check the children. Check the children! CHECK THE CHILDREN!"

I was very sleepy and did not want to get out of bed. However, the voice was loud and insistent, unlike anything I had ever experienced in the past. I finally got up, just to silence the voice. Going to the next room, where Joe and Jean both slept, I saw that Joe was sleeping. However, Jean's bed was empty! I checked the bathroom and found that she wasn't there. Coming back into the children's room, I looked under the bed and in the closet. Joe was stirring, and I asked him where Jean was. He didn't know.

Checking on the first floor, I couldn't find her—and then saw something strange. The back door was standing open, and the glass storm door was closed. A chair had been pulled away from the kitchen table and positioned close to the door. All I could think was, "Did Jean stand up on the chair to reach and unlock the high-mounted dead bolt lock?"

I went from calling for her in the house, to running outside in the 30-degree night air, repeatedly shouting her name. Staring down the long row of small, adjacent, look-alike backyards, I could see that no one was there.

It was the middle of the night. The apartment was locked up and safe. Jean was sleeping one room away from me. How could she be missing? Where could she be? Those and other thoughts tumbled around in my head as I ran back into the house deciding to call the police.

I recited my name and address, and then explained, "I just discovered that my four-year-old daughter, Jean, is missing. I last saw her when she went to bed at 8 p.m. I went to bed at 10 p.m. It looks like she pulled a chair over to the back door, reached up and unlocked the deadbolt, and went out of the house. The back door was left open. It doesn't make sense. She's never done anything like this before."

The officer asked for a description. I replied, "Jean

has light brown shoulder-length hair, brown eyes, is probably barefoot, and is wearing a yellow nightgown. We haven't lived here very long, and all the townhouses on our street look the same. If she has wandered off and makes her way back, I don't think she'll know which unit is ours." When the officer asked if anyone else was in the house, I explained that my five-year-old son was here with me. The officer said to stay in the house with my son. He would call several squad cars on patrol to look for Jean and would call me as soon as he had any news.

A thousand scenarios went through my mind. What if someone kidnapped her off the street? What if she fell into the nearby park's duck pond and drowned? What if she was hit by a car, or otherwise injured? What if she was hiding and the police did not find her, and she died of exposure?

Then feelings of guilt overtook me. What had I done wrong? Why didn't I keep my daughter safe? Why was I such a sound sleeper? Why hadn't I heard her leave? If a child is not safe going to sleep in her own bed, where is she safe? Why isn't Jon here? He is always gone when I need him! What if I had slept until my usual 5:30 a.m. wake-up alarm sounded?

Suddenly, a calm came over me. The voice had awakened me. Surely, that had happened for a reason—so Jean could be found and be safe. I waited, and I prayed.

What seemed like an eternity passed, and then the phone rang. The same policeman I had spoken with earlier said simply, "An officer found your daughter. She was walking down the nearby busy street. He said she seems dazed, is a little bruised and dirty, but looks okay. They'll be pulling up in front of your place in just a few minutes."

I put down the phone, and a sense of relief washed over me. A minute later a police car pulled up. An officer carried a barefoot Jean in her yellow nightgown up to our front porch. He gently placed her in my arms. Jean and I hugged each other tightly. The gratitude I felt was overwhelming.

"Thank you! Thank you, so much!" was all I could mumble to the policeman. He repeated what the phoning officer had told me about finding her walking several blocks away.

"Jean, what happened to you? Why did you leave the house?" I asked.

"Oh, Mom, I was so scared. I thought there was a stranger in the house, and I know they taught us at school to run away from strangers. I ran out of the house and ran and ran. Then I fell down, and when I got up I didn't know where I was. I just kept walking, until the policeman found me and brought me home."

All I could think of was how the preschool had taught the children about stranger danger several days earlier in preparation for Halloween. Jean must have been dreaming or walking in her sleep. I didn't know what to do next to keep her safe and in the house.

The officer left. I made three cups of hot chocolate. Joe, Jean, and I warmed up and calmed down after the ordeal. I cleaned and bandaged Jean's knees—which were scraped from when she had tripped—and carried her up to bed. Then I sat down in the kitchen and breathed deeply. I felt like a miracle had just happened.

Little did I know a second miracle would soon follow.

~~~~~

It was now after 1 a.m. This had been such a close call. Our daughter had been lost, and I needed to talk with Jon. Unfortunately, I had no idea how to reach him. Racking my brain, I tried to remember what scant information he had given me about his business trip somewhere in Wisconsin when he had called earlier in the evening.

Quickly, I reached for the phone book, found a Wisconsin area code and dialed it followed by the number for information.

"Hello. What city, please?" said the operator. I hesitated. I didn't know the city. What could I say? Remembering Jon's update, I responded, "Hi. I need to be connected to a hotel in Wisconsin that is next door to a restaurant owned by a Green Bay Packer." I sounded like an idiot; however, it was all the information I had.

"One moment, please."

I stood there, surprised by her nonchalant response. Then I heard a ringing sound followed by the voice of a hotel desk clerk flatly stating the name of a hotel.

I tentatively spoke, "Jon Schuch's room, please."

"Just a moment," he said. "I'll connect you."

A few seconds later, I heard, "Hello?" It was the unmistakable sound of my husband's sleepy voice.

I couldn't believe it! I didn't know what was more amazing—the whole frightening experience with Jean, or the fact that the information operator had known what Wisconsin hotel's phone number I needed in order to reach my husband. As I told Jon every detail of the past hour, the tension drained from my body—replaced by the wonder that only comes when there is a direct, dramatic, divine intervention in your everyday life.

The following day was a workday for me. I was unsure about taking Jean to Montessori preschool, but she seemed okay. I explained to her teacher some of what had happened the night before, and requested that she keep an eye on Jean and call if she did or said anything unusual. Everything went fine that day.

It was months before I could relax enough to have a good night's sleep, but Jean never had another similar episode. After nearly four decades, I have not forgotten the terror of her being lost—and how disaster was averted because I listened to the still, small voice.

Pearls from Pat

1. Listen to the still, small voice inside. It can guide you in amazing—and even lifesaving—ways!

2. Be sure a detailed itinerary with phone numbers is left readily accessible in case of an emergency whenever a family member is traveling.

3. Don't be concerned that you will sound stupid when asking for something you need. You have nothing to lose and everything to gain.

Mother Trucker

My job in Building 45 involved reviewing the heavy-duty truck quality reports that were done by hourly auditors. I also filled in as their supervisor when the regular foreman was not there. Building a strong relationship with the auditors, I learned how they determined what constituted a defect, how it was reported, and how they conducted the daily audit reviews for management.

The hourly auditors had a detailed inspection checklist that they used while visually examining every inch of the heavy-duty trucks which were pulled at random from the end of the assembly line each day. Points were deducted depending on the severity of the discrepancies found, and a perfect score of 145 occasionally occurred. Every superintendent, general foreman, and foreman usually attended the management audit review in case his area of assembly had a discrepancy which required corrective action back on the line.

The review of the engine compartment was called "Asses and Elbows," because that is what people on the ground saw when six or seven men crawled high up on the tires and front bumper of the huge truck. They had to bend over and peer into the open engine compartment to see a discrepancy under the hood, which the auditor pointed out with his flashlight. The auditors often wore white lab coats and I also wore one during audit reviews, in case there was a need to climb up on a truck. My presence was distraction enough, so I tried to dress in such a way as to minimize any display of my backside and the rest of my figure.

~~~~~

There was a lot of excitement during one particular week while I was acting as audit foreman. We were auditing the two identical heavy-duty trucks, which were ordered by the Hollywood studio that was preparing to start filming the movie *Smokey and the Bandit II*.

One truck would be used for the exterior filming and one would be used for filming the interior cab shots. Everyone was excited about being involved with trucks that would be used in a movie starring Sally Field and Burt Reynolds. These vehicles were not only to be audited—they were to leave in absolutely perfect condition, and I was responsible to make sure that happened.

One of the auditors came into the office very upset. He asked me to come out to the yard to see something. Realizing that he was moving toward one of the *Smokey and the Bandit* vehicles, I felt my heart start to race. Then he showed me his concern—there was a dent and large scrape of yellow paint right in front on the bumper. He had inadvertently hit the yellow guardrail lining the building perimeter. I felt absolutely sick. Why did *this* vehicle have to be the one that got damaged? No other truck was figuratively put under a microscope like this one was.

"I know this was an accident, and you feel terrible about it. Don't worry, we'll figure out some way to get it fixed before too many people see it." Then to show him I still had confidence in him, I said, "Why don't you go ahead and drive the truck into the audit area and start doing your audit. I'll see if I can find someone to put a new bumper on this truck as soon as possible, so we can get the management review done on schedule." I was grateful that the truck had a chrome bumper which, although more expensive, could be replaced more quickly than a bumper custom painted to match the cab body.

Once the bumper replacement was completed, both

the auditor and I smiled with a shared sense of relief. The *Smokey and the Bandit* truck was ready for the management review—and so were we.

~~~~~

A few weeks later, I gained a new appreciation for just how hard the large trucks were to maneuver. My boss said I had to learn how to drive the thirteen-speed, double clutch vehicles with hand-applied air brakes, so I could move them between the yard and the audit area.

The auditors who worked for me were charged with teaching me to drive the big trucks. Having driven four-speed manual transmission cars from the age of sixteen, I was familiar with clutches. However, getting into the cab of a huge truck with air brakes and thirteen gears to shift through using a double clutch process was a real stretch assignment for me. Perspiring profusely whenever behind the wheel, I cautiously maneuvered the behemoths around the yard and through the oversized garage doors into the plant audit area. Deeply concerned about making a mistake and damaging one of these expensive customized vehicles, I took deep breaths and worked through the fear that kept taunting me to quit.

The auditors were impressed by my persistence, and after a week, I started to feel more comfortable. This was the era when truckers used CB radios, and since we used walkie-talkie type radios to communicate with one another, everyone in the department had a "handle" or nickname. The guys realized I was the only person in the building who was a mother, and I had successfully learned to drive the big trucks. Knowing I did not use foul language, even when those around me did, they closely scrutinized my face as they very cautiously made a suggestion for my handle—"Mother Trucker!"

When the men saw me smile and nod with approval at their recommendation, they relaxed.

I became just another engineer.

1. Treat the person who makes a mistake just as you would want to be treated in the same situation.

2. Dress and move in ways that keep you from becoming a distraction.

3. Help people to feel comfortable working with you by keeping your sense of humor.

The Rolling Average Chart

My final interesting assignment while in Building 45 was developing a way to reduce transportation damage on heavy-duty trucks being shipped to customers all over the country. Some of the trucks were shipped by rail with special chains used to hold them in place. Others were shipped by road on haul-away rigs pulling three or four trucks at a time. Piggybacked at an approximately 25-degree angle, the haul-away configuration was reminiscent of a group of circus elephants, each with its front legs positioned on the back of the elephant in front of it.

A twelve-month Rolling Average Chart for tracking shipping damage was distributed to upper management every month. Each data point represented the average monthly cost the company paid to dealers for repairing shipping damage on heavy-duty trucks for the previous twelve months. The chart showed a line that was very high and relatively level for the past twelve data points. Since the first data point represented the average of the twelve previous months, the twelve-month chart essentially reflected nearly two years of data. A single good month or a single bad month did not affect the chart much since each data point also included eleven other months of data in its average value. Only a dramatic sustained improvement would get the line to go down.

To understand how, why, and what kind of damage was occurring, I analyzed where the damage costs were the highest and where they were near zero. I observed trucks being loaded on haul-away rigs and on railcars near the plant and then traveled to watch those same trucks being unloaded at railheads and dealerships.

My transportation damage study led me to make the following conclusions:

- There was no consistency in the way trucks were loaded and unloaded on haul-away rigs and at railheads. Loaders just did the best they could.

- While some chains were partially sheathed in protective plastic sleeves, many of them were not. Tie down chains were often rubbing against the front bumpers and finished surfaces of the trucks, resulting in damage.

We needed some low-cost type of protection to make sure the highest cost areas—front bumpers—would not be damaged. Working with a variety of foam suppliers doing many trials, we finally developed bumper protectors, which were inexpensive, easy to install, and able to withstand the forces of the chains that supported much of the vehicles' weight.

We also needed to establish and communicate a more effective standardized loading procedure. Consulting with all the parties involved to determine best practices, we developed a mandatory training program—with good materials and visuals—for everyone who loaded or unloaded our trucks. I taught many of the training sessions myself, and coached resident trainers at every location across the country.

Soon after this assignment was completed, I moved to another plant and reported to a new boss.

About six months later, I received an envelope in the mail from my former Building 45 boss, Vlad. Inside was a copy of the latest chart showing heavy-duty truck transportation damage costs. The first half of the line was horizontal. The last half of the line sloped diagonally downward. Attached to the chart was a note:

"Pat, here is the latest Transportation Damage Rolling Average Chart. The damage cost line has been steadily coming down for months since you left, taking a while for the twelve-month data averages to reflect all of the process and training improvements you initiated. Even though you have been gone from the department for six months, we all know the results we are seeing now are a direct result of your fine work."

I was shocked. It is always nice to get a compliment from your current boss. But it is extraordinarily thoughtful for a boss to send you a note six months after you left his department to say you made a difference—plus attach the data to prove it!

And to think, this was the same man who put a potty chair labeled "Building 45 Women's Restroom" under my desk the first week I came to work for him!

1. Realize that the fruits of your labor may not appear until months after you have completed the work.

2. Appreciate exceptional bosses who communicate praise for a job well done, even if the subordinate is long gone when the work results come to fruition.

Dispelling Myths and Fears

The title of the thesis for my first master's degree was "Women's Role in School Administration: A Comparison of Attitudes and Ambitions." At the time, I questioned why there were so many women teachers and so few women principals, especially in high schools. Articles written in the early 1970s by Dorothy Johnson and Mary Ann Carroll greatly influenced me because they succinctly captured the myths about women in school administration. Who would have ever imagined that my study about the prejudices experienced by women principals would actually forearm me with a deep understanding of men's unspoken beliefs about women foremen in a vehicle assembly plant? Here are the six myths listed by Dorothy Johnson, as well as five additional myths listed by Mary Ann Carroll, which often apply to women performing any traditional male jobs:

1. Women administrators are absent from their post more often than men.

2. Women administrators are transient because of factors such as marriage, pregnancy, home responsibilities, and spouse's out-of-town transfers.

3. Women should not aspire for administrative jobs, because they do not have the "muscle" to handle discipline problems.

4. Women are too emotional to be administrators.

5. Women prefer a man for a boss.
6. Women administrators lose their femininity (Johnson, 1971, p. 39).
7. Men administrators are easier to work with than women.
8. Women need to be protected from the unpleasantness involved in administration.
9. Women don't have the preparation necessary to become administrators.
10. Women won't give the commitment to the job that top administrative positions require.
11. Men see and generate big ideas, while women are better at following directions and doing detail work (Carroll, 1972, p. 215).

In addition to these, I added another myth based on my own business observation:

12. Women avoid business trips and out-of-town job transfers, because they disrupt their family's routine.

Although each one of these points could be elaborated on with data to show its invalidity, evidence is often not enough to dissuade men who hold such unfounded beliefs. In my master's degree thesis, I referenced Jean Way Schoonover, who wrote in 1974 concerning her premise that men's gut feelings about women administrators were actually based on their own specific subconscious fears:

1. Men fear women as peers on the job because they believe women are unable to have on-the-job relationships that are free of sexual tension.
2. Men feel a physical need for women and fear career women will exploit their need.

3. Culture has not taught men how to work with women whose only relationship is that of co-worker and professional colleague.

4. Men do not trust a woman's emotions and feel that a woman's responses to problems are unpredictable.

5. With very few exceptions, men have had no "life models" for the business relationship between man and woman. Women are narrowly viewed as mothers, wives, sweethearts, relatives, and working subordinates.

6. Men fear a woman's superiority mentally and physically in terms of her living longer.

7. Men are afraid of a career woman's ability to concentrate on and devote herself to her job, especially if she has no children.

8. Men feel that women who seek such careers are not ordinary, working women. They are extraordinary superwomen, work freaks of some kind—demented Amazons, who want to be facsimile men.

9. Men are afraid of losing their identities. In America, men often feel that they are what they do for a living. If a woman does the same job, they feel it somehow makes their work have less stature, less prestige, and less importance.

10. Men dread the fear their wives may have of the woman with whom they work—the woman who is co-worker, peer, and equal to their husbands (Schoonover, 1974, p. 415).

In retrospect, I had no women superiors to mentor me in the factory, and no male superiors or peers discussing female myths and male fears. Understanding these concerns, which were incorporated in my master's thesis on school administration, really helped me in my corporate assignments. To overcome these myths, I had to be outstanding, especially in the areas of attendance,

commitment, handling discipline effectively, not threat-
ening anyone's manhood, and not losing my femininity.
I also had to perform even the most unpleasant tasks
cheerfully, and demonstrate a big picture view, as well as
attention to detail.

Understanding their unspoken fears, I was able to be
confident and sympathetic towards various groups of
men, who had their work world turned upside down, as
they adjusted to interacting for the first time with a
woman in their department.

*1. Realize that understanding myths, subconscious
fears, and unconscious bias can help you know where
people are coming from when you are in a new environment.*

*2. Do not take prejudice or negativity personally—it
is natural for people accustomed to the status quo to
resist you and the change you represent.*

*3. Do not focus on your own difficulties when you
are the first one in an area. Be understanding—it's not
all about you.*

Perfect Attendance

The myth about women's poor attendance was of special interest to me. At my various jobs during high school and college, men could be heard muttering when a woman missed work, "It must be that time of the month." That comment used to drive me crazy.

To cope mentally with menstrual discomfort, I told myself that for three weeks of every month, my performance was very good—like that of my male colleagues. However, for one week of every month, I turned into Super Worker. The flowing blood signified fertility, potential for new life, creativity, and heightened problem-solving capability—something my male colleagues were incapable of experiencing. In my imagination, during this time, my performance would soar. I didn't mind having my periods and never missed work because of them.

My sister made me a believer in perfect attendance in 1974, after a memorable job interview. When the interviewer asked her if she had received any honors or awards that made her feel especially proud, she responded:

"I have not received any impressive academic or athletic awards. The achievement I am proudest of is a perfect attendance pin I received for being the only student in my grade to not miss a single day of classes during four years of high school." The interviewer was quite impressed. As it turned out, good attendance was very important to that particular company.

My sister got the job.

~~~~~

During my automotive career I had a perfect attendance work record for the first eighteen years—until I had to take a few weeks of medical leave for some surgery. Whenever I got sick—which didn't happen very often—I just took a vacation day in an effort to preserve my perfect attendance record. When one of our children got sick, Jon and I determined which of us was in a better position to take a vacation day to stay home. In retrospect, my obsession with my perfect attendance was probably overkill and more than I expected from anyone who worked for me.

However, when you are trying to dispel myths, sometimes you choose to go above and beyond what is expected—and overkill may not be a bad idea.

1. Strive to have an excellent attendance record. Consider the option of sometimes taking a vacation day when you or your child gets sick.

2. Address health issues promptly, especially those that impact work performance.

3. Choose to go above and beyond what is expected, especially if you are the first one in an area.

What Goes Around, Comes Around

Sixteen months after our relocation to Michigan, both children started school full time. Because Jean had done well in Montessori and was reading all the books her older brother was reading, the private elementary school tested her for proper placement. Instead of going into kindergarten, Jean started first grade along with Joe. The principal wisely assigned them to two different classrooms. Their school was fifteen minutes from home, and less than five minutes from where I worked. This made it easy for me to hop over to the school to attend a parent-teacher conference or to take my bimonthly turn for "lunch mother" playground duty, just like all the other moms.

Over the years, we were not fortunate enough to have extended family living nearby to help babysit our children on a regular basis. However, somehow we always managed to find excellent people to help us care for Joe and Jean. Mary, a wonderful stay-at-home mom whose twin boys were also starting first grade, was glad to drive Joe and Jean to and from school with her boys—and we were more than happy to pay for her car expenses. All four children became good friends. After school, Mary dropped Joe and Jean off at another nearby mom's home where the kids played until I picked them up after work.

Now employed full time and promoted to the next level with an 11 percent raise, I was finally on par with male new-hires with a bachelor's degree. Assigned to the production start-up team for a new small truck program, I reported to Herb, a congenial man with a habit that irritated me—he often came up behind me and casually put his hand on my shoulder. He made it appear harmless, but being touched by people other than my family made me feel uncomfortable. In spite of my concerted efforts to keep some distance from Herb, sometimes he'd catch me by surprise. I'd make a casual pivot move, spinning away from his hand on my shoulder, turning to face him and stepping backwards. In retrospect, I should have openly discussed the issue with him, rather than using an avoidance strategy. It might have made things easier for the women who worked for him in the future.

My job on the production start-up team was to ensure that component parts for the pilot (preproduction) vehicles met specifications, and to work with suppliers improving parts which did not meet the requirements.

One of the quality issues that arose involved the pattern on the seat fabric. The material was supposed to have the words "Truck Truck Truck Truck" repeated in numerous diagonal rows across the entire back of the seat. Because of the font type and the close spacing of the letters, the "Tr" looked like an "F" on the pilot seats, creating a very unfavorable impression. After all, people do not want to be cussed out by their new truck.

Fortunately, the supplier was able to make a change and get us seats with a revised pattern for our pilot program in a timely manner.

There was a second memorable supplier issue on the small truck pilot program. We received a shipment of instrument panels, which arrived with some air bubbles under the vinyl skin surface. I made several calls to the supplier's Mexican plant Quality Department, explaining that the instrument panels were unacceptable and needed to be replaced quickly, in order not to jeopardize our pilot assembly schedule. A second batch arrived with bubbles in a different location on the instrument panel. Again, I called, and this time talked with the plant's Quality Director. He needed to know any costs incurred for production delays due to poor quality instrument panels would be charged to his plant. The Quality Director said he would fly up from Mexico with the new parts himself.

Two days later, the Quality Director arrived. I went out to the lobby to meet him. As we shook hands, a glint of recognition passed across both of our faces—his with discomfort and mine with amusement.

The last time we had met was several years before in Ohio, when I did my first interviews for a part-time job in the automotive industry. Some of the plant interviews were only with the Personnel Department. However, one of the six facilities, which had turned me down, required me to interview with the Director of the Industrial Engineering Department. That gentleman, who stood before me now, had explained how his engineering department did not have any women in it—and he wanted to keep it that way. As his words came back to me, I enjoyed the thought of making this man sweat.

"How long have you been working at the Mexican plant?" I asked.

"About a year," he responded.

"The last time we met," I said, "you were the Director of the Industrial Engineering Department for your U.S. components division. Do you remember? You interviewed me for a job in Ohio."

"Oh, yes, I remember. I have not interviewed many women applying for engineering jobs."

"Do you still believe women should not work as engineers in plants?"

"Well, let's just say times are changing, and we all have to adjust. At least you got a job you wanted in another part of the corporation and have done well for yourself. I mean, who would have guessed then, that I would be standing here, now, having to request you to please accept the parts being made at my plant?"

We both chuckled and turned the discussion to focus on the parts issue. We looked at the earlier batches of parts, as well as the latest. He explained the problems his plant was having with equipment, material, and the curvature of the design. The parts he brought with him represented their latest process improvement—moving the surface bubbles to a location close to the edge, where they would be hidden by a trim piece after assembly in the vehicle.

I could have given him a hard time and again rejected the pilot parts for technically not meeting specification. Instead, I accepted these latest parts for the pilot, on the condition that he continue to work on improving the process to eliminate the surface bubbles altogether by the time production parts were required.

He agreed with a visible sign of relief.

1. Address the issue proactively if your boss or co-worker has a habit of invading your personal space.

2. Consider traveling to have a face-to-face meeting when there is a serious issue with an out-of-town customer.

3. Remember that, in some cases, showing mercy can be the best way to exercise power.

A Comedy of Errors

Late one Friday afternoon, I was stopped and ready to pull out of the parking lot to go home from work. A co-worker pulled up next to my van and yelled, "Your brake lights are not working!" Thanking him, I drove home and checked to see if the problem was something simple to fix, like a bulb or a fuse. Unfortunately, I could not easily diagnose the issue.

Jon came home, and I told him we needed to have a nearby garage fix the van's brake light problem. Jon replied, "I don't want you to go to the garage by yourself. Driving with no brake lights is dangerous—someone could plow right into you. I'll follow you in my car, so you can be safe."

The next morning Jean went with me in the van and Jon followed with Joe in the small car. We were less than a mile from home when I approached an intersection. The lead car stopped, waiting to turn left. The car in front of me stopped. I stopped.

Jon did not stop.

Jean and I felt a small jolt, the massive van being relatively unaffected. I knew exactly what had happened. Jon had momentarily forgotten that my brake lights were not working and had plowed into me.

I got out of the car to ensure that Jon and Joe were okay. Seeing the crumpled hood of Jon's car, I ran to the passenger side to open the door. (The car was only equipped with lap belts, not the three-point lap and shoulder restraint seat belts, which later became standard.)

Joe was crying and holding his head. I pulled his hand away and saw there was no blood. However, a goose-egg lump was starting to emerge on the right side of his forehead.

Jon was fine, but we were concerned about Joe. Since we were less than a mile from the hospital, we decided to take Joe there to get him checked out. Jon carried Joe to the van. Then Jon drove the badly damaged small car over to the side of the road.

Some people from a nearby house asked if they should call the police. We explained that we were married, and we just needed to get our son to the hospital.

Jon drove with Jean in the front of the van, while I stayed in the back trying to comfort Joe. Jon exclaimed, "I can't believe I hit the van! I was talking with Joe and didn't notice you had stopped. When I realized what was happening, I put on the brakes, but couldn't stop the car in time. I did exactly what we were trying to keep someone else from doing!"

When we got to the hospital, they took x-rays and confirmed that Joe was fine. We just needed to continue icing the lump on his head.

While we were waiting for the discharge paperwork, the police arrived, looking for us. They were upset because we had left the scene of an accident. We explained that, since no one outside of the family was involved, we didn't think we needed a police report. We wanted to get to the hospital as soon as possible.

Then they chastised us for taking Joe to the hospital instead of waiting for an ambulance. Didn't we know moving someone with a head injury was dangerous?

We explained how the accident resulted from a brake light problem. "My husband wanted to be sure no one rear-ended me." The police were going to give him a ticket and then decided that the whole situation, aside from Joe's injury, was like a comedy of errors. We had suffered enough with two damaged cars and an injured child, so they left without giving Jon a ticket.

The insurance company was not so kind. They counted the incident as two accidents—one for Jon and one for me. Fortunately, the rear bumper damage on the van was minor. When the repair shop took care of it, they noticed that the rear brake lights were not working. They fixed the brake lights.

1. Be sure all passengers use the three-point seat belts that are now standard on all vehicles—and keep children in the back seat.

2. Forgive yourself and others when mistakes are made. Learn from the experience, and move on.

3. Realize that sometimes a situation turns into a comedy of errors—so, look back on it and laugh!

Facing Fear

A year later on another Friday afternoon, I was driving home from work in a small car on a two-lane road. Another car was approaching me from the opposite direction and slowed with its right blinker flashing, indicating an intended right turn into a business driveway. A large old car, fast approaching behind the turning vehicle, suddenly swerved into my lane, hitting me head-on.

The sound of the crash was horrendous, and then there was silence. I felt nothing. I opened my eyes and could see nothing. "Am I dead?" I thought. "Is this what being dead feels like?"

Touching my head, I realized my forehead was bleeding badly into my eyes. Blinking, I regained some vision and saw that the entire left front of the car was crushed in on me, pinning my legs. I foggily understood that being 5'3" tall, and driving with the seat in the full forward position in a small car, had probably contributed to my legs being tightly wedged. The A-pillar in front of the driver's door was bent in and had blood and hair on it.

Suddenly a woman appeared at my window. She said she was a nurse and help was on the way.

Grateful to see her, I said, "I'm afraid I may pass out soon. Can I give you two phone numbers to call, while I still remember them?" She pulled out a pen and paper from her pocket, and jotted down Jon's work phone number to tell him to meet me at the hospital. I then recited the phone number for the afterschool babysitter who needed to know that there was an accident and we would be late picking up our children.

Just then, a teenager with long hair and some scrapes on his face came over to the car. He looked at me, shocked, and then ran his hand through his hair as he moaned, "Oh, Jesus, you are really hurt bad. I'm so sorry. I'm so sorry." Obviously he was the driver of the other car. I found out later that he was talking with his friend in the passenger seat and suddenly saw the car in front of him braking. Thinking he could not stop in time, he reflexively swerved to the left to avoid hitting the right-turning car in the rear. Instead, he crossed into the oncoming traffic lane and collided head-on with my car.

I felt sorry for him and was glad he was not badly hurt. I closed my eyes, exhausted and dizzy. Soon a policeman was there. Before passing out, I heard him say something about needing to use equipment called the "jaws of life" to get me out of the car.

The next thing I was conscious of was being put into the ambulance. I mumbled the name of the hospital I wanted to go to, and the attendant said we were headed there now.

My next memory was being on a hospital examination table. Jon arrived soon afterwards, having driven the 30 miles from his office to the hospital in record time. He was aghast, seeing me covered in blood. Assurances from the nurse that it looked worse than it actually was did not ease his concern.

There appeared to be no brain damage, but the cut on my forehead was deep. It took a total of 90 stitches in multiple layers to close the wound. Luckily, a plastic surgeon was on duty, so the facial scarring would be minimized. I had no broken bones, although my legs were badly bruised. It would be a few days before I could walk. After several hours in the hospital, Jon drove me home, carried me into bed, and then went to pick up the children.

I spent the entire weekend in bed. The car had been totaled, and towed to a garage. After viewing the wreckage, Jon said it was amazing I was alive. The kids were frightened, having never seen their mom incapacitated before. Jon told my boss what happened and said I would need at least three days of "vacation" (to preserve my perfect attendance record).

By Wednesday I was able to walk and we had a replacement car, identical to the one that was totaled. I looked pretty ugly, because my forehead was still swollen and starting to turn colors.

The worst part was my mental state. I was terrified to drive.

I kept thinking that a car could come from any direction and hit me, and there was nothing I could do about it. I felt completely out of control. On Wednesday I decided to practice driving the 15-minute route to work in light traffic around 10 a.m.

Getting in the car was traumatic, as memories about the accident flooded my mind. Every passing car seemed like a weapon pointed at me. The resulting fear left me shaking so badly that I pulled into a shopping center parking lot to calm down, continuously repeating a familiar scripture verse from Philippians 4:13, "I can do all things through Christ who strengthens me." Finally, the shaking subsided. I continued the drive to work and then turned around to return home, exhausted both physically and mentally.

The next day, I went to my job from 10 a.m. until 3 p.m., driving both ways while traffic was light. My colleagues were horrified when they saw me limping into the office with the head of a monster. They avoided speaking with me directly, because they could not bear to look at my face. I stayed at my desk, glad to focus on my paperwork and making some phone calls.

On Friday, things were a bit easier. By the following Monday, I was ready to resume working full days and to tackle driving in rush hour traffic. For four weeks, I would not drive with the children for fear another car might hit us and hurt them while I was at the wheel.

I still had fear and knew it was an irrational and debilitating state of mind. Jesus said, "Don't be afraid" (Matthew 10:31) and I realized that fear was really a lack of faith. I had overcome the first part of my fear because I was driving myself to work. I had to overcome the second part of my fear—driving with passengers.

Only through prayer was I finally able to drive with Joe and Jean in the car. Each time it got easier. I discovered that fear looks like a brick wall, but it's really a cloud, which you have to walk through to get to peace on the other side.

A few months after the accident, a blessing occurred when the teenager's insurance company offered me a small settlement. I contacted two lawyers recommended to me and explained, "I do not want the teenage driver to go through a court hearing or any additional grief. His insurance company has already offered me this small settlement. If you think the number is too low and believe you can negotiate more with the insurance company without going to court, I would be glad to give you a third of the additional amount of the settlement you negotiate. Would you be willing to take the job?"

The first lawyer said, "No"—he wanted a third of the entire settlement amount, including the amount I had already been offered, because that was standard practice. The second lawyer agreed to my terms.

Some good things came out of the accident. The new settlement number was more than twice as much as the original offer—and I accepted it. We used some of the money to buy materials to build a recreation room in our basement. The forehead scar was camouflaged with bangs until it faded years later.

Best of all, as a result of this bad situation, I became a stronger person—by trusting in God, facing my fears, and walking through them to the peace that was on the other side.

1. Acknowledge that fear is a very debilitating state of mind. However, it can be overcome with faith, prayer and willpower.

2. Look for the blessings, which are often hidden in seemingly bad situations.

3. Ponder this quote: "And we know that for those who love God all things work together for good, for those who are called according to his purpose" (Romans 8:28).

European Adventure

One day Jon was asked to spend three weeks visiting the company's plants in Europe to make recommendations on how to improve their energy efficiency. The trip would involve visiting Germany, Belgium, and England, with free time on weekends to do sightseeing.

Knowing I had spent one semester as a foreign exchange student in Germany at Universität Hamburg, Jon asked me if I would be interested in going with him overseas. "I have never been overseas," he said, "and it would be very useful to travel with someone who speaks German. Maybe my parents could come in from out-of-state to take care of Joe and Jean for three weeks."

"I would love to see the quality operations and audit systems of the European plants!" I said, excited by the possibility of going to Europe. "Let me check with my boss and see what he thinks."

My boss said he would definitely not consider sending me overseas on a company-paid business trip. However, if I paid for my own way and went to Europe on vacation, every day I spent in an automobile factory would count as a workday, provided I wrote a report summarizing my observations. It was a very fair arrangement.

When Jon contacted his European colleagues to make arrangements for his factory visits, he also requested them to schedule appointments for me—a company employee and reliability engineer—to meet with a representative from each European plant's Quality Department. Jon suggested I tour each plant's quality operations, while he was conducting the plant energy audits with the facility engineers.

Then Jon's boss also decided to go to Europe. He didn't want his wife on the trip, and he couldn't understand why Jon wanted me to come along. However, he agreed my ability to speak German would be helpful.

Upon arriving in Germany, I could read all of the signs, so Jon and his boss naturally gave me the job of getting us from the airport to the hotel, and then to the large assembly plant complex. When the three of us arrived, I was escorted to the Quality Department and told to rejoin my husband and his boss later for lunch in the executive dining room.

The Quality Director explained that there were no women in the plant, except cleaning women, cafeteria workers, and a few secretaries in the office. The idea of a female engineer was inconceivable. The Quality Director gave me an itinerary for the next few days. I would learn their plant's processes and also explain my U.S. plant's processes to them. It was fascinating to discover the issues we faced on both sides of the ocean were so similar, yet our solutions were often very different. My escorts were surprised at some of the process improvements we had recently implemented in the U.S. that might also work in the German plants. Identifying clever technical solutions in their plants, I took notes and requested additional information to share with my department back in the U.S.

When it was time for lunch, the Quality Director escorted me to the executive dining room, which was a very big honor. I had never even stepped inside an executive dining room in the U.S.

We had a wonderful lunch. I was the only woman in the room being served and most of the time there were two conversations going on at our table. Jon and his boss were conversing in English with the facilities executives at one end of the table, while the quality and production executives and I conversed in German at the other end of the table. When the facilities executives commented very approvingly that they had never before met an American—male or female—who spoke German, Jon was very proud.

Jon's boss did not look pleased when any favorable comment was made about me. Nevertheless, he smiled broadly when the German Facilities Director invited him, Jon and me—the three Americans—to his home for dinner. The Director said his wife could only speak German and was uncomfortable around people speaking English. However, since one of the visitors could speak German, she was happy to entertain all of the Americans. We were all delighted to experience the comforts of a wonderful German home and family.

Throughout my visit to the German facilities, I kept speaking German. Even though it hurt my pride to know I sounded like a child using simple phrases, people responded very positively to all of my efforts. A German plant tour guide shared with me a very important insight. Here is the English translation of what he said:

"Americans who come for a visit generally act very superior, expecting us to adapt and speak English. They do not even try to speak German for the basics like 'good morning' or 'please' and 'thank you.'"

He continued, "There is even a joke we like to tell, that goes like this:

What do you call someone who speaks three or more languages? Multilingual.

What do you call someone who speaks two languages? Bilingual.

What do you call someone who speaks only one language? American!"

1. Visit other facilities within your company to share ideas, compare processes, and brainstorm solutions for similar problems.

2. Cherish the relationships you build and share the lessons learned during business trips.

3. Show respect by speaking at least a few basic phrases of the native language when visiting a foreign country.

Nonverbal Communication

Up until this time, all my automotive experience had consisted of working in various component and vehicle quality departments. My next challenge was working as a production foreman in the small truck trim shop. Forty-two men who installed windshields and windows, door trim, air conditioning systems, sound insulation, and a variety of other components, now reported to me.

I was the first woman production foreman at that plant, and some of the men in my group definitely were not happy. The first day was critical and I was sure to be tested. Before the start of the shift, I introduced myself and made a few general comments about looking forward to meeting and working with them, as well as learning what each of them did. However, for the time being, my main concern was that every station was manned and ready to go when the assembly line started moving.

Besides the men assigned to do the assembly, there were several relief men who rotated through the stations on the line, doing the work of each operator as he went on break. There were also two repairmen at the end of our department's section of the assembly line conveyor who would fix any problems or missed operations identified by the inspectors.

As I walked down the line on my first day as the boss, I heard one operator grumble loud enough for his colleagues and me to hear, "I don't know why they sent us a

#^&*~%@ broad as a foreman. She probably doesn't know her a** from a hole in the ground."

When things like this happen, you know you have to do something. You just don't always know what that something is. I had to respond quickly but needed to buy myself some time. Walking over to the loudmouth show-off, I calmly looked him in the eye, very aware that at least four other operators were watching me. Fortunately, I had heard someone address this employee earlier.

"Your name's Jim, isn't it?"

He nodded.

"Well, Jim, I'd like to talk with you in my office for a few minutes, so I'm going to ask the relief man to come over here and cover for you when the man he's currently relieving comes back. I will see you then."

I turned away to speak with the relief man and walked to my office. One guy commented, "Uh-oh, Jim. Looks like she heard you, and you're in big trouble now."

In this plant, the foreman's office was a small, sound-proof room made of clear Plexiglas, located right next to the assembly line. No one could hear what was being said inside the office, but people on the line could see everything going on in there. Entering my office, I prayed for wisdom on how to handle this situation. Suddenly I knew what to do.

Five minutes later, Jim walked in. I motioned him to have a seat across the table from me. Anyone on the assembly line, who happened to look our way, would see my front and his back. I sounded cordial in my initial greeting but made sure not to smile. Then I asked Jim if he happened to see last night's basketball game. His expression showed that this was not what he expected.

"Yeah, I watched the whole thing."

Now I am not much of a sports enthusiast, but my husband is. Jon had watched the game the previous evening and had described to me every bad play, every stupid ref call, and every mistake made by the various players. It so happened that Jon's running commentary replayed in my mind just when it was needed.

"Did you see when the ref made that rotten call in the first quarter?" I began, rising from my seat in anger and recounting the incident.

"Then our defense let the other team blow right past them," I said with my teeth clenching and my fist pounding the table.

I continued with a few more game comments accompanied by animated body language. Then in a serious but calm tone, I concluded, "Jim, I'm really glad we had the chance to talk. You can go back to the line, now."

Jim left the office looking confused, since not one word was mentioned about his disparaging comments. As he departed he left the door ajar, so I was able to hear the conversation that followed.

"Hey, man, what happened in there? It looked like she was reaming you a new one."

"No," Jim said. "Nothing happened. She was just talking about basketball."

"Yeah, right. Like we're going to believe that. She didn't look like she was talking about basketball. We were watching you guys the whole time."

Looking Jim right in the eyes as I exited my office, I saw him betray a pleasantly bemused expression, conveying that he understood precisely what had just happened.

I never heard another disrespectful comment made by anyone in the group after that. There was a lot to learn, but the men taught me what was necessary. They came to appreciate my willingness to go to bat for them with people in engineering, processing, and material handling to make their jobs easier and their time at work more fun. I valued their input on improvements, and I watched as their self-esteem increased. We had a great department.

~~~~~

As a foreman, my immediate boss was a general foreman who believed the plant was no place for a woman. Every time the line shut down, he was in my face screaming how it cost the company $968.22 for every minute of my departmental downtime, and I had better shape up fast. Criticizing everything in expletives was his norm. Every day he ranted about safety, downtime, attendance, production counts at the pay point, and quality. I worked hard with the people in my department to make the necessary improvements.

Three weeks after starting that assignment, morale improved, the throughput increased, and the repair rate started to go down. The general foreman never said a single word of praise. However, on his daily inspection of my department, the only negative comment he made was, "I see two screws over there on the floor. Schuch, you need to improve your department's housekeeping."

I smiled and responded, "Thanks, I'll take that as a compliment! We must be doing a great job, if the only complaint you have is about two screws on the floor!"

1. Respond promptly to any situation requiring immediate attention, in a way that buys you some time to think through what to do next.

*2. Remember you can never be 100 percent certain that what you **think** is happening, actually **is**.*

3. Be aware that if your boss complains a lot, his way of giving praise may be by providing little or no criticism.

A Lesson in Humility

Because I was responsible for a group working on a vehicle assembly line, having everyone in my department show up for work on time was a very high priority. When the whistle sounded at the start of the shift, the conveyor started moving, and there had to be a person at every station doing the assigned operations in the allotted amount of time.

Each department had several relief men who knew how to do all the jobs on that portion of the assembly line. They could be called upon to fill in temporarily if someone was a few minutes late. If too many people were late, the line had to be shut down, causing losses in production and profit.

After having several days in a row when people were late, I called a short group meeting and explained the importance of getting to work early, so everyone could be at their stations ready to go when the shift whistle sounded. I was insistent in underscoring the importance of both punctuality and of calling in as soon as possible if something happened that would cause a delay. "It is very important to be on time!" I repeated emphatically.

Early in the morning on the very next day, I was involved in a minor traffic accident, while driving to work. People were driving slowly because the roads were icy. An approaching driver lost control of his car at an intersection, while making a left turn in front of me. Unable to stop because of the ice, I hit him. There was no damage to my car, and only minor damage to the right rear corner of his car. However, we had to wait for the police to arrive and fill out the required paperwork. Since this happened before there were cell phones, I asked a passing motorist to call the police from her workplace, which was a mile away.

As we waited, all I could think about was not getting to work early enough to be sure the assembly line was manned and ready to go. When the police arrived, I immediately asked the officer if he could radio his dispatch operator and have her call my boss to say I had been in an accident, would be late for work, and needed someone to cover for me. The policeman was surprised that this was my top concern. He accommodated my request and allowed me to speak with dispatch on his radio, providing the necessary information for her to make the call to my boss.

Completing the police report for this simple accident took nearly an hour. Finally, I was free to get in my car and drive to work. My only thoughts focused on the talk given the day before to my whole department about punctuality. Why did this accident have to happen to me on the very next day?

As I walked into the plant a half hour after the shift started and passed by my employees on the way to my foreman's desk, they began smiling and chanting, "It is very important to be on time! It is very important to be on time! It is very important to be on time!" Listening to my own words being parroted back to me, all I could do was nod my head in agreement with an apologetic look on my face.

I am convinced God has a wry sense of humor and sometimes arranges situations just to humble us and make us want to eat our words.

1. Be careful when correcting others; lessons in humility are often just around the corner

2. Let people who are expecting you know when you are running late.

Jig and Fixture

After working as a production foreman, I was given another challenge—to be the first woman maintenance foreman at the small truck plant. Being a foreman in production or quality was tough, but the macho culture of maintenance and the skilled trades during the early 1980s made being a maintenance foreman even more difficult.

I was assigned to supervise a group of skilled trades maintenance men in the Jig and Fixture Department. Their base station was a large fenced-in area in the plant, which was filled with all sorts of cutters, grinders, lathes, etc., that they used to fabricate or repair whatever was necessary to keep the production machines running. I not only was the first woman maintenance foreman—but also had a second stigma of being the first foreman in the department who had not previously worked as a machine repairman. How could this young woman, totally unfamiliar with their work, now be assigned as their boss? Such a thing had never been done before in maintenance, an organization that usually promoted its best hourly workers to the salaried foreman positions.

The guys in Jig and Fixture had their doubts about me, but they were not openly hostile, like some of the men I had worked with before. However, these men had another issue. The maintenance men from the other departments began to make fun of them, calling them sissies (and far worse!) for having a woman boss. As strong as I was tolerating abuse myself, my heart ached to see the people who worked for me being verbally abused on my account. The men said nothing in response to their colleagues' jeers. They just hung their heads in shame.

Their previous boss, an older man nearing retirement, had unexpectedly gone on an indefinite sick leave; so, it was unclear how long I would be in the foreman position. When I first met with the machine repairmen, they had been without a boss for several days. In the interim, the most senior guy was making out the daily work assignment schedule. He explained the rationale for making the assignments, which I decided to follow until getting to know the men better.

I informed the machine repairmen that having never worked in the Jig and Fixture Department, I did not have the same strengths their previous supervisor had. However, I did have my own strengths, plus a lot of experience working with different groups throughout the plant.

Looking around the work area, anyone could see it was a really depressing place to be—everything was dirty and dark. The walls had not been painted in many years, and a lot of the overhead light bulbs were burned out. My first order of business was to call the electrician foreman, with whom I had worked on a project six months earlier. I asked him to please send one of his men to replace the burned out bulbs in our area. It was not an emergency, but I would really appreciate it if he could put my request near the top of his work list.

Within two hours, an electrician was replacing light bulbs. The difference in the brightness of the area was startling. The men in my department were shocked. "Do you have any idea how long we have been asking our other boss to get some light in here, so we can see well enough to work? Maintenance always takes care of its own last. How did you get the work done so quickly?"

I replied, "I told you I have no maintenance experience, but I do have my own set of strengths. One of them is making things happen!"

The next step was getting the area painted—something I wanted to start within a week. Knowing the painters were coming soon, the men—without being told—each took some time to move things out of the way and throw out what they no longer needed.

The newly painted walls, coupled with the installed lights, and the men's cleanup made the place look like a million bucks. Now, as their buddies from other trades commented on how good their work area looked, I heard the men from my group reply, "I guess having a woman foreman has its advantages. Don't you wish you had one?"

Another milestone had been reached.

In between the physical improvements being made, I was meeting with each man to find out what sorts of assignments he liked and didn't like. I also asked what kind of new challenges or training he was interested in having. When I learned that much of their equipment didn't work, I asked why men who fixed the production equipment in the plant didn't fix their own equipment. They explained, "We've tried before to repair our equipment, but a lot of this stuff is pre-World War II. Some of the parts have been missing for years, and the manufacturers don't carry spare parts anymore."

I replied, "They may not carry the spare parts anymore, but I'll bet somewhere there are drawings of the equipment parts we need. If you had the drawings of the parts we need, do you think you could make them?"

"Don't know, but it would be worth a try," was their response.

What I really wanted was to get some new equipment. Asking to replace 40-year-old maintenance power tools seemed reasonable, but budget money was really tight. I would be able to pull some strings for a few things, but not for everything that was non-functioning.

Making an inventory of the equipment needing

parts—or at least the technical drawings of the parts—I started calling the manufacturers. I had a few successes, and my contacts agreed to send me the detailed parts drawings.

When the first part the guys fabricated for their 40-year-old equipment was installed, the machine started running. A "whoop of joy" exploded from the area that I will never forget.

1. Do not try to be a replica of your predecessor. Instead, focus on your own strengths to make a uniquely valuable contribution.

2. Make enhancements to your department's physical environment to send a strong positive message that things are noticeably improving.

When No One Needs Help

The day of my next promotion finally arrived with a 13 percent raise. As a senior reliability engineer at the medium-duty truck facility, I again faced a new plant and a new challenge. Presented with a pager, I was now on call to help any production foreman in the factory who had a quality problem that threatened to shut down the assembly line. My predecessor, who was moving to a new location, told me to introduce myself to every foreman in the factory.

Again, I was the first woman in this role in the plant. While this was old hat for me by now, it was a new experience and a big change for the men in this factory. Patience and persistence were the order of the day.

While my past experience as a production foreman was useful, in this plant there was additional complexity, which did not exist in the small truck plant where I had worked. Small trucks were commodities—customers ordered them from a limited number of option packages just as they did automobiles.

Medium-duty trucks were not commodities. While there were some standard option packages available, these big vehicles were generally used by a wide range of businesses, each having very specific needs. Essentially, an assembly line was being used to build custom vehicles—a truly challenging task. Buyers communicated to dealers the number of fuel tanks, the type of brake system, the specific features, etc., they wanted on their company trucks. The orders then went to options engineers, who customized the arrangement and location of each of the features and communicated this to the material order department and the production floor. Sometimes errors were made, and two different features were listed to occupy the same space on the truck frame. That's when someone would call my pager to resolve the issue and minimize the assembly line down time.

The first day on the job, my pager did not beep a single time. I walked up and down the assembly line talking with every foreman, receiving the same response, "I'll call you if I need you. Right now, everything's fine."

A second day went by, and there was still no pager beep. I continued to walk the line and familiarized myself with the files of prints and option configurations in preparation for a fast response. I wondered if there were really no problems occurring, or if the foremen just figured I didn't know enough to be able to help them.

On the third day, I was on the factory floor when the line stopped. Being close to the small commotion on the line, I went right to the problem area. The foreman was upset and, seeing me, said, "Building this truck is like putting five pounds of sh** in a one-pound bag. The options just won't fit."

I replied, "Let me see if I can figure this out. I'll check the paperwork, phone the options engineer, and then get with your repairman to get this truck finished before it leaves your department." I jotted down the job number and relevant information and zoomed down the aisle to the print reference office.

Between the two of us, the options engineer and I figured out a mounting configuration that would work. I was back on the line working with the repairman within a few minutes. The foreman was surprised, relieved, and grateful.

By the end of the day, my pager beeped two more times. By the end of the week, my pager was going off at a steady clip.

~ ~ ~ ~ ~

One day when I was discussing an issue with the Plant Manager's secretary, we saw the Plant Manager in his office listening to a heated discussion between two members of his staff—the Production Manager and the plant's Quality Director. The Quality Director was concerned about the daily quality audit numbers, and wanted to shut down the assembly line. The Production Manager was worried about meeting his production quotas and wanted to fix the quality issues in the repair stations at the end of the line. The Plant Manager said sternly, "Here's what we are going to do. I have decided to have you two switch jobs. Abe, (pointing to the Quality Director) you are now the Production Manager. Lou, (pointing to the Production Manager) you are now the Quality Director. Remember, I expect the two of you to work together in your new assignments and achieve the production quotas and the quality targets. I will send out the organizational change announcement immediately."

Abe and Lou both looked dumbfounded and started to protest. The Plant Manager quickly cut off their comments saying, "Both of you, get out of my office and back to the factory floor—now!"

The two men struggled in their new assignments, but the assembly line kept running. The new arrangement stayed in place for about two weeks, at which time the Plant Manager published another organizational change announcement putting both men back in their original job positions. Our production quotas and product quality numbers improved, and the two men got along better after that.

I guess the famous proverb is true: "Before you criticize a man, you must walk a mile in his shoes."

1. Use your skills to help people in trouble and you will soon become someone they want to have around.

2. Do another person's job, even temporarily, and you will understand the challenges and pressures he or she is experiencing—and become less critical of that individual's performance.

Professional Certifications

After accumulating four years of engineering experience, I became eligible to take Part 2 of the Professional Engineering Certification Exam. Passing this test would make me a state-licensed Professional Engineer (PE) in mechanical engineering. Studying for the exam would be difficult. Many degreed engineers took the state test multiple times without passing (just like some students who graduated with law degrees failed to pass the state bar exams). While some jobs required the Professional Engineering certification, most engineering jobs in the auto industry did not. However, engineers who got the license were often viewed as having initiative, professionalism, and a desire to go beyond meeting minimum requirements.

~~~~~

Thinking about the Professional Engineering Exam, I had a flashback to 1973, four years before working in the auto industry. At the time, Jon was studying to take Part 1 of the PE Exam in Mechanical Engineering. I was a stay-at-home mom taking care of Joe, who was only a few months old at the time. Barely recovered from a difficult emergency C-section associated with complications during his birth, I was already pregnant again. Seeing Jon studying, I looked over his shoulder to see what he was doing.

"I just can't figure out how to do this statics problem," he mumbled, frustrated.

"Here, let me take a look at it. Maybe I can help you." Showing him how to answer the question and looking at the other items on the sheet, I saw those also were problems I could solve.

Jon was grateful for the help and suggested, "Maybe you should try taking the PE Exam. It would be a lot more fun to study together than for me to study alone."

"Maybe you're right. I'm not working and have the time. I should at least look into it," I replied.

I applied and qualified to take the exam. Though I had no engineering degree, nor had I worked as an engineer yet, the review board determined my physics degree curriculum to be the equivalent of a mechanical engineering degree.

For several months, Jon and I studied diligently, going over problems and preparing to take the test. The day before the exam, Jon phoned after work and said:

"I just stopped by a store and saw a new hand-held device I heard guys in the office discussing. It's called a four-function calculator. You use it to add, subtract, multiply, and divide, instead of a slide rule. You just punch in the numbers and out comes the answer. I decided that getting one would really help me on the test tomorrow, so I bought one."

"How much did it cost?" I asked.

"One hundred dollars," he replied.

I went silent on the other end of the line. One hundred dollars was a lot of money for us in 1973, especially since I was home full time and we were living on one paycheck instead of two. With the price of gasoline at 29 cents a gallon, $100 was equal to nearly 350 gallons of gas! To spend so much money to do math problems when we both had perfectly good slide rules seemed absurd. However, I knew Jon was nervous about the test. For me, the PE exam was an interesting distraction from changing diapers. For him, it meant professionalism and status at work, so the test was something important to pass.

Even though every dollar-saving bone in my body wanted to object, I heard myself say after a long pause, "Okay, Jon, if it's important to you, I won't object."

"You won't? That's great! I am so happy. I know it will help me pass the PE exam. I'll pay for the calculator right now and be home soon."

"I thought you said you already bought it," I replied suspiciously.

"Well, I'm calling from the store. I told the sales clerk not to ring it up until I spoke with you. It's a big purchase and we usually discuss these sorts of things first. I really wanted to buy it, but hated the thought of having to return the calculator to the store later, if you objected. I figured if I told you I already bought it, there was at least some chance you would go along with it—and I was right!"

The next day a babysitter watched Joe, while Jon and I went to take the exam. Five hundred engineers were seated at numerous banquet tables in a large auditorium, with a dozen proctors roaming the room. Walking in more than six months pregnant, I received quite a few stares. Looking around the whole room I saw only two other women in the auditorium—and neither of them appeared to be pregnant.

On top of the table, Jon and I each arranged our respective technical reference books, which we were permitted to use during the test. Jon proudly displayed his brand new calculator, while the other engineers at our table and I pulled out our trusty slide rules. As the initial instructions were being given, I prayed:

"Dear God, please help Jon and me both pass this exam. If only one of us can pass it, please let it be him." I knew as progressive as Jon was, his ego would be shattered if I passed and he didn't.

We both passed the Part 1 Exam.

A year later, Jon qualified to take Part 2 of the Professional Engineering Exam and passed that as well.

~~~~~

Now it was 1981, and I had finally accumulated the necessary four years of engineering work experience to qualify for taking the Part 2 Exam. When I entered the large 500-person room to take the exam, I saw the total number of women taking the test had tripled in eight years—from three to nine. Everyone in the auditorium had a calculator—that cost a lot less than a hundred dollars apiece.

I passed Part 2 of the Professional Engineering Exam and received my license. The following year I took and passed national exams to become a Certified Quality Engineer and a Certified Reliability Engineer. I then joined some professional engineering and quality societies.

My resume was filling out nicely with both work experience and professional credentials. The children were doing well in elementary school, as well as in sports and music. Our whole family worked together to take care of the household chores, and Jon and I shared responsibility for carpooling Joe and Jean to their activities.

Life was good.

1. Get certifications and join professional societies to keep up-to-date and expand your career network.

2. Support your spouse who occasionally wants to buy something that is very important to him or her— even when your logical mind says it is too expensive and not necessary.

Electricity or Chemistry?

After we lived for four years in the same city, Jon was offered a new job opportunity—one that would require us to move again—this time to northeast Ohio. It had taken us a year to have our new home in Michigan built. We had spent the next three years doing our own landscaping and interior decorating, constructing a deck, and finishing the walkout basement.

The position Jon was offered was a developmental assignment projected to last eighteen months, at which time he would return to his current job location in Michigan. The housing market in our area was in the doldrums, so we knew we would incur a loss if we sold our house. Besides, we wanted to live in the custom home we had designed, once we returned to the area in a year and a half. With this in mind, we decided to get renters for our current Michigan home, and also find a house that our family could rent and live in temporarily in Ohio.

Once again I found myself in the position of looking for a job transfer, and my company had three other divisions in the new city. The first place I visited said business had slowed and they, as well as the second division, had recently done a series of layoffs. There were absolutely no job openings at the current time.

Fortunately, my husband spoke with a local acquaintance who provided the name of a director at the third division. This division made electrical components and might be looking for engineers. Instead of going through the Personnel Department, I felt moved to contact this director myself.

While we were in town for a house-hunting trip, I went to the electrical components division and told Security the name of the man I wanted to see. Security called the Director's secretary, who came down to the lobby to speak with me.

When I introduced myself, the secretary said, "I'm sorry, but I could not find an appointment for you on my boss's calendar. Why do you want to see him?"

"It's about a personal matter," I replied.

"I see. Follow me," she instructed, and then led me to the Director's office.

"Why don't you wait right here," she said, pointing to a chair near her desk. "Dan is in a meeting right now, but I'll check and see when he will be able to meet with you."

Two minutes later, Dan walked in, extended his hand, and said, "Good morning." Then taking a closer look at me, he said, "Do I know you?"

"No, we've never met. I'm Pat Schuch," I replied. I went on to say my husband was transferring to the area, and I was looking for an engineering job transfer as well. A look of total relief came over his face.

"When my secretary told me you had a personal matter to discuss with me, I didn't realize you were looking for a job. Come in and we can talk for a few minutes before my next meeting."

He looked over my resume, and we talked about my previous job assignments and the PE license I received in mechanical engineering the year before.

"The openings we have now are for electrical applications engineers. However, we sometimes take mechanical engineers and teach them the electrical engineering they need to know to do automotive wiring designs. Would you be interested in that?"

"I always welcome challenges and the opportunity to learn a new part of the automotive business," I replied enthusiastically. At the same time I was internally trying to put out of my mind the negative flashback I had. It was the face of my college electronics professor, whose class was the most unpleasant course of my life, due more to the professor than to the subject matter.

"I'll need to contact Personnel," he said, "and they will need to contact your current division. If everything is in order, we should be able to arrange for you to transfer here to an electrical applications engineering job. We'll be in touch."

I felt so blessed to be able to meet with this director without having an appointment—and then to get a job offer—especially after being turned down at the other division.

Later I learned that after speaking with me, the secretary had walked into the conference room, noting that the meeting the Director was having with his boss and some of his peers had just ended. She quietly said, "Dan, there's a young woman in your office who wants to discuss a personal matter with you. When would be the best time?" The other men in the room overheard her and began to laugh and chide Dan about this "personal matter," because of the reputation he had for being a "ladies' man." They and he had automatically assumed that the issue was much more intimate than a job interview request. Dan had promptly come back to his office to see me out of curiosity and concern.

I knew it was God who prompted me to tell the secretary it was a personal matter, rather than a job request—and, things worked out well, partially because I did.

Pearls from Pat

1. Be willing to step out of your comfort zone to find work, especially when your spouse is relocating, and jobs are in short supply.

2. Be kind to secretaries and administrative assistants—they can connect you with people you would never be able to see on your own.

3. Remember that while it is general practice to go through the Personnel Department (now called Human Resources) for job requests, it doesn't hurt to talk with someone on the inside as well.

The DWNDL Principle

On my first day in the Electrical Applications Engineering Department of the new division, I was introduced to a lead engineer named Ken. He was assigned as my technical mentor to teach me how to design automotive wiring systems. I was given a desk in a large "bull pen" of engineers, along with several short filing cabinets. These cabinets were filled with electrical diagrams and wiring harness prints for the vehicles that were now my technical responsibility. I was not sure who my predecessor was or where he went, but his old phone number was now mine. It was not long before my phone rang. The caller had a question about one of the luxury car wiring harnesses. I told him I was new on the job, would find out the answer to his question, and promised to call him right back.

I went to Ken, whose desk was nearby. Ken showed me how to pull the right print, study the drawing, and determine the answer to the question. I phoned the caller back with my response.

An hour later, a different person phoned, first requesting to speak with my predecessor, and then asking the exact same question the first caller had asked. I immediately gave him the answer.

"Wow, I'm impressed," he said. "First day on the job and you already know the design details!" He didn't realize that he had asked me the only question I could answer. I felt good anyway. This job was working out well.

Doing automotive wiring requires detailed design work to get the proper wire sizes and colors, terminals, connectors, and fusing while taking into account the myriad of electrical components in the system. Engineers go through careful validation and testing before finalizing designs, considering all of the possible option combinations, as well as the environmental conditions to which the wiring harnesses will be exposed. The last thing any engineer wants is to be responsible for a design error, which results in the possibility of something in the car not working properly.

On the rare occasion when a design flaw is discovered, there is a flurry of activity, especially if the issue is raised during vehicle pilot or production. Layers of engineering management hold review meetings. The engineer responsible for the part is involved in designing the fix, implementing it in the factory, and sometimes communicating information needed in the event of a recall. An old engineer made an interesting observation:

The best thing for your career around here is to be assigned to a vehicle having an electrical problem, which was designed by your predecessor. Then you get to be the hero, design the fix, go to all the meetings with the bigwigs, and explain how you are going to clean up the mess someone else made. The exposure you get is great, and a lot of the promotions made in the past have arisen from this sort of situation.

The second best thing for your career is to inadvertently make a design flaw yourself, and then do a good job cleaning up the mess. You still go through all the meetings with the bigwigs, and if you do a good job with the cleanup, they forgive you for the mistake and promote you because they now know you so well.

The worst thing you can do for your career is to turn out perfect designs, which create no issues. Since there is only time for bigwigs to talk about major problems, there is never time for them to discuss designs that work well, so the great engineers who do excellent designs get zero upper level exposure.

I was surprised at what the older engineer had told me. At first, it seemed a "sour grapes" attitude of one who had been passed over for promotion.

However, the more I thought about it, the more his observations seemed at least partially true, not only for Electrical Applications Engineering, but also for all the jobs I had worked both inside and outside the automotive industry. The heroes were those who could handle a crisis well—even if they personally had caused it.

Those individuals who were very proactive, who ran things so well that a crisis never happened, were generally taken for granted. They made a smooth running ship look easy, so they were not appreciated. Maybe it's a cultural thing. Could it be that when a mistake is made, Western culture rewards reactive behavior, while Eastern culture inflicts shame and public dishonor?

~ ~ ~ ~ ~

On the subject of errors, there was one morning when Stanley, the Director of Electrical Applications Engineering, held a department meeting for all the engineers and managers, and made a very memorable point. He was discussing the topic of PRNDLs. (Pronounced prindle, the acronym stands for Park, Reverse, Neutral, Drive, and Low, and refers to the gearshift mechanism on vehicles with automatic transmissions.)

Stanley said, "You all know what a PRNDL is. However, few people know what a DWNDL (pronounced dwindle) is. That is what I want to talk about today. DWNDL stands for Don't Write No Dumb Letters."

Stanley proceeded to explain the trouble caused because one young engineer had put into writing a question about the possible inadequacy of another engineer's design.

"The engineer who wrote the letter realized afterwards he had made a mistake, and his colleague's design was fine. However, the letter is still out there. The possibility exists that it could, at some future date, find itself in a court of law if any unrelated problem on the same vehicle ever arises. If you ever have a technical concern, please come and speak with your boss or me about it. Do not put the issue in writing."

The DWNDL principle is applicable to a lot of areas both personal and professional. I knew people who wrote angry or hurtful letters to colleagues or loved ones only to wish a day later they had never mailed the letter. Today in the Internet age, the DWNDL principle is even more important, given the ease with which emails—whether true or false—can be forwarded quickly to many people.

Pearls from Pat

1. Recognize, appreciate, and give positive exposure to those who do excellent work, instead of primarily paying attention to people who make mistakes.

2. Strive to be error-free in your work. If you do make a mistake, own up to it quickly and take steps to get the issue resolved with poise and efficiency.

3. Think carefully before you put something sensitive in writing.

To Coach or Not to Coach

Stanley, my boss's boss, was the head of the youth soccer program in the town where many of the managers and engineers lived. Because of this, Stanley often recruited people in his department as volunteers when he needed soccer coaches.

Periodically during lunch, there would be a huddle of engineers in Stanley's office discussing youth soccer. I never knew whether to envy the engineers for bonding with the executive or to think of them as suckers who had given in to the pressure of playing politics.

Then one day it happened—Stanley called *me* into his office during lunchtime. He said, "It's good to see you, Pat. I was just looking at the list of kids signed up for youth soccer, and I see there is a Joe Schuch and a Jean Schuch registered. Are those your kids?"

"Yes, Stanley, they are," I replied.

"That's great, because I see your daughter is in the nine- and ten-year-old girls' league, and I need both a coach and a league director for this age group. You would be perfect for the job."

My heart sank. I had never participated in sports as a kid. Reading, playing musical instruments, dancing, and acting had been my types of extra-curricular activities. Jon and I had encouraged both of our children to participate in all sorts of sports, including competitive swimming, soccer, and baseball, and Jon had been a little league baseball coach for Joe's team. My total youth sports participation had consisted of being the carpool driver, snack purveyor, and cheering spectator.

Now I stood silently before Stanley, feeling athletically inadequate and vividly remembering the pain I felt as a kid, always the last one chosen when teams were formed in gym class.

"Uh, Stanley, I have to tell you. I have never personally participated in any team sport in my life. My kids play soccer, but I don't even know all the rules. I would not be the best choice for a soccer coach."

Stanley replied, "Nonsense, Pat. If you're uneasy about some aspects of coaching, just get a parent or two to be your assistant coaches and help you with the practices and lineups. As for the league director job, that's just paperwork and phone calls—coordinating coaches' calendars, establishing teams, setting up game schedules, making field reservations, scheduling referees, that sort of thing. You're so organized, you could handle it in your sleep."

"Well, Stanley, it sounds like a big time commitment. Let me think it over and talk about it with my family tonight. I'll let you know tomorrow."

Stanley replied, "Okay. Just remember I really need your help with this, and I know you'd do a good job. I'll talk with you tomorrow."

Walking out of Stanley's office, I pondered the three key questions that have to be answered before accepting any job:

1. Am I capable of doing the job?
2. Do I want to do the job?
3. Could I take on this job without negatively impacting my other responsibilities?

Right then and there, my answer to all three questions was "I honestly don't know."

~~~~~

That evening, Jon and I sat down to talk through all of the issues.

The first issue bothering me was the pressure I felt to accept because of the positional power of the person who had asked me. I wondered about possible negative consequences to my career if I said, "No," and positive consequences to my career if I said, "Yes." On the other hand, I was not about to do this if it looked like I was sucking up to the big boss. I was angry with Stanley for making me feel uneasy, and I was angrier with myself for feeling uncomfortable.

Jon listened and then said, "Let's set aside the Stanley issue for a minute and pretend someone else from the soccer program had called and asked you to coach Jean's soccer team and be the director of the nine- and ten-year-old girls' soccer league. What issues would we have to discuss for you to make your decision?"

With this shift in focus, I went back to my three key questions. Question 1—Was I capable of doing the job? I suddenly had a flashback to my college years when I was the president of a group of kick-line dancers who performed at the half-time shows of the university's basketball games. Which was harder—leading a group of college girls doing synchronized kick-line formations, or coaching a bunch of nine- and ten-year-old girls to kick a ball down the field? The answer was clear—I had done one successfully; I could probably do the other one well. Naturally, I would have to learn the rules, research practice drills, and talk with some experienced coaches.

My confidence now restored, the answer to Question 1 was "Yes."

On to Question 2—Do I want the job? Both of the children were growing up so fast. Their athletic skill level was improving so much that there might never be another opportunity as good as this one for me to experience coaching one of their teams. My brothers had such wonderful memories of my dad being their little league coach for years. Jon had already been a little league coach for Joe's team. Suddenly I wanted to have that same type of memorable coaching experience for Jean and me.

The answer to Question 2 was "Yes."

Now for Question 3—Could I manage this job without negatively impacting my other responsibilities? That was a tough one. Our household was currently running pretty smoothly, with the children, Jon, and me each handling our share of the household chores and errands. Work was demanding, but I usually did not bring it home with me. I currently had no other outside volunteer commitments, and Jon's little league season was now over. Jon agreed to back me up at home as needed.

The answer to Question 3 was "Yes."

Then Jon said, "If you'd like to have me help you with the team, I'd be happy to be your assistant coach and learn about coaching soccer with you—maybe help out with the line-ups, or do whatever else you need. I think it would be fun for all of us. You would still have to do all of the league director work, but it sounds like most of that has to be done before the season starts."

We walked into the kitchen, where we found Jean finishing up her chores. Jon said, "Your mom has been asked to coach your soccer team this fall, and she's thinking about saying 'Yes.' What do you think?"

A big smile spread across Jean's face. "That would be great!" she said.

I knew now what to do—and the fact that the original request had come from Stanley was somehow completely irrelevant.

I took the job.

1. Do not respond on the spot when you have an important decision to make. Talk through the issue with a good listener before deciding.

2. Remember that when a person in power requests you to volunteer for an activity outside of work, ask yourself if you would do it if someone else had asked you.

3. Recruit subordinates for non-work activities only if you make it clear that their responses will have no impact on their careers—and mean it!

The Underdog

As the new volunteer soccer league director for the nine- and ten-year-old girls, I was now included in Stanley's occasional lunchtime soccer league huddle meetings. The directive to each of us in the room was brief and to the point: "Here are the names of kids and coaches for the teams from last year, as well as the list of kids and available coaches for this year. Meet with your coaches and set up this year's teams."

I was fine with being the only woman league director and the only woman coach in my league—it was just like most of my years of work with the company. And my first meeting with the coaches for the nine- and ten-year-old girls' teams went well. They were all returning coaches and had the first part of their rosters filled in with the names of girls whom they had coached the year before. Then we started filling in the rosters with the many new girls who had registered, trying to form the teams geographically by school. The coaches seemed satisfied with their final lists.

Noticing that I was the last to make my selections, one coach was quick to comment, "Pat, are you okay having your team with just three returning girls? We know your daughter is a good player, but having to coach so many new girls on your team will be a real challenge."

I replied, "If you coaches are all fine with your team rosters, I'm fine with mine. Besides, I believe youth soccer is all about the kids learning to do their very best, playing well together as a team, and having fun. If they can win a few games, well, so much the better."

A week later, I held a meeting for the parents of my team players. I explained my coaching philosophy and the importance of the girls arriving on time for practices and games. I then passed out sheets with the rules of soccer and encouraged the parents to help their girls learn about the game at home to reinforce what they would be learning at practice.

Even though Jon had already volunteered to be an assistant coach, I wanted a few more people to help out at practices, so we could work in smaller groups to teach the girls the basic skills they needed to play the game. Two dads volunteered to assist me in running the practices. One of the moms volunteered to coordinate snacks for the games. I was very pleased. The parents were getting excited and involved, which was going to help the team a lot.

After reading numerous books on practice drills for teaching basic soccer skills, I consulted with Jean and Joe. They told me about the drills their various past coaches had done that they found useful and/or fun. I incorporated them into my plans for the practices.

On the day of the first practice, I brought preprinted nametags for the girls plus the assistant coaches and myself. I knew from personal experience that people tend to shy away from interacting with individuals whose names they do not know or have forgotten. Splitting into two groups, the girls started kicking the ball to one another, each saying her own name and then the name of the girl to whom she was kicking: "Carrie to Jean," "Jean to Emily," "Emily to Allison," etc. We rearranged the groups and repeated the exercise two more times, until each girl had passed the ball to every teammate by name. Then we went on to do other drills.

Jean had, in previous years, primarily played left forward with lots of opportunity to score goals. We explained to her she would sometimes be playing defense and/or goalie this season. She would not get preferential treatment or extra playing time because she was the coach's daughter, and she was okay with that.

For the soccer games, Jon and I agreed that each of the girls needed to experience playing all of the positions. He drafted a line-up with equal playing times for which I would then suggest modifications or approve. When our first game was over, the girls were a little sad we had lost by one point. I was thrilled they had done as well as they had. I told them how proud I was at all they had learned in just two weeks of practices. We would continue to work hard, do our best, and have fun.

The next game was a tie. Again, I was pleased the girls had improved since the week before. After the game, the young referee came up to me and said he was feeling sick and had to go home. He could not ref the next two games as scheduled. Seeing he didn't look well, I told him I would take care of things. Jon had already left to take the kids to another commitment, so I would try to get another ref or ref the games myself.

I talked with the coaches for the game that was starting up and asked what they thought we should do. "Well, neither one of us should ref, but we would sure appreciate it if you would ref our game."

Acting as referee for that game and for the next one, I developed a real appreciation for the stress the refs are under having to stay extremely focused and make the right calls. I had only come to know the rules well myself for about two weeks, especially those involving "off sides" calls and corner kicks. Running up and down the field continuously for two games in a row was mentally challenging and physically stressful.

Then things got worse. The ref that was supposed to work the last two games didn't show up. Again, I talked with the coaches involved and decided to go ahead and keep acting as referee. There were no cell phones back then, and the games were so tightly scheduled that there was little time between games to try to get to a phone in a far away building to make other arrangements.

Finally at home later after coaching one game and refereeing four games in a row, I lay down on the bed. I had never been more exhausted in my life.

I planned to make sure a referee scheduling issue like this one never happened again on my watch.

~~~~~

The girls were learning how to handle the ball and move it down the field, but a few were still a little hesitant when they came face-to-face with a member of the other team. I thought of a principle I had always believed to be true: if you can do something unusually hard or really scary as an individual or as a team, then going back to doing normally challenging activities seems easy by comparison. (Jon utilized this principle while golfing, when he put weighted rings on his driver to take practice swings. After removing the weights, his driver felt light and he would tee off with ease.)

The girls needed to experience something more difficult than playing a game against another girls' team.

Then it came to me—how about playing a short practice scrimmage against a boys' team? This would be pretty scary for them, but once they learned from the experience, I was sure they would feel confident playing against any girls' team.

Approaching the coach of Joe's soccer team, I asked if my girls' team could scrimmage his nine- and ten-year-old boys' team, who practiced at the same time on an adjacent field. The coach thought the idea was a bit unusual, but agreed to do it.

At first, the girls were a bit intimidated. However, Jean assured them she had played against her brother before, and it was no big deal. I reinforced that they should just do their very best and pass the ball to open players as we had practiced. I knew overcoming fear and mastering the mental game was more important than mastering the physical game.

The scrimmage was difficult, but I could see many of the girls toughening up with determination and gritting their teeth as the playing progressed. A few of the girls made some faking moves, and were delighted as they evaded the boys who were their foes. We halted play after twenty minutes, and teams went back to their respective practices. Overall, the boys had been superior, but the girls had played with determination.

Compared to scrimmaging the boys' team, the next girls' team they faced did not look daunting at all. My team played with such resolve—they just refused to give up—and won the game!

As the season progressed, I was so proud of them. Their confidence increased, their ball handling skills improved, and their teamwork intensified as they each felt comfortable playing a variety of positions on the field. They were having fun.

The girls won every game for the rest of the season and then went on to win the league championship—not bad for an underdog soccer team whose female head coach had grown up being the last kid picked for every team in gym class.

~~~~~

Decades later, I was on the phone with Jean (who in high school was named "Athlete of the Year" lettering eleven times in four different sports, and as an adult ran a marathon in 3 hours, 11 minutes, 32 seconds). She was talking about coaching her own young daughter's soccer team and made a surprising comment to me:

"You know, Mom, when I think back to playing soccer as a kid, all of the coaches and all of the seasons kind of blend together. The only one that stands out is when you and Dad coached my soccer team. You made the big blue and white team banner, and we won the league championship. You gave each girl a certificate saying what she had done for the team that was special. It was really a memorable season."

Being deeply touched by what she said caused tears to well in my eyes. We said our goodbyes and, hanging up, I remembered my initial anger when my boss's boss pressured me—a non-athlete—to coach girls' soccer. I suddenly realized Stanley had done for me what I had done for the girls—challenged me to be more than I thought I could be.

More importantly, coaching Jean's soccer team provided our family with a season of treasured memories.

Thank you, Stanley.

1. Volunteer to help with your child's extracurricular interests. The time you spend together is invaluable.

2. Set up a mechanism for a new group of people to learn each other's names quickly to increase the team's comfort level and cohesiveness.

3. Have your team do a difficult exercise together. Facing normal challenges will then seem easier.

4. Assemble a coaching team that shares your core values and works well together to model the behavior you want the players to adopt.

On a Wing and a Prayer

As part of designing and validating wiring harnesses, electrical applications engineers traveled to the car assembly plants with prototype harnesses to make sure the lengths, routings, and functionality all worked on prototype cars. We made these customer visits flying there and back on the same day. The eight-passenger company plane, which transported us between Ohio and Michigan, was affectionately called the "puddle jumper," because our flight paths were generally over Lake Erie. There was no wall between the pilots and the passengers, so we observed everything the pilot and co-pilot did and said. These intimate flights so close to the instruments, where we could listen to the pilot lingo, really fueled my interest in flying. I decided to take lessons and get a pilot's license.

We lived only a few miles from a small airport, and when I signed up for flying lessons, Jon decided to join me. First we had a series of classes to attend and books to read. I was surprised at how much pilots had to learn. Besides knowing about the plane and the instrumentation, there was a new language to learn in order to communicate with the tower, protocols that had to be followed, weather patterns to comprehend, landmarks to watch for, and courses to chart.

When the time finally came for me to log some hours flying a plane with an instructor, I was thrilled. Even practicing coming out of a nosedive stall did not scare me. Instead, it provided me a sense of satisfaction to be able to return the plane to level flight. It was intriguing that pilots used the steering wheel to make turns in the air but had to use foot controls to make a plane go left or right while on the ground. I was like a sponge, learning everything possible, especially while in the air.

We had initially thought that learning to fly would save us money when it came to visiting out-of-town extended family members or going on vacations. It was not long before we discovered that flying small private planes is far more expensive than being a passenger on a commercial flight. The costs of renting or owning a plane coupled with the costs of fuel, airport charges, hanger charges, maintenance, and a host of other related expenses, made us rethink our whole endeavor. Jon and I realized we loved to fly, but not enough to make the financial sacrifices needed to continue. We stopped our flying lessons after a few months.

The first good reason to learn to fly a Cessna is because you love to do it. You are willing to pay whatever it costs to feel the sense of power and freedom you experience when you are piloting your own plane—at least in good weather. The second reason to take flying lessons is to understand what happens during airplane emergencies. Whenever watching one of those airplane disaster movies, I thought, "I want to know enough, so I could— with coaching—land a plane in an emergency."

Ironically, shortly after discontinuing flying lessons, I was a passenger on a flight that was not routine. I was doing some paperwork aboard the "puddle jumper," returning from a customer visit along with several other engineers. The weather had been overcast and foreboding when we left, but the pilots said they thought they could skirt the bad weather and get us home for dinner.

Because of my interest in flying, I always sat as close to the pilots as possible. On this stormy day, I was right behind the co-pilot, so I had a great diagonal view of the pilot's face. The storm unexpectedly shifted direction.

Instead of skirting the wind and rain, we were suddenly right in the middle of it.

I have often been on large planes when we encountered turbulence. The bumping and jostling is annoying and sometimes a bit scary. However, when you are in a very small plane in the middle of a big storm, it feels like the entire plane is literally going to be torn apart.

The pilot was doing his best to keep the plane on course and was perspiring profusely. Rain was pelting the windshield faster than the wipers could clear it. All of the engineers on board were perfectly quiet, some silently praying, while being tossed to and fro. My abdomen hurt from the barrage of jerking forces being applied by my seatbelt.

Many thoughts passed through my mind: my children and how much I wanted to see them grow up; Jon and how great a team we were, sharing the adventures of our life together; my parents and how upset they would be, if anything happened to me.

Through it all, however, I personally felt a sense of calm, reflecting back to being near death as a preschooler.

~~~~~

I vividly remembered being healed from meningococcal meningitis as a young child while lying alone in a hospital bed. I experienced a sense of overwhelming and all-encompassing love, and the powerfully peaceful presence of Jesus. Even at a young age, after that life-changing experience, I understood three things:

1. God has a special purpose for each of us, and He does not call us home until we have been given a chance to fulfill our purpose.

2. Once we understand the infinite, unconditional, and specific love God has for each one of us, we realize there is no reason ever to be afraid, for He is always with us.

3. When we have a relationship with God, we listen to His still, small voice within us, and experience peace during the course of our lives, no matter what happens around us.

~~~~~

The plane was getting closer to our destination airport, and the co-pilot shouted to us to brace for impact, remove any eyeglasses, and put our heads down while we held our knees. As I put my head down, I saw the runway approaching. The plane appeared to be coming in with the right wing lowered about 20 degrees, probably to offset the wind. I prayed the pilot would be able to control the plane well enough to have the wings level at the moment of touch down.

The landing was rough. We bounced several times. As the plane was brought under control and slowed to taxi to the gate, all of us aboard cheered and clapped, again and again, thankful to God and to the pilots, grateful to be on the ground in one piece. Looking at one another with a sense of shared relief, the pilot said to the co-pilot, "I hope I never have to fly through anything like that again."

In the terminal, each of the engineers went to find a pay phone. We had to call our loved ones and tell them that, though we were running late, we were safely on the ground and would be home for dinner. Because the weather on the ground in town was only moderately rainy, our families did not even realize there was a reason to be concerned. Only those of us who shared that flight knew how close we came to meeting our Maker that day.

1. *Take some flying lessons if you really want to appreciate all that pilots have to know to do their jobs.*

2. *Celebrate every day of your life, and live it as fully as if it were your last.*

3. *Consider this quote: "Be strong and courageous. Do not be frightened, and do not be dismayed, for the Lord your God is with you wherever you go" (Joshua 1:9).*

1988: Jean, Jon, Joe and Pat Schuch

PART II

ACCELERATING TO MIDDLE MANAGEMENT

(1983-1991)

The GMAT

Sometimes you meet people who are doing something which ignites a spark in you, making you think, "Gee, I'd really like to do that." Such was the case when I met a few smart, single people in their mid- or late twenties, who were heading off to Harvard Business School on a company-sponsored fellowship program.

The company awarded a limited number of fellowships each year for master's programs in engineering and business at specific prestigious schools—such as MIT, Harvard, and Stanford. The first step was to take the Graduate Management Admission Test (GMAT). The next step was to apply and get accepted at one of these top schools. With a university acceptance letter in hand, the last step was to fill out a form for a corporate fellowship.

Going to business school was not an early goal of mine. Science, engineering and technology were what excited me. However, after spending years in quality, manufacturing, and engineering, I repeatedly observed that money drove nearly every decision made in the corporation. Engineers seemed to be at the mercy of the business and financial people. Learning the language of business would help me communicate better with the company's decision makers.

The oldest of six children, I was born in Cleveland as the offspring of a die maker and a housewife, whose parents were all Polish immigrants. I was now 33 years old, married, with two children. Was there even a ghost of a chance of being accepted by a business school like Harvard? Everyone knew it was filled with privileged, rich kids—mainly single men, who had attended prep schools and graduated from Ivy League universities at the top of their classes.

It seemed like such a long shot. However, after talking with Jon, I decided it wouldn't hurt to take the GMAT and see how well I did. I bought a study book with sample tests to work on before the exam was held in October.

The day of the GMAT arrived and I had completed only part of one practice exam from the study book. Even without proper preparation, I hoped for a good outcome. In completing the preliminary personal information section, I confirmed Harvard, MIT, and Stanford as the schools to receive the test results. When the proctor said to begin, I proceeded through the multiple-choice exam, filling in the appropriate circles for the questions I could answer with certainty. For every question I couldn't answer, I narrowed the responses down to two choices, putting a small mark above the two possible answer circles. Reaching the end of the test booklet, I had two minutes left, and thirteen unanswered questions.

There was a guessing penalty on the GMAT. Correct answers were each given one point. Blank answers were given zero points. Wrong answers were given minus one-fourth of a point. It seemed better to leave an answer blank than to make a mistake. On the other hand, if out of every five uncertain questions, I answered one right and four wrong, I would break even. Nervously I prayed, "Dear God, if you want me to go to Harvard, please guide my hand and let me choose correctly."

Randomly selecting one from each pair of likely choices, I quickly filled in the answer circles without re-reading the remaining thirteen questions. Then I went back and erased my preliminary consideration marks,

eradicating the last one just as the ending buzzer sounded.

~~~~~

Weeks went by, and finally the GMAT mail arrived.
Remembering my prayer during the test, I gingerly
opened the envelope. The results were not what I had
expected.

Seeing my "99+ percentile" score, I felt overjoyed,
totally humbled, and completely in awe. It was God who
had guided my hand in answering those thirteen uncertain questions. With a GMAT number that high, my
chances of getting into Harvard had just increased significantly.

*1. Don't waste energy thinking about all of the rea-
sons why you will not reach your goal. Instead, take
the first step.*

*2. Believe: "With God, all things are possible" (Mat-
thew 19:26).*

Dual Career Synergy

Wanting to live in the Boston area, I was pleased to receive acceptance letters from both Harvard and MIT. If I was awarded a corporate fellowship, there was a factory outside of Boston Jon could transfer to while I worked on my degree.

Taking my Harvard acceptance letter and recommendations from my superiors (including Stanley), I applied for a corporate fellowship. When I went for an interview with the corporate fellowship committee, they said my GMAT score was the highest ever received in the company's history of reviewing fellowship applicants.

Several weeks later I was notified that I had received a corporate fellowship. According to the terms of the fellowship contract, I would be placed on a two-year educational leave. During this time, the company would pay for tuition, moving expenses, and half of my salary, which would cover most of my housing costs. During the summer between my first year and second year, I would work full time for my sponsoring division at full pay. I had to sign a legal document promising to remain with the company for at least two additional years after graduation or reimburse the company for all expenses associated with my degree.

After signing the fellowship agreement document, I sent my acceptance letter to Harvard. Jon and I celebrated. We were excited about the adventure awaiting the family in Boston. The next step was for Jon to secure a position at the company's Boston area facility.

For the past two years, Jon had been an energy facilities manager, running the corporation's energy supply division which handled the gas well drilling operations for a natural gas field located adjacent to the company's car assembly complex. This small division also arranged for the acquisition of natural gas and other fuels supplied to all of the corporation's U.S. plants.

Here came the snag. When Jon talked with the people at the Boston area facility, they said there were no manager level job openings. If he really wanted to transfer to Boston for two years, the only work available was designing a waste treatment facility, a job Jon had done ten years earlier. They would keep his pay at its current level, but responsibility-wise, this would be a demotion.

Jon was crushed.

By this time, we had been married twelve and a half years. Each time Jon had relocated to advance his career, I had been the "trailing spouse." However, I had always found a position equal to or better than what I had before. This time I would be moving, and Jon would be the "trailing spouse." This time, the work of the "trailing spouse" would not be equal to or better than before.

"Well, Jon," I said regretfully, "I can't let you take a big step backwards in your career. I will just notify the company and Harvard that I will not be using the fellowship. There is no way I am going to listen to you say, for the rest of my life, how you allowed your career to be ruined, so I could go to Harvard."

"Hold on a minute," said Jon. "There is no way I am going to listen to you say, for the rest of *my* life, how you sacrificed a Harvard fellowship for the sake of *my* career. We have to go to Boston."

We both stood there in silence. We had come so far in this long process, overcoming overwhelming odds. We just could not be defeated now. There had to be a win-win solution somewhere; there had to be alternatives to explore.

We began to brainstorm. After an hour of considering many different ideas—including Jon interviewing with other companies for a comparable position in Boston—we narrowed our focus to the following options:

Option A: Keep things as they are. Pat gives up the fellowship for now. Reapply next year if Jon can get a corporate manager job in Boston.

Option B: Move to Boston. Jon takes the facilities engineering job he was offered. Hope a manager position opens up soon at the Boston plant, and he returns to his current corporate manager responsibility status.

Option C: Have a commuting marriage and leave the kids in our current home with Jon. Pat flies home from Boston on weekends to be with the family.

Option D: Have a commuting marriage and have the kids move to Boston with Pat. Jon flies to Boston on weekends to be with the family.

Before we delved into the pros and cons of each option, we agreed that maintaining the integrity of our family was our highest priority. Options C and D were the best choices for both of our careers. Looking closely at those last two options, we realized C would have more problems than D, mainly because Jon's job required some travel. Since I would be in Boston, there would be no one to watch the children at night while he was out of town on business trips. Plus, I was unsure about my ability to travel home on weekends with the school workload I anticipated.

Option D seemed more doable. The kids would move to Boston with me, since I would not be doing any traveling while in school. Jon's work schedule could be arranged to accommodate frequent weekend flights to Boston. We hated to uproot the children again; however,

Joe and Jean had already demonstrated their ability to adapt well to new schools and towns, so this was not a major concern. Here was the bigger issue—could this commuting marriage arrangement be structured in such a way that the family relationships remained intact?

In 1984, I knew of no one who had a commuting marriage, so there was no one to advise us. We would have to figure this out on our own. In order for this separate living arrangement to work, Jon needed daily contact with the children. We planned to have him call Boston every day and talk with Joe for ten minutes, Jean for ten minutes, and me for ten minutes. If Jon did this and also spent two or three weekends each month in Boston, we would have a good chance of maintaining the strong family ties which were important to all of us.

Next, we had to look at our budget. The eighteen-month duration of Jon's "temporary" assignment at the gas field had already passed; Jon and his boss both preferred for him to stay in his present Ohio job assignment indefinitely. We still had a mortgage on the Spanish-style house we had built in Michigan, but the rent from the people living there covered that house's expenses.

Estimating plane fares, long distance phone charges, and the expensive Boston housing costs, we would not have enough money without making some drastic lifestyle changes. First, we could sell our new customized van and buy an inexpensive used car for me to drive in Boston. Second, since our current Ohio house lease was almost up, Jon could move into a much less expensive condo near his office. I'd rent the least expensive, small house I could find in a good school district close to the Harvard Business School campus.

We looked at each with hope. "Do you think this plan could work?" I asked tentatively.

"It sounds wild, and other people—especially our parents—will think we're nuts. But we've done crazy things before, and it's always worked out. Let's do it!" We kissed to seal the deal.

By working together synergistically, we had generated multiple alternatives, selected the best one, and then designed a strategy to strengthen our family, keep Jon's career on track, and achieve one of my goals. We believed we could develop a plan where each party got what he or she wanted, and we did it. It was not a compromise. I later found out Stephen Covey would call what we did "synergizing," or finding "the third alternative" (Covey, 1989, p. 284).

1. Find a way to support your spouse's dreams without totally sacrificing your own—both are important.

2. Create a third alternative based on your deepest values whenever you have a decision to make and you don't like the obvious alternatives.

3. Don't let other people's concerns weaken a decision you feel strongly about as a couple.

Harvard Business School

We executed our plan for a commuting marriage—and things turned out even better than we expected.

We found a small, furnished house to rent in Belmont, Massachusetts, a town with an excellent school system. It was close to public transportation, and about three miles from campus. Jon decided to buy a small condo in Ohio at a good price because the mortgage payments were actually less than rent. On moving day, everything was marked with one of three different colored stickers, indicating what went to Boston, what went to the Ohio condo, and what went into storage until the end of the Harvard adventure.

Arriving in Boston, I went to register for business school classes taking Joe and Jean with me. While we waited in the registration line, people made comments, assuming the children, ages eleven and ten, were registering for MBA classes. That a 34-year-old woman with middle-school aged children would be going to business school with a bunch of mostly 20-something single guys never occurred to anyone. It was easier to believe Joe and Jean were the business school students!

Every class at Harvard Business School was divided into nine sections, each with around 90 students, 25 percent of whom were women. After the first week of classes, each section held an election to select a section leader, called the Educational Representative or Ed Rep. This individual would attend council meetings, be a liaison between the section and the administration, and mediate class issues with professors. I was elected the Ed Rep for Section F, an honor that overwhelmed and humbled me, since I greatly respected the talent and intelligence of my section mates. People told me afterwards that the first two sentences of my brief speech differentiated me from my competitors and had gotten me elected. Four other candidates each told why he or she should be elected. Being the last one, I spoke from my heart something like this:

"After hearing all the other candidates speak, I believe you can not go wrong in voting for any of them. Each one has a wonderful background and would make a fine section leader." Surprised looks came across the faces of my competitors. Then I continued, "As a working mom with two children, I have a lot of experience juggling multiple responsibilities, and remembering what is most important in life. The one bit of experience I do have, which would prove useful to an Ed Rep, is I previously taught college physics classes in a 90-person tiered classroom much like this one. I can personally relate well to the professors, as well as to the students."

I was happy to be elected Ed Rep. Being a few years older than most of the rest of my classmates was an advantage. I believed that God wanted me here to help the people in this class.

Harvard Business School in 1984 was a boot camp intended to push people to their limits. High anxiety was the result of putting a room full of young adults—who were all among the top students in their high school and college graduating classes—into an academic environment based on too much work and a forced curve for grades. This was especially true for students who had never experienced, or had not learned how to handle, academic "failure"—i.e., getting a B or a C. At Harvard Business School, it was not enough to reach a set standard of excellence—you had to also perform better than your super-smart classmates. Even if everyone in the class did "A" work in a course, the professor was still re-quired to give the lowest nine A's (bottom 10 percent of the class) a grade of Low Pass (LP). Students who got too many LP's (or "Loops," as we called them) were dropped from the program. This grading system—coupled with the professors' procedure of "cold calling" random students to open class discussions with their prepared case analysis—contributed to the intimidating boot camp environment of the classroom.

Having children, I had a perspective on life priori-ties, and I worked to alleviate some classmates' fears and concerns about potential failure. Yes, Harvard Business School was important, but it needed to be understood for what it was—a learning adventure, not a life or death crisis situation. I viewed my classmates as extended family members, and invited those who did not already have plans, to celebrate Thanksgiving with the Schuch family at our home.

My classmates said I gave them a sense of hope dur-ing their dark moments of doubt. They saw me working to survive the curriculum, perform my Ed Rep duties, and still keep my sanity while caring for a house, a commuting husband, and two children in the sixth grade. They knew they had it easier by comparison, and had less reason to worry or complain. If Pat could do it, surely they could, too.

~ ~ ~ ~ ~ ~

At the time, there were very few computers in my company, so I was excited that our "Class of 1986" was the first at Harvard Business School to use computers for coursework. The equipment was called a "portable computer" only because it had a carrying handle. In real-ity, it was a large, heavy, elongated box that contained a very small screen, and was very difficult to move. Be-cause Joe and Jean had a computer class at their new middle school, they mastered the basics quickly and were able to help me learn how to use my new equip-ment.

Every evening Jon phoned, and spent ten minutes speaking with Joe, ten minutes with Jean, and ten to fifteen minutes with me. The results surprised us. We discovered that Jon knew more about the details of the children's lives while he lived 600 miles away, than he did when we were all together in the same house. He realized that he had not spent ten minutes of daily one-on-one time listening to Joe and Jean at home before our move to Boston.

Jon worked very long hours during the week, so he could leave his office in northeast Ohio at noon on Friday. He drove to Pittsburgh, flew to Boston via Newark on People Express Airlines, took three subway trains and a bus, and arrived Friday evening for dinner with the family. Jon stayed the weekend and then, early Monday morning, reversed the process, arriving at work shortly after noon. Some of Jon's most significant career accomplishments occurred during those two years of our commuting marriage. To complement the gas well drilling activities, he established a small group to run a natural gas brokering operation that was extremely profitable. Jon became recognized as a well-respected expert in the natural gas industry.

~~~~~

When Jon was in Boston, he attended Joe's middle school basketball practices and games. The second week of the season, the coach asked Jon if he would be the assistant coach for Joe's team. Jon explained he did not live in Belmont, and was only in town two or three weekends a month.

The coach replied, "I asked every other father to help, and they all turned me down. Our practices are on Saturdays and our games are on Sundays. If you would be willing to help me on the weekends when you're in town, that would be great!"

Jon agreed, and became the assistant coach for the boys' basketball team, and also led the team when the head coach was gone. He got to know many of the students at the middle school. When he walked down the streets of Belmont, Massachusetts, kids would wave and shout, "Hi, Coach Schuch!" bringing a smile to Jon's face.

Our first year in Boston went very well and our adventures brought the family closer together. The children and I adjusted to our respective schools and Jon's career flourished 600 miles away.

1. View working in an intimidating and competitive environment as a learning adventure—not a life or death situation.

2. Dialog with each of your children for at least ten minutes a day. What you learn will surprise you.

3. Understand that a commuting marriage can be a positive experience if you make communication a priority. Absence (and abstinence!) makes the heart grow fonder.

Three Mortgages

In between all the marathon study sessions, Harvard Business School held three or four formal social events throughout that first year; Jon purchased a used tuxedo to avoid repeated rental charges. We went skiing as a family and took some other wonderful weekend trips throughout New England, knowing that our time in Boston was passing quickly.

When spring came, I found myself thinking about houses in Belmont for the next school year. We had been notified that the house we were living in would be available to lease again the following year, but the rent would be increasing from $1300 per month to $1500 per month. Housing purchase prices in Belmont had increased 20% over the previous eight months from $150,000 to $180,000 in the neighborhood where we were renting. That was a lot of money for a small, 60-year-old, three-bedroom house with a one-car garage on a 50' x 100' lot. It looked like Boston area housing would continue to increase for the next few years.

It was crazy to think about buying a house in Belmont. We were strapped for money and already paying on two mortgages—the Spanish-style house we had built in Michigan and Jon's small condo in Ohio. Nobody in the MBA program even thought about buying a house while in school. Yet I found myself looking at the real estate section of the Sunday paper and even stopped by a few open houses to get a feel for the market.

Then an opportunity presented itself. It was time to sign up Joe and Jean for the spring season of Belmont little league baseball. I went with the children to the address listed on the registration form to drop off the paperwork and pay the application fees. Driving down the street looking for the designated house number, I was immediately enchanted by the neighborhood. After knocking on the door and handing the homeowner the little league registration form, I commented, "You live in a really great neighborhood! Are there any homes for sale nearby?"

He responded, "As a matter of fact, I heard that the house right across the street may be going on the market soon. If you're interested you may want to talk with the owner before she contacts a real estate agent."

I walked across the street, rang the doorbell and was greeted by a middle-aged woman and a barking dog. When I expressed my interest in buying a home in the area, especially after hearing that hers might be coming on the market soon, her face brightened. She had not yet contacted a realtor and was very interested in selling her home, so she could move to Cape Cod to start a bed and breakfast business. I made an appointment for the following day to see the house with our children and Jon, who would be back in Belmont by then.

Occasionally, Jon thought I had some crazy ideas. This time he was absolutely sure of it. What was wrong with me? I had always been ultraconservative, especially about money, never allowing our family to incur any kind of debt except a home mortgage. Now I was thinking about having not one, not two, but three mortgages? Well, there was no point in discussing it, because no bank would agree to such a thing. However, Jon did agree the Boston real estate market was experiencing a real boom, and it would not hurt to look at the house in the enchanting neighborhood.

It was immediately obvious that the three-bedroom, two-bathroom house needed a lot of work. The single mother of three had done practically no maintenance on the house since her divorce several years before, and her large dog had done some noticeable damage. Jon and I had lived in many places so we both saw the potential of this neglected house and its two-car garage, located in the wonderful neighborhood. We knew with a lot of our own work and a small amount of money, we could do wonders with the house. Joe and Jean really liked the home and were already choosing their bedrooms.

The still, small voice inside was guiding me to buy this house. After serious deliberation and a lot of number crunching, we determined we could tap into Jon's stock savings retirement plan money for a down payment. To make the mortgage payments, we would need to cut the food budget in half, bring the clothes budget and entertainment budget to near zero, and eliminate all non-essential spending. We thought we could survive being "house poor" for a year, but we knew the chance of getting a bank to give us a third mortgage was somewhere between slim and none. Together we prayed about this big decision and finally decided to go for it and leave the mortgage to God. If we did not get the mortgage, then we were not meant to get the house.

I got a copy of a real estate purchase agreement form and filling it out we made a low-ball offer contingent on getting financing. The owner countered with a higher offer, and we finally compromised on a price. Signed purchase agreement in hand, I was off to the bank in town offering the best interest rates on "jumbo mortgages" of $200,000. I said a prayer before entering the bank, "Dear God, if it is Your will that we buy this house, please move this bank to lend us the money."

After the loan officer received the information on our family income and the loan amount, he started to ask questions, which I quickly answered, as he wrote down some notes:

Did we have any outstanding debt? Yes.

Car loans? No.

What kind of outstanding debt—mortgages? Yes, two mortgages. I gave him the loan amounts and monthly payment figures for each.

Did we plan on selling either of the two properties we owned in the next few months? No.

Was there any other debt? No, just two mortgages.

He started shaking his head and began to say how he was sorry, but he just could not give us a third mortgage. Then he continued to ask questions.

Would the house be in both my name and my husband's name? Yes.

Why isn't Mr. Schuch here?

I explained how my husband worked 600 miles away and we were in a commuting marriage. This was making matters worse. He continued to shake his head.

Then came what turned out to be the magic words, "...and I am currently attending Harvard Business School." He stopped shaking his head. His demeanor immediately changed, and he said, "Did you say Harvard Business School? Well, then, I think we may be able to work something out for you."

I sat stunned as he left the room to confer with his boss. Once again something, which seemed to be highly unlikely, had just been made possible, all because we had followed the guidance of the still, small voice inside.

We got the mortgage.

~~~~~

In June, the children and I moved our things into storage, and drove back to reside in Jon's small condo in Ohio for a few months (along with my college-aged brother who lived with us while employed nearby for the summer). I worked full time for the company as an international marketing analyst for electrical components.

Two weeks before fall classes started, we drove back to Massachusetts with some extra furniture, and moved into the house in the enchanting neighborhood.

1. Pray often and listen to the small voice inside. You will be amazed at the extraordinary blessings you will receive.

2. Attend a university that is prestigious—or favored by a key decision maker—and you'll find doors opening which might otherwise be closed.

Finance 101

Hoping someday to have a very demanding auto executive job, it was important for me to practice having a happy work-life balance while still in the high-stress world of Harvard Business School. Essential to achieving that was living one day at a time and promoting certain family values. In our household we emphasized:

- The importance of God
- The importance of family
- The importance of good health
- The importance of service to others
- The importance of hard work
- The importance of education and learning
- The importance of wise financial choices

~~~~~

We had started teaching the children at an early age about financial responsibility. By the end of first grade, when Joe and Jean could add and subtract, I had given each of them a checkbook register. They used it to keep track of the cash they received as gifts and allowances, and to record how they spent it.

In second grade, when they had wanted to get their first video game (an Atari which cost over $100), Jon and I set up a special box for them to use as a savings bank for the video game. Every week after they received their allowances, they decided how much they each wanted to contribute to the Atari savings box. Jon and I would individually match the same amount. If Joe and Jean each contributed 50 cents, the money in the savings box increased by $3.00—i.e., $1.00 from the children and $1.00 from each of their parents. Money they received for Christmas and birthday gifts helped to accelerate the process. Still, it took months of sacrificing small purchases they would otherwise have made, in order to save for something important to both of them.

One day they finally had enough money to buy the Atari. I suggested that they shop around by phoning various stores to find the merchant with the lowest price. They looked up the phone numbers, made the calls, and wrote down the information they received. The children were surprised at how much the prices varied from store to store. At the least expensive retailer, they could buy not only the video game console, but also an additional game cartridge for the amount of money they had saved. Joe and Jean took their Atari savings box to the store and emptied its contents for the cashier to count. We took a picture of them proudly holding the game in the checkout line.

~~~~~

Four years later, we naturally discussed at a high level with Joe and Jean the financial sacrifices we needed to make for me to attend Harvard. Now, in our second year in Boston, we were going to buy a house, so they would be impacted by our increased belt-tightening.

We explained that just as they had been willing to sacrifice their normal purchases in order to buy the Atari game, we all had to sacrifice our normal purchases in order to buy this house. They were happy we were going to buy the bigger house in a nice neighborhood, but it meant they would not receive allowances for the next year. If they wanted any spending money, they would have to figure out how two seventh graders could earn it from sources outside of our household.

Jean had been babysitting for some neighbors the previous year and could do even more in this new neighborhood. Both children wanted money arriving weekly like their allowances had done. Their incomes needed to provide cash for a few small pleasures as well as savings for the bigger things they wanted, including college. (Jon and I told them they would each pay for a third of their college education, and we would pay for two-thirds, just like the Atari savings plan.)

Then they saw it—an ad in *The Boston Globe* saying newspaper carriers were needed. Excited, they both applied. Fortunately, they were both assigned newspaper routes adjacent to each other—and only a few blocks from where we lived.

Deciding to do both routes together before school, they each took one side of the street and worked out a system using a wagon to pull the papers during the week. Jon and I agreed one of us would drive on Sunday mornings so they could load the heavy Sunday papers in the open hatchback of our old car. They could both run behind the car pulling the newspapers out one at a time from the back and dashing to each customer's front porch for the delivery. They designed and printed their own homemade business cards on a computer, providing them to their customers who could then call Joe and Jean directly if there were any delivery issues.

During this year, the children learned to handle barking dogs, late-paying customers, and bad weather. When *The Boston Globe* held a contest to see which carriers could sign up the most new subscribers, Jean was one of the winners, and got an all-expense-paid trip to Disney World with the other high-subscribing carriers. Best of all, Joe and Jean had spending money to buy what they really wanted, and both added $1000 to their respective savings accounts from their earnings and tips. This was a real accomplishment for two seventh graders in 1986.

Our family ate a lot of macaroni and cheese that

year. We bought very little and found we were still as happy as ever. I worked hard on schoolwork during the week. On weekends, Jon and I did a lot of house cleaning, painting, and minor repair work. Ten months after we bought our home, we put it up for sale by owner, hosted one open house, received three offers, and sold it without a realtor for $123,000 more than we paid for it, netting $117,000 in profit after improvement expenses!

When I graduated, my extended family—my parents, five siblings, one brother-in-law, and three nieces—flew in from the Midwest. They saw me presented with a diploma plus the Harvard Business School Dean's Outstanding Service Award (engraved on an impressive pewter bowl). The Boston area plant that refused to give Jon a manager job was kind enough to loan me a 15-passenger company van to transport my entire immediate and extended family around Boston for three days, celebrating the blessings God had bestowed on us.

I received job offers from three different divisions in the company, and decided to accept a job assignment in Ohio near Jon's office. We sold at a profit both the Spanish-style home we had built in Michigan as well as Jon's condo, paying off those two remaining mortgages. Then we bought a nice home within walking distance of the middle school and high school in another wonderful Ohio community, midway between the plant and my parents' home—about 45 minutes drive from each. Making the large profit on the Belmont house near Boston enabled us to accomplish another one of our goals: to be mortgage-free homeowners by our fifteenth wedding anniversary.

Jon and I were determined not to pay another penny of interest for the rest of our lives.

1. Realize that how much money you have has nothing to do with how happy you are.

2. Reinforce the idea that financial choices have consequences. Good choices generally have good consequences.

3. Encourage young children to save money and pay part of the cost for expensive things they want.

The Angry Interview

In researching where to work after Harvard, I had done some exploratory interviews with companies outside the auto industry. Some job offers included signing bonuses large enough to reimburse my sponsoring company for my educational expenses. However, none of the companies had products that excited me like automobiles did. The reality was I liked working in the auto industry, so my job search started to focus on various divisions within my own company.

I interviewed with and received offers from some divisions doing innovative work that attracted MBAs. My most interesting interview, however, was at a traditional compact car assembly plant with a dynamic young plant manager named Harvey.

Following interviews with several older members of the Plant Manager's staff, I was now sitting in Harvey's office. He was about four years older than I was and had a winning combination of intelligence, ambition, and charisma. We reviewed my resume and discussed my education and work experience.

When he asked why someone with a Harvard MBA would interview at an automotive assembly plant complex, I responded that I found manufacturing to be extremely difficult and challenging. I believed I could make a difference.

Harvey explained how this was an exceptionally difficult plant, with few women in salaried positions, and none at the superintendent level. I replied that this was not a problem since I had frequently been the first woman in various facilities; the men generally changed their attitudes over time.

Then his line of questioning changed. Harvey started asking various questions about my husband's job. Specifically he asked, "Isn't there a chance Jon could be transferred out of the area sometime in the next few years?"

"Sure," I responded. "I suppose so. There's always a chance my husband could be presented with an opportunity out of state. That's true of anyone. I mean, you yourself could be transferred out of state within the next few years. Right?"

Still Harvey persisted. "Can you guarantee if I offered you a job here, your husband will not accept an opportunity to leave the area?"

Something inside of me snapped and my cordial, smiling, polite interview persona disappeared. Controlling the anger rising within me, I spoke in a very quiet and serious tone, saying, "Look, Harvey. I have one final thing to say. You can decide not to hire me because you don't think my personality will fit in with the culture here. You can decide not to hire me because you think a woman—any woman—can't cut it here. You can decide not to hire me because your production staff may fear a Harvard MBA could expect special treatment and fast promotions and that could adversely impact morale. However—you should never, ever decide not to hire me because of what future choices my husband might make."

We both stared at each other in silence for several long seconds. Then we both stood. The interview was over.

I left the room thinking I really blew that interview. Although I wanted that job more than any of the others, it didn't really matter to me anymore. I knew there would be consequences, but didn't regret my words.

Several days later, much to my surprise, Harvey called. He explained how he and the other members of his staff who had interviewed me, wanted to offer me a shift superintendent position. However, one staff member, who had not interviewed me, was opposed to the whole idea. I would need to speak with that director and convince him to accept me as part of the team.

I talked on the phone with the dissenting director named Zach, and he had two concerns: first, a woman superintendent might evoke a rebellion and/or be a distraction on the factory floor and thus adversely impact production and profits; second, a Harvard MBA might expect special treatment and annual promotions. By the end of our talk, Zach reluctantly agreed to go along with the rest of the plant manager's staff and support the job offer they wanted to extend to me.

Unlike my earlier advancements, getting a promotion to an assistant superintendent level was a very big deal. The job offer included a 29 percent raise and a long-awaited middle management perk—the use of a new company car for product evaluation purposes. The product evaluation program would provide me with a different vehicle every three months, as well as provide the gas, insurance, and vehicle maintenance. In exchange, I was required to do several evaluations on each car and quickly report any operational or quality issues that needed to be addressed. It had taken me nine years of hard work, but I had finally reached a significant degree of success, not only for myself, but also as a representative for all women in the automotive industry.

I took the job.

~~~~~

I had many adventures as a shift superintendent at that facility. However, one of the most memorable and touching moments occurred some months later at Zach's retirement party. As I shook his hand and wished him well in his post-retirement endeavors, he said, "I am never wrong. However, though I hate to admit it, I was wrong about you. You know I opposed the Plant Manager when he wanted to bring you aboard. I have to say you turned out to be an excellent shift superintendent; you have made a real contribution to our operations here."

Looking into his eyes, I glimpsed a man who seemed to have a rare need to ease his conscience on this, the last day he would ever see me. I replied, "Thank you for sharing that with me, Zach. Coming from you, it really means a lot."

Over the years, I have been the catalyst to change many men's attitudes about women. To this day, no one's words ever surprised or touched me as deeply as Zach's did that day.

1. Let people know you're angry when it's appropriate. However, control the way you express your anger.

2. Realize that the people who oppose you the most initially can end up being your biggest supporters.

Being Second

After a brief plant orientation period, I was told to report to the Body Shop superintendent named Burt. He planned to teach me everything I needed to know before turning me loose to run the Body Shop on second shift.

Burt was a pleasant, hands-on guy, who could fix any non-functioning welding equipment as fast as the machine repairmen assigned to do the job. I soon discovered Burt was fine with having a woman as a shift superintendent. He quickly explained that he had a talented wife, and a smart daughter who was studying to be a doctor. He fully understood how capable women could be and was a real believer in equality of the sexes.

Burt cautioned, however, that I had to be aware of what I was walking into in this facility. He explained:

> *First, there is a female plant engineer, who is married to a man who is also a plant engineer. She is viewed as somewhat unprofessional, because every time she has a fight with her husband, she removes the nameplate on her desk displaying her married name and replaces it with her old one showing her maiden name.*

> *Second, there was a woman in the plant several years ago who had been promoted from foreman to general foreman. Her performance had been adequate as a foreman, but*

as a general foreman, she ran into all sorts of problems. The men resented her promotion, because she was viewed as inferior to the other candidates. She was prone to screaming sessions on the floor, and there were a host of other issues.

I hate to tell you this, Pat, but there is one thing harder than being the first woman superintendent in the plant. It is being the second woman in a supervisory position, when the first one did not perform well. Besides proving yourself, you are going to have to overcome her negative legacy.

Burt's words shook me with their importance. It had been years since I had thought about what it would be like to be the second woman in an area, where the first one had provided the employees with a negative experience. This last consideration happened when I decided to marry Jon and turned down a job offer to be the first woman sales engineer at a welding equipment company. Industrial companies were concerned about hiring women who might get married, have babies and then quit working. I definitely intended to do all those things—and, I did not want to establish a negative precedent making it harder for a second woman engineer to get a job at the company.

Instead, I had taken a job teaching middle school physical science, being very upfront during the interviews about my intention to only work for a year or two. I had made a conscious decision not to start working in corporate America until after my children were old enough for me to work continuously with no plans of quitting or taking extended leaves.

Now I began to wonder about the women who had come after me at the various automotive facilities over the years. Did they have an easier time because of the path I made for them? Did any of them have a harder time because of any mistakes I might have made? The woman general foreman who did not perform well at this plant probably did not know her issues could make a problem years later for me—someone she had never even met. Maybe she learned from her mistakes and went somewhere else and did very well, or, maybe she moved on and did not do well, again creating issues for her female successors.

We don't fully know what legacy—whether positive or negative, helpful or hurtful—we leave behind. This is especially true when you are the first of your kind to do something.

1. Attempt to make things easier for those who come after you, especially when you are the first of your kind in an area.

2. Understand that the only thing harder than being the first is being the second—when the first one did not perform well.

The Body Shop

"Grueling" was the best word to describe my job as a second shift Body Shop superintendent. Hourly workers, maneuvering large D-shaped weld guns on balancers, did most of the welding required to assemble the sheet metal on automobiles. Sparks flew everywhere and a pungent burning smell filled the air. I quickly learned that weld sparks burn tiny pinholes into clothing, especially the shoulder areas of shirts. Any sparks that still had some energy left after burning through your clothing would burn tiny brown dots into your skin. The good news was, by the time these sparks flew through the air and landed on you, they generally did not hurt. Protective goggles with side shields were required for anyone walking through the Body Shop, as a single flying spark hitting one's eyeball could do significant damage.

As the Body Shop second shift superintendent, I was responsible for 350 production people on the line, a few dozen skilled tradesmen, salaried supervisors and engineers—and eleven robots. The number of robots was slated to increase, as one by one they replaced operators doing the least desirable jobs on the assembly line.

Robots were a wonder to behold. They were accurate and efficient and reduced the number of welding operators needed. However, keeping robots running required highly skilled (and highly paid) maintenance repairmen with a sophisticated knowledge of electronics and programming techniques. This was new territory for our plant, and we only had a few maintenance men on each shift capable of doing this work.

Fortunately, I had a fine group of welder maintenance and production people working for me. While most were leery about working for a woman, only a few of them were really hard cases.

One such person was a general foreman named Carl, who reported directly to me. Carl was about ten years my senior and believed women served only one purpose—sex. Carl also had an unusual fetish when it came to women. I overheard him speaking with a group of men explaining that while hot babes were great, he personally preferred fat women, because they were more appreciative.

My relationship with Carl was a real challenge. I thought since I was thin, I would not be his type. I soon found out if fat women were not around, Carl would settle for thin ones. Talking with Carl was like walking through a minefield because, while he never said anything inappropriate to me, his eyes always looked like he was mentally undressing me.

I always kept the conversation focused on the job, directing his gaze to papers filled with production statistics, manpower issues, the equipment status, the quality sample checks, the number of jobs through the pay point, the size of the bank, and special orders expected on the line during the shift. As I got him more deeply engrossed in discussing work issues, the awkward sexually tinged gazes faded as his concentration on business topics increased. He was an excellent general foreman when his mind was not drifting to the subject of women. It would take Carl longer than the other guys to be reprogrammed to see me as a Body Shop professional first and a woman second. However, it had to happen. The department needed to run well, and it was going to take both of us working together and staying focused to make the improvements that were necessary.

During our initial conversation, Burt had explained that the Body Shop was a tough place to work. It was considered both the "armpit" of the assembly plant and the production bottleneck. Rather than increasing efficiency, the advent of sophisticated robots had increased Body Shop downtime in the short term. We often had to pay expensive overtime premiums to build up the Body Shop's depleted bank of production units needed to keep the rest of the plant running, and we wondered if the robots' benefits really outweighed the costs.

Second shift work gave real meaning to the saying, "It's hard to drain the swamp when you are up to your eyeballs in alligators." Every day was a fight for survival, and a struggle to keep the line running. It was hard to carve out time to do the proactive systems analysis needed to make significant production improvements.

While in my elevated office at lunchtime on one particularly tough night, I surveyed the Body Shop and recalled my wish many years before as a foreman in the Truck Plant. I imagined one day becoming a production superintendent—so I would have the power to make things happen. At the time, the superintendent was some important leader I never even saw. He was often quoted by my general foreman, but was far too busy to interact with production foremen.

Coming back to the present, my wish had come true; now I was a superintendent. Unfortunately, I didn't feel like a powerful leader. In fact, I had the horrifying realization that I, personally, did not have the ability to control even the basic metrics like production counts and quality.

The only people who did were the production foremen and the people on the line! Why had no one explained to me when I was a foreman, how powerful I was, and how much my superintendent *needed me* to do my job well and get good numbers, so *he* could look good?

The impact of this "ah-ha" moment surprised me. Could it be true that the higher up in the organization you go, the more dependent you are on the people under you to accomplish the work for which you are responsible? I felt as if I had stumbled upon some unspoken secret, some terrible truth no one in upper management wanted anyone to know—the big guys are totally dependent on the little guys.

In reality, the guys at the bottom are also dependent on the guys at the top, who do all the hiring, and firing, and assure the paychecks and health benefits keep coming. Intellectually, I know there is a balance, a symbiotic relationship, a mutual dependency existing between the top and the bottom of any organization.

However, the concept of mutual dependency is not talked about in hierarchical circles of power. In any organization governed by control, dependence of subordinates on superiors is emphasized; dependence of superiors on subordinates is a well-guarded secret.

Previously, I had been a leader in other kinds of organizations, both educational and non-profit, which successfully used a leadership methodology based on motivation and inspiration, rather than control. I had seen great results come from getting people to *want* to do their best, because they saw themselves as an important part of something meaningful—something more significant than their own individual desires. This type of inspirational leadership, combined with the communication of genuine appreciation for extraordinary individual and team contributions, was the style I wanted to use. I just did not know how the Body Shop organization would respond to the kind of cultural change this leadership style might produce.

Although a believer in the chain of command, I made it a point to speak every day with each of the foremen, as well as with the general foremen who were my direct reports. I did not provide the foremen with direction, since this was the job of their general foreman. However, I wanted to understand their problems, and know what each one needed to be able to improve performance and identify trends and common issues requiring system changes. I also tried to nod and make eye contact with all of the hourly welding operators and maintenance workers when walking through the area, stopping to talk briefly with anyone who waved me over to chat.

In December, I felt moved to do several things that had never been done before in the plant. First I designed a Christmas card that combined both a plant and religious theme. I made nearly 400 copies—one for every second shift salaried and hourly employee in the Body Shop. Following the verse were the words, "May God bless you and your family in the coming new year."

I personally signed each card, and said a specific prayer as I handwrote an employee name on each envelope. While doing all the handwriting at home, I set up a little assembly line—with Joe and Jean's willing assistance—to fold cards, stuff envelopes, and insert a candy cane in each. Bringing the cards in to the plant a few days before Christmas, I asked the foremen to distribute them later in the day, when they passed out the paychecks to their employees.

On the last day before Christmas break, I did a second unusual thing. I brought in my accordion, some song sheets, and several Santa hats. I asked the general foremen if any of them would be interested in strolling along the Body Shop assembly line with me during the annual Christmas potluck lunch buffet. They could sing the Christmas carols whose lyrics were on the song sheets, while I supplied the music on the accordion. I did not want anyone to feel pressured into participating in this unusual and potentially undignified performance. What a pleasant surprise it was when several of them enthusiastically volunteered, including Carl—who had a loud, wonderful, singing voice.

We all wore Santa hats and had a lot of fun, walking down the aisles of the Body Shop singing. People were laughing and joining in the carols as we went by. Years later, I ran into people who worked in the Body Shop for decades. They said it was the most memorable and spirited Christmas at work they ever experienced.

I have heard it said that people do not care how much you know, until they know how much you care. My department knew I cared about each one of them, and when I asked for their best work, they gave it.

1. Focus on behaving professionally and expecting others to do likewise, especially around men who view women as sex objects.

2. Remember that upper management needs those at the bottom of the hierarchy, as much as—or more than—those at the bottom need upper management.

3. Show the people who work for you that you care about them as individuals.

What the Cat Dragged In

Shortly before I became the Body Shop second shift superintendent, the entire plant made a transition from having regular production running five eight-hour days, Monday through Friday, to working four ten-hour days, Monday through Thursday. Under the new schedule, the Body Shop first shift ran from 6:00 a.m. to 4:00 p.m., while the second shift operated from 4:30 p.m. to 2:30 a.m., four days a week.

The bad news was I was not at home in the evenings Monday through Thursday. On those days, my only face-to-face contact with Jon and the children was in the mornings, before they left for work and school. The good news was I had off from 2:30 a.m. Friday morning until 4:30 p.m. Monday afternoon. This was a nice block of time for family, trips, projects, chores, etc. In reality, I generally slept all day on Fridays until the kids came home from school, to compensate for insufficient sleep during the workweek.

Second shift had a big advantage—a near zero amount of meetings, visitors, politics, and upper level red tape. The planning and production strategies were determined during the day by the Plant Manager, the Production Manager and the Area Superintendents. Second shift superintendents were expected to simply run the line, achieve the quality and production targets, get the maintenance done, and leave the production unit banks between major areas filled for first shift.

On the downside, second shift had far less support. You couldn't phone a product engineer in the middle of the night with a design question, or call a supplier about an issue with his last shipment of parts. This all had to wait until day shift came in to do the follow-up. On second shift, you were on your own, having to deal with whatever came up, with the resources you had on hand. As a result, there was a special team ambiance and self-reliant attitude, focusing only on what was important, and leaving trivial matters to be handled by first shift.

My ten-hour workday, in reality, turned out to be twelve to fourteen hours. I was at work by 3:30 p.m. to review with the first shift superintendent any issues needing follow-up on second shift. I often did not leave the plant until 3:30-4:30 a.m. At the end of the shift, I wrote a log of what happened during the evening, and listed what equipment or parts issues needed to be understood or addressed when first shift started.

Instead of the Body Shop shift always ending at 2:30 a.m., overtime was often necessary to fill depleted banks. The conveyor between the Body Shop and the Paint Shop contained a bank or buffer of welded bodies. This bank would be reduced, if robot malfunctions or other causes of Body Shop downtime occurred during the shift. Because there was only 30 minutes between first and second shift—barely enough time to change some weld tips and do other mandatory daily maintenance—first shift couldn't fill significant depletions in the bank by working overtime. If they had a lot of downtime and left the bank very low, we were in a potential bottleneck situation. Having any significant downtime on second shift would end up shutting down the rest of the plant, jeopardizing overall plant production counts and profits. No matter how good or bad the state of the bank was at the start of my shift, it was my responsibility to work my department overtime to ensure the bank was full for the start of the 6 a.m. shift.

One night was especially difficult. I had spent quite a bit of time with maintenance after the shift ended, reviewing some equipment issues. By the time my log was finished, it was nearly 5 a.m. I was totally exhausted. Knowing Jon's alarm clock rang for him to get up at 5 a.m., I decided I had better call him before leaving the plant for my 45-minute commute home.

I heard his voice on the phone mumble, "Hello."

"Hi, it's me. I'm still at work. I knew you would be getting up now. I thought you might get worried if you turned in bed and saw I wasn't home yet."

"Why would I be worried?"

"Well, you know, I thought you might be concerned if I was not home at my usual time. Someone might have attacked me in the parking lot or something."

"Pat, have you ever taken a look in the mirror to see your appearance at the end of a shift? You usually look like something the cat just dragged in. Don't worry, no man in his right mind would want to attack you at the end of your shift; at the beginning of your shift, when you look cute and perky—maybe—but not at the end."

At first I was surprised by his comment and momentarily a little hurt by Jon's lack of concern. Then I turned and faced the glass panel window of my elevated office overlooking the Body Shop. Seeing the reflection of the tired, bedraggled face staring back at me, I started to laugh. "I see what you mean. Just so you know, I'm getting ready to head home now."

"See you then. Love you," Jon responded.

"Love you, too."

As I hung up the phone, the first shift superintendent entered the office. "What are you still doing here?" he asked in surprise as he started to take off his coat.

"Let's just say we had a rough night. I've got it all in the log, but since you're here now, I'll take a few minutes and give you the highlights of what we took care of and what you'll have to address right away."

At 6:10 a.m. I walked through the door at home just as Jon was picking up his briefcase to leave for work.

"Where were you? I expected you home twenty minutes ago," he said with a hint of concern.

"The first shift superintendent came in the office right after I hung up with you. I decided to tell him what was going on in case he had any questions."

"Why didn't you call me to say you would be late?"

"I thought you said you didn't worry about me when I was late."

"I said I didn't worry about some guy attacking you at the end of your shift. But I do worry about you getting hurt in the plant or being in an accident driving home. Next time, call, so I know what's going on."

"Okay."

He gave me a fast kiss and went into the garage. I smiled as Jon pulled his car out into the driveway and pushed the remote button to close the garage door.

Jon had just reaffirmed that he did care about what might happen to his wife—even if she did look like something the cat just dragged in.

Pearls from Pat

1. Focus on the positive aspects when you work second shift—such as the self-reliant culture with no formal meetings, visitors, or upper level interference.

2. Let the folks who love you know where you are at night, even if they seem not to worry about you.

Emotions

Six months after I started at the assembly plant, Harvey brought in another woman as a shift superintendent in a different area. He then moved me to the fabrication plant next door where the shift superintendent position was called an assistant area manager. Having succeeded in getting men at the assembly plant to accept having a woman shift superintendent, I now needed to do the same thing at this other plant. After running the Body Shop, I was familiar with—and hopefully could improve—the occasionally problematic deck lid, hood, and door assemblies made at the fabrication plant.

My first week there, at the start of a meeting with my peers and superiors from other departments, one area manager, named Vince, tried to provoke me. "You know, Pat, women really don't belong in a plant. Everyone knows they're just way too emotional." I simply smiled, not uttering a word. I was patient, knowing these men were having far more trouble adjusting to me, than I was having, adjusting to them.

Midway through the meeting, the issue of the plant's high scrap rate came up. Vince started banging his fist on the table and shouting with a red face, "the #^&*~%@ scrap rate is too high! What the #^&* are we going to do about it?" As the slew of profanity continued, I calmly said, "You know, Vince, men really don't belong in a plant. They're just way too emotional."

The room broke into laughter. With the tension dissipated, we got back to business formulating an action plan to address the scrap problem.

When things become tense, both men and women can get emotional. However, they manifest their emotions in different, culturally influenced ways. When men are angry, they tend to raise their voices and swear; women sometimes cry. The way both sexes are wired predisposes them to these respective responses, making them almost reflexive. The problem is that angry swearing is viewed as a sign of strength, while crying is viewed as a sign of weakness. This is a significant challenge for a woman in an authority position working in a macho culture environment. The only thing that counteracts these programmed responses is focused self-control.

I had an important personal unwritten rule: "Never, never, never let them see you cry." Here is where the breathing exercises from childbirth classes came in handy. Taking a deep breath—while simultaneously calling on God for strength and wisdom to respond calmly—was the approach I used to keep the infrequent tears at bay, at least until I got into my car to go home.

Sometimes women in all male environments try to imitate men. They condition themselves to yell and swear as a response to tension. In my opinion, this generally does not work as well as the calm, controlled approach; the latter demonstrates respect both for the one being spoken to, and for the speaker.

At the fabrication plant, I had an outstanding boss named Earl, who used to say, "People are like tea bags; they don't show their true colors until they're in hot water." When we really respect others and ourselves, we demonstrate respect even while we are under stress. Earl had an even temperament, was consistent and fair, and was the epitome of "an iron fist in a velvet glove." When he was angry, his eyes blazed, however, he kept his voice eerily calm and measured. People respected him and responded faster than they did to the yellers.

I learned a lot by observing Earl.

~ ~ ~ ~ ~

Over the years, I've come to realize that being the first woman requires a great deal of understanding, because the people you're working with are going through a grieving process—they have suffered a terrible loss of the status quo. This work-related grieving process has distinct steps, similar to the Kübler-Ross five stages of loss associated with death or divorce: Denial, Anger, Bargaining, Depression, and Acceptance (Kübler-Ross & Kessler, 2005, p. vii).

People who are the first of their kind in an area have to help their colleagues get through these stages as quickly as possible. It is important to know the adjustment period may vary from one day to many years. The more time the new person spends with colleagues, the more the colleagues become accustomed to the emerging reality. Finally, a state of acceptance is reached. Some people even move beyond acceptance—to *value* the differences that accompany the new normal.

This is how organizations evolve.

1. Accept that men and women have different ways of handling stress; both should exercise self-control.

2. Demonstrate respect for yourself and others when stressful situations occur, and neither swear nor cry.

3. Give people some time to grieve the loss of the status quo, which accompanied your arrival.

Who Has the Balls?

Having a woman in a middle management position was a big adjustment for the salaried people with whom I worked. It was an even bigger adjustment for the union officials. When hourly people did not like something their supervisor did—especially if some specific work rule had been violated—they called their union official, and he wrote a grievance. These grievances were collected, reviewed with lower management, and either settled or passed on to the next step of the review process. Eventually, the tough ones were delivered to me. If I couldn't settle them, they went to the next step or sometimes were set aside—to be used as bargaining chips in the next major contract negotiation.

There were all kinds of union committeemen. Some were good and decent and fair. They would defend their constituents when the complaints were valid and gently counsel them when their complaints were not. One such exceptionally ethical committeeman, named Larry, had thirteen children—all born to the same wife. Whenever someone asked Larry how his family was doing, he would answer, "With thirteen kids, it's statistically impossible for me to say 'Fine.' There's always at least one kid who is sick, in the hospital, recovering in a cast, or in some kind of trouble at school!"

Another interesting committeeman named Frank was secretly helpful to me. He gave me advice on how to guide the foremen and general foremen to handle certain difficult employees. He explained how sometimes he, as a committeeman, had to put on a show, and yell at management in defense of his people. However, he always worked things out behind the scenes in a way that would save face for all parties involved.

The plant's lead committeeman, Neil, was best described as a political animal. Fiercely defensive of all workers, even when they were completely wrong, he generated more grievance paperwork than everyone else combined. Neil also spoke very disparagingly about me.

Most of the people on the line were decent folks who just wanted to do their jobs and get paid. A few were troublemakers, who wanted to do less than a fair day's work. Some people expected to get paid, even when they knowingly produced defective parts that had to be scrapped. Union representatives liked their elected positions because they did not have to do any manual labor in the factory. They stayed in comfortable offices, until someone called wanting them to write a grievance.

Some union representatives believed it was their job to make the people who voted for them happy by keeping the daily production count requirements as low as possible. In auto assembly plants, the conveyor belt speed was set; everyone had to get the assigned work done within a window of about a minute per vehicle. Fabrication plants, on the other hand, made smaller parts on many short subassembly lines. Each line had a unique average hourly throughput requirement; this was determined by run capability of the various machines, the downtime needed for changing steel stock, the maintenance schedules, etc. In a given eight-hour shift, various lines in the fabrication plant might complete their scheduled work in seven hours—or even in as little as four hours. The people were then free to go to break areas, play cards, read books, etc. until it was time to clock out after their eight-hour shift. Committeemen were not tied to the line, but were required to be in their offices or in the plant for the entire shift.

Some people were tempted to leave the plant early, asking their buddies to illegally pick up their time cards and punch them out later at the official end of shift. This was considered fraud. People caught doing this were suspended without pay for several days. Generally, grievances were then written. If the evidence was not strong enough, it eventually got settled, and the employee was reimbursed for any lost pay.

One day, just such a thing occurred on second shift. One of the foremen working for me happened to be near the exit at quitting time. Observing a worker placing two separate time cards into the time clock, he went up and grabbed the punched time cards from the employee's hand before they were returned to the timecard rack. After putting the worker, whom he knew by name, "on notice," the foreman saw that the second time card belonged to the man's second shift committeeman, named Storm. The employee explained how his committeeman had asked him to do this favor for him today. Storm told the worker that he had people do this for him in the past, and nothing bad ever happened. He convinced the employee that no one would get into trouble, because "committeemen and their friends never get suspended."

Storm was known for unethical behavior and not highly regarded by many people in the plant. The foreman met with his general foreman, and then both of them met with me. Disciplining committeemen was rare and generally considered an unwise thing to do; they could generate a lot of written grievances and cause other trouble in retribution.

However, the foreman and general foreman were so fed up with the past behavior of this committeeman, that they wanted to discipline both him and the employee. They also wanted to be sure that I would stand behind them, and not cave in as the expected grievance went through the process. The suspensions would mean loss of pay, plus disqualify both men from the $500 year-end bonus for hourly worker perfect attendance.

The foremen and general foreman felt strongly that this unwritten assumption—that committeemen were above the rules—needed to be stopped. I agreed. Since the evidence was so compelling, this was a good case to use as an example for everyone. I discussed the situation with my boss and the Plant Manager when the first shift started, to ensure their concurrence with the suspension.

It took some convincing, but Earl and the Plant Manager agreed to support my decision to proceed with the discipline. They made it clear, however, that the monkey was on my back, and any complaints they received would be forwarded directly back to me. Storm was shocked at the suspensions. He immediately complained to his union buddies on first shift to try to fix things for him. The foreman had given the incident report to Labor Relations, with the detailed account of what happened. Other day shift committeemen ranted and raved, but the decision stood firm for the employee and the union rep—a three-day suspension with no pay, and the automatic forfeiture of the annual perfect attendance bonus.

I knew that this grievance could possibly get settled in the following year, when the contract talks heated up. Until that time, the discipline would be on the record. An example had been set for the whole plant, including all the committeemen.

A few days later, I came into my office at the start of the second shift, and found a small wrapped box sitting on my desk with a card. In the box was a sleeve of three shiny new golf balls, and a card with the following note:

"To our boss Pat—a person who has more balls than any man in this plant. Thanks for supporting us." The general foreman and all of the foremen had signed it.

My eyes started to dampen as I looked at the three golf balls. I had received many awards and honors in my life, but no tribute had ever touched me as deeply as this one did. Another milestone had been reached.

1. Learn to work well with union representatives.

2. Take a stand for the people who work for you, especially when they need your support for something they consider important.

3. Act to correct unacceptable behavior, especially when the evidence is incontrovertible.

Hugh Hefner vs.
the Boy Scouts

In the early days when the first women started working in plants, there were no such terms as "sexual harassment" or "political correctness." You quickly learned that if you wanted to work in a plant, you had to survive long enough in the culture that was there to be able to change it. If you really wanted to make things different, you had to be patient and exploit every opportunity to further your own agenda.

What exactly was my agenda? Well, I wanted to make the workplace a fair and ethical environment, free from ethnic jokes, foul language, and personal attacks of any kind. I wanted a workplace where people were judged by the quality of their performance, rather than by their gender, race, or ethnicity. I wanted people to work together to solve problems, to care about one another, and to enjoy coming to work, because they were reaching their full potential.

Okay, so maybe this vision was considered a tad bit unrealistic in those days. However, I relished every baby step of progress made towards this goal and recognized the chance for a major advance when I saw it.

Just such an opportunity happened one week after a bad incident occurred while I was working on first shift. I had received an intra-office mail envelope, which could have been sent by anyone—hourly or salaried—with this note attached:

"Pat, this picture was posted in the men's john all week. I thought you should know." It was unsigned. Attached to the note was a page torn from a *Playboy* magazine with a photo of a topless, well-endowed brunette, with her hair styled similar to mine. Her face was in a shadow, and hand-written across the bottom were the words, "Pat Schuch—Hubba, Hubba!"

The photo did look somewhat like me. The thought of that photo being posted in the men's restroom just made me sick. I was trying so hard to be an outstanding assistant area manager; some days, it just seemed I could not get past the "woman" thing. Tearing up the photo into a hundred tiny pieces, I decided to forget about it for the time being. There was nothing I could do. After all, the plant was filled with soft porn. If a skilled tradesman had a toolbox, chances were fifty-fifty that a semi-nude woman's photo from Hugh Hefner's *Playboy* magazine was taped inside. At various workstations along the subassembly lines, similar photos could be seen. The soft porn had always bothered me, but I had chosen not to fight that particular battle. I had other, more important issues to address. On this day, however, the issue had become personal.

I needed a plan.

Seven days later, an opportunity presented itself—a troop of Boy Scouts was coming to tour the plant. With this personal porn issue fresh in my mind, I went to talk with the Plant Manager. "I hear a Boy Scout troop is going to tour the plant next week. As you know, there is a lot of soft porn, plus some foul language graffiti throughout the plant. Maybe it would be a good idea for you to send out a memo to everyone. It could state that, because there is a Boy Scout tour of the plant next week, all inappropriate pictures and graffiti need to be removed from the plant. You could even mention doing a quick inspection the day before."

Although I had never complained about this issue before, the Plant Manager looked right through me, and said, "Those girlie calendars really bother you, eh?" When I did not respond right away, he continued, "I guess you're right, though. I wouldn't want any of those Boy Scouts telling their folks they saw something inappropriate displayed in my plant. I'll send out the memo."

The day before the Boy Scouts came, all of the graffiti, girlie calendars, and *Playboy* pictures were gone. The plant looked great. I quietly celebrated a small victory.

The day after the tour, some—but not all—of the pictures started showing up again.

Fortunately, two weeks later a junior high science class of both boys and girls wanted to tour the plant. Again a memo went out, and again the pictures disappeared. I overheard some men on the line commenting about how they liked having no girlie photos around. They wished it would stay this way permanently.

A few days after the science class tour, a much smaller number of photos were returned to their previous locations. Again, I celebrated a private victory.

Then came a new memo: because there would be periodic public plant tours in the future, it was important for the factory to maintain a professional environment at all times.

I'm sure the plant was never completely and permanently cleared of all girlie magazines. There were probably closed toolboxes and lockers somewhere that still had secret photo galleries. However, I continued to support the good public relations generated by the periodic public plant tours. I also celebrated the private victory that took place in that plant, in the days before people were instructed about the unacceptability of a concept called "sexual harassment."

As I saw it, it was Hugh Hefner versus the Boy Scouts—and the Boy Scouts won.

1. *Celebrate even small progress toward your goals.*

2. *Take action if you are personally attacked, to prevent others from experiencing what you have experienced.*

3. *Exploit a situation if it provides an opportunity to advance your agenda—even if it's only temporary.*

I Always Hear You

For several months, both shifts' production at the fabrication plant operated on an exhausting 58-hour workweek—ten hours a day Monday through Friday, and eight hours on Saturday. Foremen, general foremen, and hourly employees were paid time and a half for everything over eight hours daily, and double time on Saturdays; assistant area managers were required to work the same long hours, but were only paid their standard salary for a 40-hour week. As a result, during this period, the assistant area managers (including me) were the lowest paid employees in the plant.

Most days I worked through lunch or grabbed a bite of a sandwich brought from home. So when my mom invited me out to lunch on a Tuesday to celebrate my youngest sister's birthday, I checked my calendar, noted a 2 p.m. plant meeting, and readily agreed. Spending even a short time with two women I loved would be a refreshing break from working with men all week.

After informing my boss about my lunch plans, I went to my parking spot and got into my company-assigned sedan to leave the plant. Just then, Matt—the man responsible for delivering company cars to managers and executives—approached me. He said it was time for me to do a vehicle exchange. He had pulled up with my next vehicle, a shiny new blue cargo van with dark tinted windows. I was expected to drive the van for the next three months and formally evaluate its performance. Taking my few personal belongings out of the sedan, I moved them to the van, and handed Matt my car keys. Matt then gave me the keys to the new van. I got in, started the engine, and drove to the restaurant.

It was wonderful being with Mom and my sister, whom I had not seen in a while. We were all in a happy mood and thoroughly enjoyed our lunch together.

Looking at my watch, I said it was time to get back to work and we all walked out to the parking lot. Going up to the blue van, I put the key into the door lock, but it wouldn't turn. Puzzled, I went to the other doors; again, the key wouldn't turn. Seeing my dilemma, my sister took the key and also tried to unlock the van doors with no success, saying a prayer as she tried each one. She returned the key to me and the van remained locked.

My heart sank as I tried to come up with some logical explanation for my problem. During the trip to the restaurant, the ignition key had worked just fine. When I arrived at the restaurant, I had pressed the lock button on the inside of the door as I had exited the van, instead of using the door key. Maybe when Matt gave me the keys to the van, he had given me the correct ignition key but the wrong door key. Looking again at my watch, I tried to think what else could be done.

"Let's all pray together and ask God to unlock the door," my sister suggested. Desperate, we held hands and formed a circle next to the right sliding cargo door. The three of us said a short, earnest prayer, praising God, and asking Him to please unlock the van. Then I tried again. At first, the key behaved as before, unable to turn. Then, all of a sudden, the key turned and made an unlocking sound. As the side cargo door easily slid open, we were all happy and started dancing around! We were relieved and rejoicing because the door, which originally refused to open, now unlocked so quickly after our heartfelt group prayer.

Then I stopped and peered into the van—and my heart sank. There in the back were some items that didn't belong to me.

This was somebody else's vehicle.

Horrified, I pointed inside the van. "Those aren't my things!"

"What do you mean, those aren't your things? They *have* to be your things," said my sister.

"I'm telling you, this is not my van," I said. Then I quickly pushed down the lock button and pulled the sliding side door closed. Concerned that the van's actual owner would come out of the restaurant and see all of us fiddling with the vehicle, I urged everyone to move away immediately. We quickly stepped in front of the van and onto the sidewalk.

Looking around the parking lot, I suddenly saw it— an identical blue cargo van, located several parking spaces away. Running to the second van, I tried the key and it immediately unlocked the door. Checking inside, I confirmed that *this* van was definitely my vehicle.

Laughing and crying and shaking our heads, we all hugged one another, relieved and amazed at what had just happened. I got into the van and drove back to the fabrication plant for my meeting. As I drove, I suddenly had this image in my mind of Jesus laughing as he watched our facial expressions, especially when I looked into the first van and saw the unfamiliar items. Now that we no longer wanted what we had so earnestly prayed for, I found myself asking, "Why did You say, 'Yes,' to *this* prayer, when You knew it was stupid?"

Then it dawned on me. Jesus loves us so much. When He unlocked the van, He was essentially saying, "I want you to know that *I always hear you*—even when you pray for simple, unimportant, and sometimes stupid, things."

I have prayed for many important things during my life, and have frequently not received what I earnestly requested. When it came to prayer, I asked myself, "Why would God unlock a van that wasn't mine, but not save the life of someone dear to me?"

I was moved to reread the Bible story about King David when he was crying, fasting, and pleading with God to save his dying baby son (2 Samuel 12:14-23). After David spent seven days at home in constant prayer and fasting, the baby died. To everyone's surprise, David's calm response was to get up, eat something, and go to the temple to worship God. He accepted God's answer, even though it wasn't what he wanted. Time passed, and God gave King David another son—Solomon—who became known as one of the wisest men in history.

I have heard it said that God has three common responses to prayer: "Yes," "No," and "Wait, not now." However, I believe if we listen very closely, we will find when God doesn't say, "Yes," His most frequent response is this: "I hear you. I love you. I will give you something that will *eventually* turn out to be even better than what you requested. Keep praying and have faith."

1. Know that God always hears you when you pray.

2. Appreciate that when you don't get what you pray for, God may be doing what is ultimately best for you.

3. Reflect on this scripture verse: "And whatever things you ask in prayer, believing, you will receive" (Matthew 21:22).

Just Ask the Customer

Every factory has an Achilles heel—some product or station that is more problematic than all the rest. Our troublesome operation was the metal assembly door line. Manufacturing coupe and sedan doors—rights and lefts, fronts and rears—meant six different changeovers and set-ups to keep the assembly plant next door running smoothly.

Door assemblies are complicated. Besides joining inner and outer panels, and welding all the necessary structural reinforcements, doors have to meet tight dimensional specifications. Poor door fits mean water leaks and wind noise; both issues are very noticeable to the car owner.

I was a staunch advocate of high quality, and preached it all the time to the people who worked for me. Because of this, I found myself in a real dilemma when the skilled trades foreman responsible for changing over the door line contacted me. He could not tweak the production equipment to make a door that was within specification, despite hours of effort. Now there was less than three hours of just-in-time inventory of this particular door part number. If we did not start the line soon, we would cause the car assembly plant next door to shut down.

I went to the line to look at the sample door in the dimensional checking fixture. It was out of specification by one millimeter in the top rear corner. I did not want to deviate from my convictions and say, "Run the line," knowing the part was out of specification. However, I did not want to shut down the assembly plant, either.

One year earlier, I had been responsible for the Body Shop of the plant next door. I knew very well how doors were installed. There was a finessing tool similar to a rubber mallet, which a skilled operator sometimes used to make adjustments if an unusual stack-up of assembly tolerances kept the door from fitting properly, especially in the top rear corner. If I were still running the Body Shop, and someone called me with a choice, "Receive doors one millimeter out of specification in the top rear corner, or, don't receive doors and shut down the assembly plant," I knew what I would have said.

Turning to the skilled trades foreman and production foreman, I said, "I'm going to call our customer next door, explain our situation, and see what he says. If he says he will accept parts with the discrepancy, then we will run the line. If not, we'll keep working on it, and hope we get it right before too much assembly plant production is lost. Once we get through this crisis, we have to get some technical help to find out the root cause of our equipment adjustment problem."

We phoned my former colleague from a speakerphone in my office to find out what he wanted us to do. He said he would alert his operators that the parts were slightly out of specification in the top rear corner. They could make the adjustments needed to assure good door fits on the assembled cars. "Just put a tag on each rack of doors, noting the problem. Start up your line and keep those doors coming. I don't want to shut down the Body Shop over this issue—especially since we can adjust for it so easily here, and still deliver a quality vehicle."

My two foremen were stunned. One shook his head and said, "We never would have thought to call the customer. In the past, with other assistant area managers, we were told to just run the line with the parts not to spec and hope no one complains. But I guess if you're really serious about quality and you run into trouble, calling the customer is the only thing that makes sense."

I could not have said it better myself. After all, I used to be the customer.

1. Walk the talk and insist on meeting quality standards.

2. Put yourself in your customer's shoes whenever you are in doubt, and the right decision becomes more obvious.

Fifteen Minutes of Fame

It has been said we all get our fifteen minutes of fame. In my case it's true, because there were a few times when my photo appeared in the newspaper during my automotive career.

The first time was as part of a large cover article entitled "Dream Homes" in the Sunday supplement of a major newspaper in Michigan. There was a photo of Jon, six-year-old Joe, five-year-old Jean, and me, standing on the driveway in front of our brand new Spanish-style home, without any grass or landscaping. Reporters driving around new developments had chosen our custom home as one of several to include in the article. Because we had designed the house ourselves, they were especially interested in us. The article was nicely done.

The next two newspaper articles with my photo were work-related.

Shortly after starting work at the fabrication plant, I received a call from my childhood hometown newspaper. The reporter was doing a series of articles called "Finding the Whiz Kids." She was interviewing people who had been National Merit Scholarship Finalists from local high schools twenty years earlier, to see what they were doing now. She had contacted my parents, who had provided her with my married name and out-of-town phone number. Most of the former "Whiz Kids" she interviewed were accomplished professionals working in clean, quiet environments. Interviewing someone working in a factory would provide a nice contrast.

The young reporter, who made the long drive to the plant to interview me, had never been inside a manufacturing facility. She was surprised when I handed her safety glasses and earplugs. She was overwhelmed by the size of the plant's equipment, and especially surprised by the din on the factory floor.

"Doesn't the noise bother you?" she shouted while readjusting her earplugs.

"You get used to it," I replied. "Noise is good. It means the lines are running well. There's a rhythm to the plant that is almost like music. When things get quiet, we become concerned. It means something is wrong, and the issue has to be addressed right away."

She took some posed photos of me as we walked through the factory. Then I stopped briefly to speak with two foremen, who needed to update me about a problem. After the reporter talked with me for a few additional minutes, she spoke with my boss for five minutes, and left to make the long return drive to her office.

Three weeks later, a copy of the published article arrived in the mail. The first thing I noticed was the contrast in the "then" and "now" photos. The first was the senior year picture from my high school yearbook, where an optimistic, sixteen-year-old girl who had been voted "most likely to succeed" and "most well-rounded" smiled, wearing a pretty sweater. The second photo was a candid shot showing a profile view of a short woman, looking up, while talking with two tall men in front of some big equipment. She had an odd, serious expression and was wearing a plain shirt and pants, safety glasses with side shields, and a pager attached to her belt. In short, the photo was very unflattering. The article had some decent quotes, but understated my position, calling me the first woman supervisor in the plant. It didn't mention I was an assistant area manager responsible for more than 300 people.

~~~~~

My favorite news photo and article appeared on the first page of a section in the Sunday edition of the major newspaper in the city where we worked. The title was: "Fast Lane Families—Busy Couples and Children Find Time to Stay Together."

The photo showed Jon in a shirt and tie sitting on a chair behind his desk in his Energy Supply Division office. I was shown in a pants suit sitting on the corner of his desk. It looked like we had been casually chatting with each other, and had both just turned our heads to look and smile at the camera. This time, the caption under the photo *overstated* our positions:

"Jon and Pat Schuch both hold top management jobs while raising their son and daughter." (Jon and I actually held middle management positions.)

This article focused on the topic of work-life balance. In it, Jon and I talked about the two years we had spent in a commuting marriage, living 600 miles apart. We agreed our family life was much easier now, since we were all living in the same home. Even though our individual careers were demanding, we and the children (Joe, thirteen, and Jean, twelve) all had our own chores to do at home to keep things organized and running smoothly. The Fast Lane Families article had a concise concluding sentence: "Although there are sacrifices to be made, tight schedules to keep, and long days to endure, the Schuch family has made it work."

~~~~~

Jon's career was much more newsworthy than mine. Being the head of the company's Energy Supply Division had its pluses and minuses. The minus was it was not considered a "core business" of the company, because its operations were not automotive. On the plus side, because it was not a core business and because his supportive boss was located more than 200 miles away in Michigan, Jon could run the division without interference—as long as it continued to be profitable.

The Energy Supply Division had been established in 1975, when the country was plagued with historic energy curtailments. The corporation wanted to have its own supplies of natural gas to keep its factories running. In the past it had completely relied on local utility companies, who curtailed gas to industrial consumers when the supplies were limited. Now the company drilled gas wells on a well-situated plant site, and leased acreage from adjacent farmers and landowners for additional wells. The company could do more than supply its factories in the immediate area; it could put natural gas into the pipeline to benefit its remote factories as well.

While Jon was running the division with a staff of seven—plus ten field personnel—the number of operating gas wells increased to over 300, and his small division made more annual profit than the nearby car assembly plant employing more than 6000 workers. Jon had a real entrepreneurial spirit. This job enabled him to be an "intrapreneur"—an innovative entrepreneur operating semi-independently within the framework of a large corporation.

When natural gas became deregulated, Jon had an idea, which further propelled him into the energy industry spotlight. To supplement the natural gas obtained from company-owned wells, he developed a process to broker natural gas for the corporation. Buying supplies of natural gas from around the country at low prices, he then brokered deals with pipelines to transport it for low rates, resulting in tens of millions of dollars of annual savings in the corporation's natural gas costs!

Even the U.S. military heard about Jon's success. The Brigadier General responsible for all of the branches of the U.S. military services traveled to Jon's office to meet with him. The Brigadier General asked for Jon's advice on how the U.S. military could write and execute contracts with suppliers and pipeline companies to buy and transport natural gas to military bases and facilities across the country.

While well recognized in the energy industry, Jon was virtually invisible within our automotive company. He had limited promotional opportunities in a corporation focused on the core business of automobiles. However, Jon loved his job and enjoyed contributing significantly to the company's profitability.

Because the company used more natural gas than the quantities handled by many utility companies, Jon was treated like an energy industry executive and was frequently asked to speak at natural gas conferences at resorts around the country. A full-page color photo of Jon conversing with a pipeline executive appeared on the front cover of the pipeline company's annual report, which was distributed to all of its shareholders.

There was no doubt about it. Jon had his fifteen minutes of fame.

Pearls from Pat

1. Prepare for talking with a reporter by bringing some memorable sound bites, a written summary of your title and responsibilities, and a flattering photo.

2. Understand that members of the press are attracted by expertise and personal passion—and so are the people who select conference presenters.

3. Work in an area that is not part of your company's mainstream product focus, and you could end up with limited career options.

No Extensions

Enjoying opportunities to mentor people at work, both formally and informally, I was pleased to be assigned as the fifth year project advisor for a female co-op student assigned to our complex.

Nicole was working on a B.S. degree in electrical engineering, a five-year program at an out-of-state university. As a co-op student, she spent alternating terms going to school and working for the company. Nicole had done well at a variety of rotational assignments throughout the plant over the previous few years. Now she was doing her fifth year project on a new type of computer-controlled welding system our plant had under study.

Nicole had done a great job of overcoming the anti-women prejudices of the mostly middle-aged men who worked in welder maintenance. The men were having a difficult time adjusting to the increasing sophistication of the new computerized systems. I, for one, was glad to have a young person around like Nicole, who was quick to grasp the new technologies. The wiser men from the welder maintenance group were slowly realizing they had as much to learn from Nicole, as she had to learn from them. They informally established a synergistic quid pro quo, exchanging the wisdom of their work experience for her understanding of new computerized welding equipment programming techniques.

Nicole and I would meet every two or three weeks to discuss the progress of her fifth year project. She had completed the introductory research section of the paper and was part of the way through the data collection portion, when she surprised me with a special request.

"I have been having trouble collecting credible data, and I'm falling behind schedule in my project work. I would like to relieve some of the pressure I'm feeling right now, so I want to apply for an extension. If I spread the work out over an extra term, I think things will go much better, and my end product will be perfect."

I sat there for a full thirty seconds without speaking.

~~~~~

During this interlude, I was mentally transported back to my own college undergraduate days when I was several years younger than Nicole. I had been carrying a particularly heavy course load, and my biggest problem was one particular class—Advanced Thermodynamics. With two weeks left in the term, I was concerned about not being able to finish all the work in a good enough fashion to keep my grade point where I wanted it to be. Going to my professor, I asked for a one-month extension. He could give me a grade of incomplete, and change it a month later when I finished the work.

The professor looked across his desk at me, shaking his head. "Pat," he said, "In my experience, academic extensions seldom work. If I give you the extension, you will walk out of here with a sense of relief and temporarily slow down or discontinue your thermodynamics work. One month from now, you will find yourself in exactly the same position you are in today, only more stressed. I would like you to consider doing the best you can on this course with the time remaining in this term, take whatever grade you get, and then move on with your life. You need to strive for excellence, not perfection."

Instead of taking the professor's suggestion, I continued to persuade him how everything would be fine if he just gave me the extension. He finally agreed.

One month later I was in exactly the same position—only more stressed. In my own mind the completion standards were even higher, because of the granted extension. New courses and other responsibilities were vying for my time. I was getting behind in the new courses, as I tried to do the thermodynamics work from the previous term. In the end, my finished work was no better than it would have been a month earlier, and my new courses had suffered. My professor had been right.

~~~~~

Now, looking across the desk at Nicole, I finally opened my mouth, and said firmly, "No extensions."

She looked shocked. I had always been so supportive of her—a constant encourager and her advocate. This response from me was the last thing she expected.

"What do you mean, 'No extensions'? You *have* to give me an extension! I want this project to be great, and I just won't be able to finish it by the end of the term."

The professor's words from years ago came out of my mouth: "Nicole, in my experience, academic extensions seldom work. If I give you the extension, you will walk out of here with a sense of relief and temporarily slow down or discontinue your fifth year project work. Next term you will find yourself in exactly the same position you are in today, only more stressed. Consider doing the very best you can do on your project with the time remaining in this term, take whatever grade you get, and then move on with your life. You need to strive for excellence, not perfection."

Then I continued, "Nicole, by taking an extension, you will have to pay tuition for an extra term, and you won't be able to graduate with your class. I am confident you can do a terrific job completing your project and end up with results that will make us both proud. Instead of an extension, let's brainstorm how your supervisor and I can relieve you of other responsibilities. What additional plant resources can you draw on to finish your project? What line scheduling changes or extra manpower do you need for the data collection? How can we eliminate the distractions? Would doing some of the work on night shift make things easier? Do you need more quiet time at the library or at home to do the writing?"

By answering these questions, we began formulating a concentrated effort action plan.

Nicole did complete a splendid fifth year project on time. I was so proud of her. At the end of the term, she graduated with her class, and then started a good-paying full-time job—working for us.

The special words she spoke to me then still resound in my heart, "Pat, I am so glad you didn't give me that extension when I asked for it."

1. Avoid academic deadline extensions—they seldom work. Instead, do the best you can in the time you have, and move on with your life.

2. Aim for excellence. Insisting on perfection wastes time and you usually do not achieve it anyway.

3. Remember that sometimes the best way to help someone is to say, "No."

The Deming Way

Right before I graduated from Harvard and began working as a production shift superintendent at the assembly plant, the corporation underwent an organizational shift and eliminated all quality departments. Instead, all inspectors and quality engineers reported to their respective production area managers. Now, the pendulum swung back and the corporation decided to reestablish separate quality departments. During the earlier era, the person in charge of the department had been an executive, called the Plant Quality Director. The same job would now be a lower level position, called the Quality Manager.

The Plant Manager at the fabrication plant where I now worked approached me and asked if I would undertake the challenge of reestablishing the Quality Department for the metal fabrication plant. As the plant's Quality Manager, I would not get a raise, but would move up two reporting levels on the organization chart. Instead of reporting to my current boss—who reported to the Production Manager, who reported to the Plant Manager—I would report directly to the Plant Manager and be part of his staff.

This new opportunity and the leadership challenge of building a department with vision and drive excited me. I had always preferred starting up new organizations or processes, to stepping into preexisting ones. Years before while working in quality, I had been nationally licensed as a Certified Quality Engineer (CQE) and a Certified Reliability Engineer (CRE) by the American Society for Quality Control (ASQC). This new position would bring with it some significant additional training opportunities.

I took the job.

~~~~~

My boss sent me to the Institute for Productivity through Quality at the University of Tennessee in Knoxville. I would be in Tennessee for one week during each of the next three months. My classmates were quality, production, and plant managers from all over the country and from a myriad of industries, all focused on how to improve their company's product quality. It was fascinating that people from such diverse industries and plant sizes could have such similar problems. After the first week, I found myself looking forward to seeing my classmates again the following month. Each of us reported on the progress we made at our home plants implementing the principles learned in class.

In addition to the University of Tennessee program, I was sent to a four-day seminar conducted by Dr. W. Edwards Deming. I had long been a fan of the famous quality expert. At the age of 50, he had left a government census job to help industries improve their products using process control techniques. Initially ignored by companies in the U.S., Dr. Deming had traveled to and consulted in Japan. He was considered to be one of the main reasons the Japanese auto industry made significant quality improvements, resulting in their world market success. I looked forward to hearing his lectures.

Initially the sight of the 88-year old Dr. Deming surprised me. Because he had a great deal of difficulty walking, two beautiful young female associates escorted the famous quality guru to his chair on stage. As frail as he looked, his voice was strong and passionate. For four days, he talked about statistical process control, the importance of understanding a systems view of production quality, and the need for continuous improvement of the systems design and processes. During breaks, Dr. Deming autographed copies of his books purchased by seminar participants.

Waiting in line for him to sign my copy of his book *Out of the Crisis* (Deming, 1986), I carefully formulated the question I wanted him to answer. When it was my turn to be face-to-face with this living legend, I pulled out a camera and asked the person standing behind me to take a photograph of Dr. Deming and me. Overhearing this, the quality master grinned broadly and seemed pleased about the photo request. Then I asked him the question I had prepared, "Dr. Deming, out of all of the things you've taught us over the past four days, what is the most important thing you want me to remember?"

I expected him to reference one of his famous "Fourteen Points," or to elaborate on one specific aspect of statistical process control. Instead he paused for a moment, and then said these memorable words: "The most important thing for you to remember from my lessons this week is this—always find joy in your work!" To reinforce the point, he neatly wrote on the title page of the book he was autographing for me, "My best wishes to Pat. May she have joy in learning and joy in work. W. Edwards Deming 23 May 1989."

I thanked him and walked away, pondering his unexpected words. Here was an 88-year-old man who loved his work so much, who believed in the importance of his message so passionately, that it was a still a joy for him to teach the principles he espoused. Health issues, uncooperative joints, personal wealth—none of these were enough to stop his pursuit of happiness.

To this day, I am still inspired by Dr. Deming's quality concepts. However, even more inspired by the man who found joy in learning and in work, I often reflect on this most important concept.

Dr. Deming would be pleased.

1. Recognize that the fundamental issues of quality processes are amazingly common across a broad spectrum of products and industries.

*2. Realize that what you do for a living is not nearly as important as finding joy in doing it—whatever **it** is.*

3. Consider this scripture quote: "You will show me the path of life; in Your presence is fullness of joy; at Your right hand are pleasures forevermore" (Psalms 16:11).

Bumps in the Road

Jon and I had always worked well together on all of the big things in our lives—children, careers, relocations, balancing household responsibilities, etc. We both knew we were blessed to have no major issues in our marriage like addictions, infidelity, domestic violence, financial discord, etc. I also knew whenever I asked Jon to take on a home improvement project with me, he might grumble a bit—but he generally did what I requested, and he never stopped working until the project was completed. Likewise, I was always there to help him when his job presentations needed a review or when his home or community projects needed an extra hand.

Despite our mutual love and outstanding teamwork, frictions about little, everyday things surfaced several times a week. Within days after our wedding, Jon started reacting to my imperfections by yelling and cursing. He had never responded this way while we were dating or engaged. (This was especially difficult for me because I had never heard my father swear or complain.) Jon used profanity for a variety of reasons, such as when I didn't put his tools back in the proper location, or when he saw cobwebs in the corners, or when I asked him to move a newly planted shrub a foot to the left.

Most days I overlooked his harsh tone and comments, realizing the substance of his objections had some merit. Nevertheless, there was no justification for the unrelenting criticism and the bad language coming out of his mouth, and I sometimes verbally lashed back at him. I hated it when our children saw the two of us behaving badly, even though neither Jon nor I stayed upset or angry for long.

In the early years of our marriage, Jon and I had gone to couples counseling. The answers were simple, but not easy to implement: neither of us could change the other; we each had to change our own behaviors while being more tolerant of each other's shortcomings. Jon and I would make promises and progress—and then slip back to our old habitual actions.

One day when we had been married for nearly 18 years, Jon realized I had moved his comb and he couldn't find it. His typical loud verbal barrage followed. I found the comb and returned it; however, at that moment, something inside of my spirit broke. Every curse out of his mouth was an affront to the God I loved. The years of Jon's complaints seemed like a river slowly eroding the rock of my spirit and self-esteem. I felt like a grand, empty canyon.

Before Jon had proposed marriage, I had prayed for days, asking God for His guidance concerning this important decision. I was sure God wanted me to marry Jon, and I happily accepted his proposal when it came. If I was doing God's will for my life, how could He allow Jon to behave so badly?

In my completely broken state, I called out to God for help—and He finally answered me. "If you leave Jon, he will come to Me." After much prayer, I became more convinced that Jon and I needed some time apart.

The children were away from home for two weeks working as counselors at an academic summer camp for gifted children, so I decided to spend some time with my parents. I came home from work about 90 minutes before Jon was expected to arrive, and packed my suitcase. I quickly vacuumed and dusted the house, and left a note: "Jon, I'm going to stay with my parents for a while. I just can't take the complaining and cursing any more.

You should be happy—I left the house in perfect order. Enjoy your time alone. May God bless you. Love, Pat."

My parents' house was an hour and 20 minutes drive from my job, but the extra commute time was worth the peace of mind. My parents knew every marriage runs into rough patches and they were there to listen.

When Jon phoned, I briefly told him that things had to change. I needed time to think and so did he. I did not want to talk with him until he met a few times with a Christian counselor. He could call back then.

Jon sought out counseling from a minister in my sister's church located 35 minutes from our house. When Jon phoned me, he explained how inspiring the minister had been in his counseling sessions. We both knew we needed more than two weeks to address our issues, so Jon agreed to move to a place nearby temporarily so I could be home when the children returned from camp.

Jon and the minister continued to meet and pray together. The minister emphasized the importance of both spouses having the same order of priorities:

1. God
2. Spouse
3. Children
4. Extended Family
5. Work/Household Chores

Jon explained how his heart had been changed. He really understood how I was more important than our household aggravations and how God was even more important than I was. If Jon truly embraced the order of those priorities, he wouldn't swear or complain anymore. If I truly embraced the order of those priorities, I would change my habits to avoid doing the behaviors that annoyed Jon. We also discussed praying together regularly. ("A Gallup Poll in 1997 by the National Association of Marriage Enhancement showed the divorce rate among couples who pray together regularly is 1 out of 1152"— less than 0.1%!) (Smalley, 2008).

Three months later, we attended a church-sponsored marriage weekend retreat. After much praying and discussion, we finally understood and experienced God's presence in our marriage and both felt moved to live once again under the same roof. After that, things at home were much better—although not perfect. There were still a few bumps in the road from time to time. However, Jon and I knew as long as we both had God as our top priority, we would receive enough strength and grace every day to forgive each other and try again.

Marriage is a lifelong commitment between two imperfect people and a perfect God. It's not always easy, and it requires a lot of work.

It also helps if you both maintain your sense of humor. Comedian Rita Rudner explained it this way: "I love being married. It's so great to find that one special person you want to annoy for the rest of your life!"

1. Understand that even good marriages go through rough periods, especially when small, unresolved aggravations build up over time and cause a marital rift.

2. Remember that a period of separation can provide the time and space necessary for counseling, for reflection, for healing, and for spending time with God.

3. Ponder the husband-wife-God union: "A three-ply cord is not easily broken" (Ecclesiastes 4:12).

The Nine-Foot Razor Blade

While I was the Quality Manager at the fabrication plant, my responsibilities included a group of technicians, who manned the new, large, air-conditioned, high-tech, computer-controlled, metrology space known as the Coordinate Measuring Machine (CMM) Room. The technicians recorded three-dimensional coordinates of key points on the surfaces and perimeters of the metal parts manufactured at the plant, to assure they met the specifications. They had previously worked in the plant as inspectors, setting parts in mechanical fixtures and using gauges to take measurements. Now they were considered the prima donnas of the inspection world; they worked in a clean, temperature-controlled environment, running sophisticated computerized equipment only they and their supervisor knew how to operate.

Their supervisor was Vicky, a determined, intelligent, hard-working, beautiful young woman about twelve years my junior. Like me, she was one of the few salaried women in the plant. She viewed me as a mentor as well as a boss, often getting my views on how best to navigate the treacherous waters of the male-dominated plant environment.

On this particular day, Vicky came to me with a problem. We were ramping up the quantity of part numbers being checked in the CMM Room and it was time to add the extended van roof as one of the regulars. The problem was the CMM technicians were refusing to take measurements on this large component, considering it too unsafe to handle.

The extended van roof was an ominous metal part, nicknamed the "nine-foot razor blade" by the guys on the press line who manufactured it. As the part came off the line, two men—one on either side, wearing Kevlar gloves, arm coverings, and aprons—would lift the van roof from the press line conveyor belt, rotate it from a horizontal to a vertical position and then place it on a rack. The rack was specially designed with long pins at the top, which fit into holes in the forward edge flange of the roof part. The parts would hang from those pins, each succeeding part nesting vertically onto the preceding part.

Vicky explained, "Harry and Sam say they won't get an extended van roof part and bring it into the CMM room for a dimensional check. They think it's too difficult and unsafe to move such a large part. They've called for their committeeman and the union safety representative. How do you think I should handle this?"

After reflecting on the situation for a moment, I asked her, "Do you believe, as a supervisor, you should never ask the people who work for you to do something you are unwilling to do yourself?"

"Yes, I do," Vicky responded.

"So do I," I said. "One way to resolve this is for you and me to volunteer to demonstrate to the guys how to do the job safely. We could put on all the safety gear, remove an extended van roof from the rack, and put it on top of the largest parts cart we have. Then we could wheel it carefully down the aisle and into the CMM room without damaging the part. If two petite women, like you and me, do this in front of the committeeman and the safety rep, the male egos of Harry and Sam will make them stop complaining. After all, they're each over six foot tall and weigh more than 200 pounds. They definitely are physically stronger than we are."

"Do you think the two of us could actually lift and

rotate an extended van roof?" Vicky asked. "It's the biggest part in the plant!"

"I don't know for sure if we can or not. I do know in order to do this, we would both have to be very determined and would need to pray for divine assistance. The decision is yours to make. I'm only letting you know that this is one option you have as a last resort, if other negotiating fails. I'm here for you, if you need my help. If you decide to do this, remember the union would have to agree to permit us, as salaried employees, to handle the part, and do what is considered union work this one time."

The committeeman and the union safety representative had arrived, and were talking with Harry and Sam. Vicky left my office to be available once they were ready to talk with her. Fifteen minutes later she was back in my office.

"I tried talking with them to resolve the issue, but Harry and Sam are insisting they can't work with the extended van roofs. The union guys both backed them up. When I finally mentioned you and I were willing to demonstrate to them how to do it, they all started laughing. They readily agreed if we could do it, they would do it. 'I can hardly wait to see this. This ought to be good,' were their exact words."

"Okay then," I replied. "Let's say a prayer, and go do this. Remember, we have to smile while we're working. We have to make it look easy even if it takes every ounce of strength we have."

We rolled the largest part cart we had to the extended van roof press line, and donned the necessary cutproof Kevlar protective accessories. Then we discussed what we would do and pantomimed the motions several times to practice how we would lift the part from the rack pins, walk several paces, rotate it 90 degrees, and place it on the cart. We practiced the route we would take to move the cart that would hold the oversized part; we had to be sure nothing would be in the way on route to the CMM Room. Once we felt fully synchronized, Vicky and I were ready to start the process for real.

By this time, about a dozen hourly people had gathered to watch the show. The committeeman must have called his buddies in the union office because most of the onlookers were union representatives.

Vicky was 5'4" and weighed 110 pounds. I was 5'3" and weighed 120 pounds. Standing on either side of the van roof rack we felt dwarfed by the "nine-foot razor blade." We each pantomimed fully extending one arm to reach the six-foot mark and then moving the other arm out from our waists to reach the three-foot mark. Hopefully with these two handholds on both sides, the nine-foot part would be balanced as we moved and rotated it. We counted on the sharp edges being unable to penetrate the Kevlar gloves as we grabbed the part.

Vicky and I faced each other on either side of the vertical part rack, positioned our hands, and slightly lifted up a van roof from the two hanging support pins. Through her safety glasses, I could see Vicky's soft brown eyes open wide, as both of us felt the full brunt of the unsupported weight. It was heavier than we had expected. For an instant, our eyes met. Filled with prayer and determination, we felt the adrenaline rush we needed to lift the part completely off of the pins. Time slowed down; we were completely focused only on each other and the van roof. As planned, we smiled and took a few steps. Synchronizing our movements, we rotated the huge part 90 degrees to a horizontal position, slowly walked forward, and placed it on the part cart.

A momentary rush of relief rolled over us. Only then did we hear the applause. Harry and Sam were not clapping, but everyone else was, including the committeeman and union safety rep. We smiled at each other and winked, as if to say, "No big deal." However, we both knew it *had* been a big deal—and divine help had made it possible. Then as we had practiced, Vicky and I carefully moved the cart down the aisle and around the corner to the CMM Room entrance, and then safely through the doors.

After that, Harry and Sam never complained about doing CMM dimensional checks on extended van roofs.

1. Do not ask the people who work for you to do something you are unwilling to do yourself. Instead, lead by example.

2. Practice doing something difficult by mentally visualizing every detail of the process, walking through it in pantomime, and then actually doing it.

3. Reflect on this scripture verse: "He gives strength to the weary and increases the power of the weak" (Isaiah 40:29).

Influencing Design

In every plant, there are key metrics that provide manufacturing people daily feedback on how well they are performing. At the fabrication plant, those metrics included how many of each part were produced, how much scrap was generated, and what the quality audit score was.

The quality audit reviews were held in a centralized area called the Green Room. In addition to meeting all dimensional specifications, it was important to have good surface quality, especially on a finished Class A surface part (one very visible to the owner of the vehicle). The Green Room was the best place to view sheet metal parts due to the special green lights mounted on the ceiling and on the walls. This special lighting reflected off of the oil used to wipe down the parts and revealed any surface flaws. The quality auditors recorded all imperfections—such as low spots, splits, or dings—on important exterior parts such as doors, hoods, deck lids, quarter panels, etc.

The manufacturing supervisors, inspectors, tooling engineers, and upper management from the plant attended these reviews; a poor audit score was a source of embarrassment for everyone involved with the part. Sometimes there was shouting and cursing as defects, which were not visible under regular plant lighting, became obvious under the Green Room lights. Usually the people responsible huddled together, trying to decide what tooling adjustments should be made to correct the issue. Sometimes action plans were made to repair certain parts by "bumping out" depressions or sanding down surface roughness before shipping the parts to the assembly plant next door.

After one of these audit reviews, our plant's most experienced and talented tooling engineer stopped to talk with me. George was a big man possessing a slight German accent, white hair, and a firm handshake. He was considered a real craftsman and a master at figuring out how to finesse dies and tools to transform a flat piece of sheet metal into a stylized part. On this day, George was obviously frustrated.

"No matter what I do, certain parts are inherently problematic because of their surface design. Round gas tank openings present no problems, but square ones generally have lows in the corners; curved feature lines on body sides and doors are fine, but sharp feature lines inherently have splits; deck lids with shorter waterfalls (rear vertical surface from the top of the trunk to the bottom edge) are fine, but those with long waterfalls present problems. Why can't the car guys at Design Staff just give us a break and create cars with features we can manufacture easily?"

I looked at George with sympathy. He was right. I had once visited the corporation's Design Studios. Talented young designers were making bold sketches of new future concept cars and then turning their best drawings into full-scale clay models.

"George, you have to understand when the designers make models of these cars for the first time, they do it in clay. They can mold clay into any shape whatsoever. They have no idea how easy or difficult it will be to make the same car out of sheet metal. They don't think about how the car panels get shaped by going through a series of dies on a press line. Designers in Michigan have no idea their creations will cause a metal fabrication plant in Ohio so much grief for years. They are as separated from manufacturing as east is from west."

George replied, "I wish I could just speak with all of them for fifteen minutes and make them understand a few things. Increasing a radius just a little could have minimum impact on the appearance, however, it would have a huge positive impact on the quality, manufacturability, and cost of hundreds of thousands of vehicles produced each year."

Suddenly an idea began to form in my mind. "George, maybe you can do just that."

"What do you mean?" he asked.

Thinking aloud, I said, "Maybe we could make a short video of you describing problematic sheet metal part features right here in the Green Room. You could explain how simple design modifications could significantly improve the quality of manufactured cars. We can title the film, *World Class Quality Vehicles Begin With World Class Quality Design.* You have so much passion about this subject that you could easily speak from the heart, without even using a script. Ted does a lot of the presentation work for the Plant Manager. I'll bet he could videotape you and make any necessary edits. As the plant's Quality Manager, I can prepare a short introduction. Ted could use my voice over some brief film clips of the plant showing running press lines and metal assembly operations. Once the film is complete, I could arrange for you and me to make a trip to Michigan and meet with the designers. We'll show them the movie, answer their questions, and leave copies of the film for them to use as reference in the future. We could even prepare a one-page handout summarizing our recommended design tips for quality vehicles."

George's response was enthusiastic. "It's a wild idea, but I would be willing to give it a shot. Trying to do something sure beats standing around complaining. Do you think we could get through to them?"

"Well, designers don't like to have anything cramp their creativity, and some may respond negatively. However, I believe some would be grateful for the enlightenment our film and presentation would provide. Their understanding and awareness is key to any potential behavioral changes they make. At least it would be a powerful first step towards bridging the gap between design and manufacturing."

We began our little film project. It didn't take long to finish. Ted filmed George, who did a great job reviewing each of the problematic parts in the green room, articulating the issues and his recommendations. Ted took a few film clips of the outside of the plant and of operators handling parts on the press lines and metal assembly operations to provide the visual footage for my brief voice-over introduction. Very little editing was needed. The final version was about ten minutes long, however, it effectively conveyed all of the surface suggestions we wanted designers to consider.

When the film was completed, I showed it to the Plant Manager and the rest of his direct reports at a staff meeting. They loved the film. However, the Plant Manager was a little uncertain about how the corporate politics of the whole thing would play out. A couple of "plant rats" like George and me trying to tell the prima donna corporate Design Staff what not to do could turn out to be a real disaster. It could reflect poorly on our plant and the Plant Manager. We, as manufacturing, needed to know "our place" in the pecking order of perceived corporate importance.

Unabashed by the Plant Manager's hesitancy, I explained how a friend of mine in product engineering had provided me with the name of a design staff manager. I just wanted to call him about the film, and our willingness to speak with him and his designers. If they were interested, George and I would travel the 230 miles to see them. If they had no interest, we would drop the whole idea for now. Finally, the Plant Manager agreed, and gave me the go-ahead to make the call.

Two weeks later, George and I were standing in front

of a large group of designers and their managers from several of the studios. As expected, a few of the designers balked at some of the ideas presented in the movie, but most of them were intrigued by how simple design changes could result in vehicles manufactured with inherently higher quality. After the meeting, George and I walked through the Design Studios with their respective managers and designers and pointed out the clay model features that were good—and not so good—for manufacturing quality.

George and I returned to the plant in high spirits. We were even more pleased when we got feedback from the Plant Manager that his boss's boss had "heard good things" about our presentation to Design Staff.

We don't know how big an impact our particular project had on the manufacturability of future designs. However, we knew for certain we had made a step in the right direction. As George so aptly put it, "Trying to do something sure beats standing around complaining."

1. Relieve high levels of frustration by converting negative energy into positive action.

2. Communicate your concerns to the people who are creating the problem—you can't expect them to resolve an issue they don't know exists.

3. Be aware of—but do not be paralyzed by—the politics of your situation.

The New Plant Manager

The atmosphere in the fabrication plant was buzzing. A new plant manager was moving here to our Ohio location from Pennsylvania. People realized that the factory leader set the tone for the entire facility, so the secretary was nervous, the plant staff was nervous, and the union representatives were nervous. Everyone knew things would change—but no one knew exactly *how* they would change.

When Chuck arrived at the plant, he created a powerful first impression. He was 6' 6" tall, lean and strong, with long limbs, white hair, and a very pale complexion. Frowning, he looked stern, but when amused, his smile warmed the room. His penetrating eye-to-eye gaze seemed to peer into the very center of your soul. His appearance was just how I imagined the archangel Gabriel might look.

Cordial but serious, Chuck shook hands with everyone he met. He made it clear he would "eat lunch in the plant cafeteria every day from 12:00-12:30, come hell or high water." Anyone was welcome to join him. We later learned Chuck was a diabetic and a regular eating schedule was an important aspect of his life. Most of the salaried workers were accustomed to skipping lunch because of work issues, or generally grabbing a bite of a homemade sandwich or vending machine candy bar. The thought of sitting down and actually eating lunch for half an hour was completely foreign to us.

On the first Monday after Chuck came to our plant, he sent out an unusual memo. In an effort to get to know us quickly, he scheduled a two-hour meeting on Thursday starting at 9 a.m. During the meeting, he wanted each member of his new staff—and the people who directly reported to them—to prepare a presentation of five minutes or less, using no more than one or two slides to convey the following information:

- The presenter's name, education, and past work experience
- The presenter's job title, job responsibilities, and why his work was important to the plant
- One idea on what could be done to improve the plant

The assignment was a simple one. It involved writing down information each of us already knew about ourselves. Yet each of us spent every spare minute during the next three days writing and rewriting the bullet points on the two slides we were about to present. Having to articulate briefly why our work was important motivated each of us to step back from the routine of our daily tasks. We had to think about the essence of our work and its value to the plant as a whole.

Thursday arrived, and all of the invitees assembled in the large conference room. The plant manager's secretary—who was first to present her own two slides—manned a five-minute timer. When the timer dinged, the presenter had to stop speaking, even if in mid-sentence.

I sat there amazed by what I was learning as, one by one, people I had worked with for several years shared information about themselves and their jobs. Embarrassed by how little I knew concerning the vastness of everyone's past work experiences, I also realized the only familiar aspect of everyone else's job was the part that touched *my* responsibilities directly. When my turn came, I calmly went through my information, finishing right before the timer sounded. Later I heard other peoe were as surprised by my presentation, as I was by theirs.

After one hour and 55 minutes, twenty-three people had presented. Then the plant manager spent three minutes going through his two slides, one minute articulating his vision for the plant, and the last minute thanking us for providing him with such a complete picture of the plant, its people, and its operations. Promptly at 11 a.m. the meeting ended.

It was one of the most informative and interesting meetings of my life. I enthusiastically looked forward to learning everything our new leader had to teach us. Everyone knew then that things were definitely going to change—for the better.

Pearls from Pat

1. Consider having the members of your new team and the people who report to them present succinct overviews of their experience, their job responsibilities, the value they bring to the organization, and their ideas for improvement.

2. Don't assume just because people have worked together for years that they really know one another well.

3. Remember that the leader sets the tone for the entire organization and its culture.

The Core Team

After he had been the Plant Manager for a month, Chuck asked me to meet him in his office. Once I sat down, he began a long monolog:

I have a letter here from my boss in Michigan explaining how the corporation is starting a new concept for vehicle development, called a Core Team, beginning with the next generation of compact cars to be built in this complex. The team will meet one day a week at divisional headquarters in Michigan and will be led by an executive from product planning. Members of the team will include a manager from each of the main functional areas—design, engineering, metal fabrication, vehicle assembly, finance, personnel, marketing, material handling, etc. I have to select a person to be part of this new Core Team—someone knowledgeable about our plant operations—to represent our facility in these future product development meetings. This person has to be willing to travel and also assist me doing strategic planning and developing a five-year business plan for the plant.

For this reason I am establishing a new position called the "Future Product and Business Planning Administrator," which will re-

port directly to me. It will be the same pay
scale as a manager level position. With your
plant and engineering experience, MBA, and
personal passion for having manufacturing
priorities reflected in product design, you are
my first choice for the job.

Seeing me trying to process all he was saying, Chuck clarified: "The up side is it would provide you with a chance to get some corporate exposure outside of the plant and learn a lot about product design. The down side is you would be traveling every week to Michigan— 3½-4 hours each way, and would no longer have anyone reporting to you."

My head was spinning with the pros and cons of this new opportunity. I had spent nearly a year getting the new Quality Department up and running and the people were working well together as an effective, cohesive team. We had made outstanding progress in a very short time. Since graduating from Harvard, I had always managed sizable departments, the largest being nearly 400 people. To return to being an individual contributor would feel in some ways like a step backwards. However, the learning potential of being part of the corporation's first product development Core Team was very enticing.

"Chuck, this sounds like a really interesting position, and I'm glad you're offering it to me. Before responding, I really need some time to think through the implications this would have on my family, as well as on the Quality Department. Can you give me one or two days to talk it over with my husband, and then get back to you?"

Chuck agreed and then handed me a copy of the letter his boss had sent him, which explained the Core Team portion of the position.

Jon and I spent the whole evening going over the pros and cons of the new assignment. I was excited about the prospect of working with a product development team on the design of a brand new vehicle. The biggest issue was the weekly travel. Some weeks I might be able to drive to the engineering center, attend meetings for four to six hours, and then drive home the same day. Other weeks would require an overnight stay, with extra responsibility for taking care of the children and their activities falling on Jon. It also meant any business trips Jon had to make would need to be arranged around my schedule.

Jon was supportive, as usual. Then I talked with Joe and Jean. "We'll be fine, Mom. If you want the job, take it," was their response.

It was unclear whether this move would help or hurt my career. A small voice deep within me said to walk forward towards the unknown.

I took the job.

~~~~~

At my first Core Team meeting, I was filled with a sense of excitement. Looking around the room I saw I was, at least for the time being, the only woman. Caleb, the executive leading our team, was a young, intelligent, handsome, articulate man who possessed a good sense of humor and a firm handshake. He was also the first African-American company executive I had ever met.

African-Americans, like women, were slowly starting to ascend the corporate ladder. I'm sure Caleb was feeling the pressure that usually comes from being the first of his kind in an area. Fortunately, Caleb's boss was also his mentor, enthusiastically coaching him in the ways of being a successful corporate executive. It was important to Caleb, his boss, and the company that the next generation vehicle be a "home run." The new Core Team model presented a unique challenge as a structure to design, manufacture, and bring new cars to market.

Caleb did a great job of being a hard-working, dedicated leader who set an example of excellence for the entire team. When conflicts arose, he not only facilitated compromises, but also inspired the team to look for third alternatives, which were better than our original conflicting proposals.

Driving to and from the weekly meetings was quite a chore. A wide variety of audio books made the time spent in the car educational—a sort of "Automobile University." Attending the Core Team meetings, I learned about the other functional areas and the integrative design approach, which more than made up for the travel inconveniences. My contribution helped steer the group towards manufacturing-friendly options.

~~~~~

Most weeks, the meetings started at 8 a.m. I would get up early, leave home around 4:15 a.m. and drive three and a half hours to get there on time. On one particular day, a heavy snow was predicted. Normally when bad weather was expected I would drive up the night before. However, this time Joe was performing in a high school band concert. I went to his performance, got a few hours of sleep, and left home at 2:30 a.m. Fortunately, the drive through the snowstorm, though treacherous, took just one hour longer than usual—due mainly to the small volume of cars on the road.

I arrived at the meeting site one hour early. Feeling stressed and tired, I pulled into a parking spot at the far end of the lot, set a travel alarm for 7:45 a.m., reclined back my car seat, and snuggled up with the pillow and afghan I had brought along. I slept soundly for 45 minutes, and then awoke feeling refreshed just before the alarm went off.

When I walked into the meeting, the team leader was surprised to see me arrive on time, knowing I had traveled hundreds of miles to get there. Caleb used that information to chide three of my teammates, who lived nearby, but arrived late because of the bad driving conditions!

Pearls from Pat

1. *Work as part of a cross-functional team to get broad insight about completing an important project on time and on budget.*

2. *Consider making a lateral move from a supervisory position to a non-supervisory position, if it enables you to learn new skills and work with people who can help you advance your career.*

3. *Discuss with your entire family any proposed job assignment that will impact the household routine, so potential difficulties can be identified, and possible solutions proposed.*

4. *Consider the time you spend in your car as an opportunity to listen to audio books and expand your knowledge.*

GPS

The following spring, there was another Core Team meeting business trip that was memorable. Because the corporate engineering center and the divisional engineering offices were about 90 miles apart in Michigan, sometimes the Core Team meetings were held at one location, and sometimes at the other. On one occasion, it was decided to have a three-hour dinner meeting at a restaurant mid-way between the two regular meeting locations.

I worked half a day at the factory and then made the long drive to the designated eating establishment, arriving an hour before the 5:00 p.m. dinner meeting. Walking around the restaurant, I noticed framed photos of beautiful homes on the walls, and questioned a waitress about where the pictures had been taken. She explained that the houses in the photos were all located in a new subdivision located right around the corner. My watch confirmed there was enough time before the meeting started to drive around and look at these lovely residences.

Turning into the subdivision, the first things I noticed at the entryway were the impressive center boulevard and a small, but elegant, unmanned guardhouse. Driving farther, I saw a beautifully manicured golf course on the right, and a pair of tennis courts on the left. Continuing to drive, I passed an expansive treed area and then glimpsed a large lake situated behind stunning homes, each with a unique design.

Then I saw it—a very appealing house with a For Sale sign on the front yard. It was the smallest home on the street—a simple, elegant and symmetrical, red brick Williamsburg colonial residence—with a back yard overlooking both the lovely lake and the last hole of the perfectly manicured golf course.

I don't know why individuals feel attracted to some things and not to others. Up until then, Jon and I had moved twelve different times in the nearly twenty years we had been married. We had liked and learned much from every place we had ever called home. We had become somewhat attached to most of those places, mainly because of the time and sweat equity we had invested in each. However, looking at this house evoked a strong emotional response in me. I suddenly recalled whimsical conversations between Jon and me—Jon said someday he'd like to live on a golf course, and I said someday I'd like to live in a brick house on a lake.

Here I was, staring at a For Sale sign in front of a brick house that overlooked a lake *and* a golf course. What were the odds of that?

I drove around the rest of the neighborhood, and then went to the restaurant to attend the dinner meeting.

Arriving home the next day, I could hardly wait to tell Jon about the house on the golf course. "Just think," I said, "if you got offered a job transfer soon to central office, we might be able to buy the brick house."

The idea, while initially crazy, was not really so farfetched. There had been rumors that the company was closely reevaluating all operations not considered to be part of the "core auto business." The energy division that Jon ran, while small and very profitable, was definitely not automotive in nature. If the company adopted a strategy of divesting itself of all non-automotive businesses, Jon's days at his Ohio location were numbered.

Personally, I was feeling a little restless. I had been at the same manufacturing and car assembly complex in a variety of lateral assignments for five years since graduating from Harvard Business School. Promotional opportunities in the plant were very rare, and I could see none on the horizon.

From a family perspective, Joe and Jean were finishing the last quarter of their senior year. After twelve years of attending grade school and high school together, they had decided to go to different colleges in different states. Joe planned to attend the University of Michigan, which happened to be less than 30 minutes from the brick house overlooking the lake and the golf course. If, by any chance, we could move there, Joe could pay an in-state rate, a savings of nearly $12,000 a year!

The down side was that we were now living in Ohio, within 45 minutes driving time of my parents and four of my five siblings. If we were to relocate, I would miss the ease of attending the frequent extended family celebrations I had come to enjoy for the past five years.

~~~~~

A month later, while attending a Core Team meeting at the divisional engineering office, I spotted a job posting for a die engineering group manager, a position that for me would be a promotion from a low manager level to a high manager level salary range. My engineering background coupled with my work at the fabrication plant provided the experience necessary for the job. I told my boss, Chuck, that I felt moved to apply for the posting. When asked to come in for a job interview the following week, I scheduled it early in the afternoon, after the next Core Team meeting.

I already knew Steven, the Die Engineering Director who had initiated the job posting, from his past visits to the fabrication plant. The interview was going well, when Steven said something unexpected.

"Pat, knowing you live hundreds of miles from here, I was both surprised and pleased when you sent me an application for the posted die engineering group manager position. However, I think that with your background, you would be perfect for a different die engineering group manager position that was going to be posted next week. This second position is for someone overseeing die engineers working at the Vehicle Launch Center on the next midsize car program the corporation has under development. This person will have to spend some days each week here at the divisional engineering offices and some days at the corporate engineering offices 90 miles away. This manager will also be part of the future midsize vehicle's engineering systems management team that includes engineering group managers from interiors, exterior/structures, chassis, electrical, powertrain, heating/ventilation/air conditioning (HVAC), die engineering, and manufacturing engineering.

With your engineering background, Core Team experience in product development, and years at the fabrication plant, you would be a great fit for that position. The job is yours if you want it. I contacted your boss before asking you to come in for this interview, telling him chances were good I would be offering you a job."

Thanking him and affirming my interest, I asked Steven to put the offer in writing, including the small promotion and raise. I would need to speak with my boss and my husband. If Jon were agreeable, he would need time to ask his boss if he could transfer to Michigan. Steven understood I might need as long as a week to respond to the offer.

I walked out of his office on a cloud. The job responsibilities sounded exciting, and the position being offered was a promotion to a high manager level with a 10 percent raise. If we moved to Michigan, Joe would get the in-state tuition break—plus we would be about 150 miles closer to Jean's college, Purdue University, in Indiana.

I happily realized that the house on the lake and the golf course was located midway between the divisional engineering offices and the corporate engineering offices—and it was the same distance away from Jon's boss's departmental office. Its location was perfect. Hopefully, it was still on the market.

I thought about the importance of being in the right place at the right time. Within the span of a month, a Core Team meeting in one city had brought me in the vicinity of a house where I wanted to live. A Core Team meeting in another city had brought me in the vicinity of a bulletin board with a job posting for a promotional opportunity that I wanted to pursue. Some people call it luck or being in the right place at the right time. I call it GPS or God's Positioning Spirit—guiding me down a path of blessings that He wanted me to follow.

I said a silent prayer of thanks.

1. Realize that occasionally a well-timed relocation can be very beneficial for your family, as well as for your career.

2. Give thanks whenever GPS—God's Positioning Spirit—guides you to be in the right place at the right time!

The Win-Win Realtor

Before driving all the way home after the job interview with Steven, I decided to swing by the neighborhood with the house overlooking the lake and the golf course. Pulling up in front of the house, I was relieved to see the For Sale sign still on the lawn, with the name and phone number of the listing realtor. Using the bulky mobile phone unit designated for plant staff business trips, I called the realtor, explaining I was in town for the day from out-of-state and wanted to see the red brick house as soon as possible. The agent, named Denise, said she was nearby and would call me right back. Five minutes later, she called and said the owner was home; it was fine to come now and tour the house.

We walked up to the front door, which was opened immediately by an attractive woman named Kim who appeared to be in her mid-to-late thirties. Smiling, Kim said she would take the dog and wait on the back porch while we toured the house. Her four children would start coming home from school in about thirty minutes.

With four bedrooms, two and a half baths, and a den, the house had the same number of rooms as our current residence. This home was three years old, had been professionally decorated, and had beautiful hardwood floors throughout the main level. The floor plan was perfect for entertaining, with multiple circular traffic flows from room to room. The kitchen had a cooktop stove on the butcher block island, as well as a double wall oven. The dining room was spacious and open, enabling family gatherings of twenty or more to sit around a long table extending into the living room, if necessary.

The best part was the breathtaking view. The lake and the golf course were visible from every room facing the back of the house and, because of the open floor plan, the lake could be seen from some of the rooms in the front of the house as well.

While touring the house with Denise, I noticed a specially decorated basket, prominently displayed, that surprised me. On its handle was stenciled the name of the small Ohio city where we currently lived. When we went out onto the covered back porch to view the back yard, I saw Kim moving to and fro on a white porch swing and asked her about the basket with the city name on it.

Kim replied, "We used to live in that city before we moved to Michigan. In fact, we liked it there so much, we custom built this brick home based on the Williamsburg colonials, which are popular there."

I told Kim we currently lived in that very same city. It explained why I was so drawn to this house. Among all of the beautiful modern-style residences in the subdivision, only this traditional brick house felt like home to me. I experienced an instant connection to Kim, as well as to her house. She went on to explain that her husband had already been transferred to San Francisco. She and the children would join him in a month, once the school year was over. I explained how I had just been offered a job in the area; my family and I had a lot of details to work out before I officially accepted it. If things progressed, I wanted to come back this weekend and bring my husband to see the house.

~~~~~

The next few days passed quickly. When I went in to see my boss, Chuck laughed and said, "See, Pat, I told you being on the Core Team would provide you a lot of exposure and opportunity. However, I expected you to be on the assignment longer than sixteen months." Since the new job meant a promotion for me, Chuck supported the move.

Jon and I had already been talking hypothetically about a potential lateral transfer for him the month before. We had discussed all of the advantages of moving nearer to corporate headquarters, both for our jobs and for our family. Because of this, Jon and the children were already mentally prepared to make the move. We had spent five years in this city—longer than we had lived anywhere—and the children had been able to attend eighth grade and all of high school there. Since they would be graduating in a few weeks and starting college in the fall, it was the perfect time to move.

We planned to drive to Michigan for the weekend to do some preliminary house hunting. Jon arranged to meet with his boss, Henry, on Friday evening to discuss his job options. He wanted to speak with Henry face-to-face, to inform him of my promotional offer, and to explore alternatives for Jon's next assignment at the central office location.

Jon's meeting with Henry went well. Jon had gone into the meeting with a job description of the work he wanted to do. Since the Ohio gas well operation would continue for six to eighteen months, Jon believed he could oversee things from Michigan provided he was on site one day a week. (He proposed to make the same weekly drive I had made for the past sixteen months, but in the opposite direction!) Because Jon had been at the forefront of the deregulation of natural gas, he saw the possibility of something similar on the horizon for electricity. He wanted his responsibilities expanded to include a proactive role in developing a corporate strategy for the deregulation of electricity. Henry was impressed with Jon's proposal and said there was office space available for him at headquarters, so the transition could take place any time. Jon was glad an opportunity for me prompted him to design an opportunity that was good for him, too.

Now we could spend Saturday and Sunday house hunting. Despite my enthusiasm about the house overlooking the golf course and the lake, Jon was unfamiliar with the city where it was located and not especially interested. He wanted to first check out houses in the prestigious suburbs where his boss's work associates lived.

We spent all day Saturday house hunting in the well-established suburbs where Jon wanted to look. Home prices were definitely higher there than where we currently lived in Ohio. Most of the homes in our price range were older and could best be described as "dumpy." At 9:00 p.m., we pulled into our hotel, exhausted. Jon was disappointed.

"How about if we call the realtor who showed me the house overlooking the lake and golf course?" I asked. "I'll give her a price range and have her show us homes in various subdivisions. I know you don't know much about this little city, and it's not as prestigious as the well-established suburbs. However, it is perfectly situated close to two major freeways and is a 50 minute drive from your future office and from both of mine."

Jon agreed, and we called Denise.

The next morning, Denise did a great job of taking us on a tour of the city, showing us the downtown, the schools, the park, the lakes, and the best restaurants. Then we looked at homes in various subdivisions. Her last stop was the red brick Williamsburg colonial overlooking the golf course and the lake. When we stepped out of the car and walked to the back of the house, it was obvious that Jon was blown away. The golf course was beautiful; we overlooked the last hole, which wrapped around the lake like a mini-version of Pebble Beach. Beyond the green, the lake curved in front of a community park, beach, and marina.

Denise said, "There are two golf courses here and an all-sports lake connected by a canal to another larger all-sports lake."

"Just wait until you see the inside," I said, anxious to go into the house and glad the owners were not at home. As we walked through the house, I pointed out to Jon not only the house's current features, but also possible future changes—like enclosing the large back porch and constructing a spacious deck—that would make the place even better. Jon attempted to visualize them in his mind as clearly as I did in mine.

Jon looked over all the information sheets on the house including the taxes. The asking price was more than we wanted to spend. "We'll think about it and let you know," Jon said. "Pat has to formally accept the job she was offered, now that we know I have a job here as well. Right now we have to get on the road. We have a three and half hour drive home and work tomorrow."

Denise said, "You have my phone number. Just don't wait too long, if you're serious. You should know there have been four offers made on this house in the past six weeks—all were less than the asking price, and all were turned down."

We got in the car and started driving towards downtown and the nearest freeway. Jon said, "I see what you mean about the house and its location having everything we ever wanted."

"I know I want to live there," I said. "So if you like it, too, why don't we just stop the car, call Denise, and make an offer?"

"Are you kidding?" Jon said. "Right now?"

"Why not?" I replied. "We can go into a restaurant, and call Denise to meet us with the paperwork. While we are waiting, we can pray about what the offer should be."

We did just that. We had been going over numbers for the past few days, estimating what we could get for our house, and what additional cash we could pull together. After praying in the restaurant, I heard the offer number in my head.

It was a sellers' market and the amount in my head was $46,000 less than the asking price. In reality, it was the highest amount we could offer without taking out a mortgage. I believed it was the right thing to do, and felt a peace about it. Jon agreed.

Denise wrote up the contract and told us we would hear from her the following day. "It's less than what they want," she said. I explained that it was all the cash we could raise. We had two children starting college and we were determined not to take out a mortgage. We drove home excited and full of hope.

The next morning I called Steven to talk about his job offer and told him the good news about Jon's Friday night conversation with Henry. Then I gave Steven my official response.

I took the job.

An hour later, Denise called. "I have good news and bad news," she said. "The bad news is your offer was lower than two of the four other offers Kim and her husband already turned down. They feel the selling price has to be higher than all the offers they rejected."

She then said cheerily, "The good news is Kim really likes you, Pat, and felt some kind of connection, because their family used to live in the same Ohio city where you live now. They put a lot of themselves into this house and they really want you folks to be the next owners."

Denise continued, "However, they are insisting on a recorded sales price higher than the offers they have already refused. I came up with an idea. You talked about some improvements you wanted to do to the house. We could rewrite the contract with the price being $7,000 higher than your original offer. We would include the stipulation that the sellers return $7,000 to you at closing to be used on the home improvements you want made. You end up paying the net price you offered, while the record of sale will show the higher price that the sellers want. This is not a problem since the house appraised at more than the original asking price, and no mortgage is involved. When I proposed this to the sellers, they agreed. What do you think?"

We were impressed with Denise's clever solution to a sticky situation. She was skillfully designing a win-win agreement for both parties—as well as securing her own commission. "It sounds acceptable to me. The higher recorded sale price may have a small impact on our property taxes. However, it shouldn't be too bad. Fax me the revised contract. I'll run over to Jon's office and review it with him. If he's okay with it, we'll both sign it, and fax it back to you."

All parties signed the contract and we received a fax of the completed version around 11 a.m. We later found out that another couple, whose earlier bid had been rejected, came back that afternoon wanting to increase their offer. They were told the house had been sold that morning to some automotive people from Ohio.

Against all odds, we had the house we wanted, at the price we wanted, and the jobs we wanted. By following the still, small voice within, we were once again blessed by God.

Pearls from Pat

1. Proceed immediately, once you know what you want and feel moved to act. "He who hesitates is lost."

2. Look beyond what both parties say they want and understand why they want it in order to design a creative win-win agreement.

Farewells and Toilets

The first few weeks of June passed quickly, as Joe and Jean graduated from high school and started their summer jobs. The company provided a bridge loan equal to the officially appraised value of our Ohio home, so we could close on the Michigan house on June 30th. I officially started my new job July 1, 1991. The plan was for Jon and the children to stay in the Ohio house and work with a local realtor to sell it, until college started. Once we moved Joe and Jean into their respective college dorms, Jon would move all of our belongings to Michigan, and settle in to his new office. The company would buy our home for the amount of the bridge loan, if it didn't sell by then.

Wrapping up things at work in the fabrication plant was a big job. The Plant Manager had chosen my replacement, a bright man he had worked with at a fabrication plant in Pennsylvania. I had updated the five-year business plan, which served as the roadmap for the upcoming start of the plant's next fiscal year. The new guy would have a few months of breathing room on that part of the job. Bringing him up to speed on the Core Team work was more complicated. However, I had confidence he would work out just fine, once he moved his family and transitioned his own replacement in Pennsylvania.

I was surprised and touched to see the Plant Manager's secretary busy preparing a farewell party for me—drinks and hors d'oeuvres on the patio of a nice restau-

rant after work on my last day. I had never known anyone from my plant to transfer—retire, yes; but transfer,
no. I thought at most there might be lunch with the rest
of the Plant Manager's staff. Plant people generally were
not interested in socializing with one another after work.

~~~~~

When Jon and I arrived at the party, I was shocked
to see 50 people in attendance. My former boss and
some former associates from the assembly plant were
there, as well as a large contingent of people from various fabrication plant departments. The biggest surprise
was seeing the committeemen, including Neil and a few
others who had provided me with my biggest challenges.

After some eating and socializing, the speeches and
storytelling began. Vern, the Director of Plant Engineering and Maintenance, was a smart, good-looking man
about my age, who had this story to tell:

> *One night around 7:00 p.m., everyone in
> the administration building was gone, except
> Pat and me. Suddenly Pat rushed into my of-
> fice, talking excitedly, "Vern, you've got to help
> me! I just went to the john, and when I flushed
> the toilet, my pager slipped and went down the
> drain. I put my hand in but couldn't feel the
> pager. Do you think there's a chance it's caught
> in the trap in the wall? I sure hate to ask Chuck
> to get me a new pager because mine was
> flushed down the toilet."*
>
> *Well, it struck me as really funny, but I
> tried to keep a straight face and said, "Pat,
> show me which toilet swallowed your pager."
> After leading me down the hall to the women's
> restroom, Pat held open the door to the second
> stall. I unbuttoned the right sleeve of my long-
> sleeved white shirt, and shoved my hand and
> arm in as far as possible.*

"I can't feel a thing," I told Pat. "I'll call a second shift plumber to take a look, and remove the toilet from the wall. Maybe we'll get lucky, and he'll find it in the wall trap. My guess is it's well on its way to the sewer line."

Grabbing some paper towels, I wiped off my wet arm. Pat opened the door to the hallway and I rolled down my shirtsleeve as the two of us walked out of the restroom. While I was buttoning my shirt cuff, we heard a noise nearby, in what had been the deserted hallway. Staring at us was one of the second shift lady janitors. By the shocked look on her face, I could see she had jumped to the wrong conclusion about what the two of us had been doing in the women's restroom. Pat saw her expression as well, and quickly tried to explain about how she had flushed her pager down the toilet, and how I was trying to help. The lady janitor walked down the hall, shaking her head, not believing a word of Pat's story.

The plumber removed the toilet but never found the pager. We decided to get Pat a gift that will prevent such an accident from happening again. We designed a special toilet seat with a pager holder built right into the cover.

The audience had been laughing throughout Vern's story. When he pulled out a standard wooden toilet seat that had been modified to include a special compartment—complete with a pager—the audience roared and clapped. I also laughed, especially remembering how beet-red Vern's face had turned when that lady janitor was staring at us.

The Plant Manager gave a very heartfelt speech, talking about all of my contributions. He explained that my going-away gift was just what I had been asking him to get me for the past sixteen months—my very own mobile phone. The contributions of the party participants had been used to purchase the phone and my future boss Steven had agreed to pay for the monthly usage charges. It was the perfect gift since my new job required me to be in the car a lot covering two offices 90 miles apart.

The other speakers told stories of the fabrication plant's first woman assistant area manager and how she had turned the facility upside down. They said her presence had made them clean up their language, take down their girlie calendars, and try to be better people, as well as inspire them to produce world class quality products. They had discovered that a woman could be a good boss. They would never be the same again.

Tears clouded my eyes as I tried to keep from breaking my own "never let them see you cry" rule. They had given me the best present of all.

They showed me I had made a positive difference.

Pearls from Pat

1. Keep your sense of humor when your most embarrassing moments are revisited at your farewell party.

2. Realize that even people who hassle you the most, can sometimes come to like and respect you.

3. Appreciate people who say you've made a difference.

2003: Dr. Pat

PART III

DECELERATING TO EXECUTIVE

(1991-2007)

A Systems Approach

Starting my job as a die engineering group manager, who was part of an engineering systems management team, was an exciting prospect. My functional boss already had a talented woman named Helen working as one of his engineering group managers, so the "first woman" trail had already been blazed. However, there had never been any female engineering systems managers at the Vehicle Launch Center where the next generation of mid-sized cars would be developed. I welcomed the challenge with enthusiasm. Cassie—an engineer assigned to a different future vehicle program, and the only other woman working at the Vehicle Launch Center—warned me about the male environment of product engineering.

"Pat, you worked in various plants, and I am sure the men there gave you a hard time. They probably cussed and said you didn't know what you were talking about. When you are in a predominantly blue-collar environment, men will openly criticize you and you can deal with it on the spot. Now you are in a totally white-collar environment, surrounded by men who are educated and polite—and sometimes duplicitous. Instead of insulting you to your face, they will undercut your credibility behind your back. Your male peers subconsciously believe their manhood is somehow diminished if a woman does the job as well as—or better than—they do. Because they try to hide this from you, it is much more difficult to deal with it."

Cassie had just done a great job of articulating something I had sensed amid all of the product engineering professionalism, but could not quite put into words. It was going to take time, persistence, and a lot of excellent results to become really accepted by these engineering systems managers.

The die engineers who were assigned to report to me at the Vehicle Launch Center had their own concerns. Though I had worked around dies for four years (and my dad was a die maker), I had never worked as a die engineer and didn't have the specific technical experience their previous bosses had. These die engineers were among the very best; they were selected for the Vehicle Launch Center assignment because of their expertise.

However, our job there was not only to design dies, but also to influence automotive exterior design; we needed metal surfaces contoured in a way that they could be stamped without splits, depressions, and other imperfections. To make matters more challenging, we had been given a high-level corporate mandate: on this program, no more than four "hits per panel" were allowed—meaning we could use no more than four presses (and consequently four dies) to make any given part. Currently in production there were a number of car parts requiring seven presses. The corporation was now mandating that we shorten the press lines in the plants and decrease the budget for dies.

We all knew one way to play the die game was to divide one complex part into two simpler parts, which could each meet the four hits per panel criteria; unfortunately, this usually increased the total number of dies. If this happened too often, we would not meet the reduced die budget target. Plus, more parts would mean increased welded subassembly costs. We had to have the fewest number of sheet metal part numbers, each requiring four dies or less.

Getting an idea, I searched for and found the video George and I had made several years before while working at the fabrication plant in Ohio. I also found the one-page summary sheet we had compiled on vehicle features that contributed to split-free, high-quality sheet metal parts. In my mind, a two-phase strategy started to form. I needed the die engineers to buy into my strategy.

Phase 1 involved expanding the feature summary sheet into a small handbook on metal part features. This would support not only quality manufacturing, but also the corporation's four hits per panel requirement.

Phase 2 of the strategy required working closely with Design Studio during the next six to twelve months—while they were creating the sketches and exterior clays of the future car. It was not enough to have die engineers walk across the street to Design Studio every few days. I wanted a die engineer to be physically located there in the studio, desk and all. It was a crazy idea that had never been done before. However, I honestly believed a die engineer with a "schmoozing salesman" personality could infiltrate the artistic kingdom of Design to increase radii and reduce metal draw depth, while still ensuring an eye-catching exterior appearance. Two of the guys working for me, Victor and Sean, had personalities that fit the bill. If I could convince Design Studio to allow it, we would assign Victor to move into a desk near the designers, using Sean as his backup on vacation days.

I met with the die designers and reviewed the two-phase strategy looking for their feedback. They quickly became excited about the ideas. They had spent their entire careers in a reactive mode, doing the best die engineering they could to get the sheet metal to form and produce the designated exterior surfaces. They wanted to make a mind shift—to be proactive and influence the exterior design. This would make the die engineering and manufacturing easier and less expensive, while yielding higher quality parts. The concept was very empowering. They were more than willing to write the handbook, and they liked the idea of having a desk by the clays. However, they were very doubtful that Design Studio would ever approve of a die engineer actually residing near the models.

My response was, "If you guys agree this idea has the potential to yield positive results, then I'll see what needs to be done to make the move happen. You start writing down what exterior feature constraints are necessary for your respective parts to meet the four hits per panel requirement."

I next met with two key executives from the new mid-sized car program—the Vehicle Chief Engineer and the Core Team Leader. Failing to meet the four hits per panel requirement and the die budget would reflect poorly on them, as well as on me. They seemed impressed by the two-phase strategy. I suggested that the best way to get a generally autonomous group like Design Studio to accept a new way of doing things was to sell it as a "three-month pilot program." If it proved to be disruptive, everything could revert back to the previous way of doing things in 90 days.

Design Studio agreed to the idea of a three-month pilot program. One week later, Victor moved his files into a desk near the clay models. I had briefed Victor on the importance of building relationships with the designers and modelers. He needed to suggest alternative ideas in a subtle manner, rather than telling them what needed to be done. Victor was an artful schmoozer; he knew the best way to get a change made was to make a designer think it was his own idea.

The other die engineers frequently visited Design Studio. They let Victor know when they had any concerns about how the clay sections for their parts were developing. The second schmoozer, Sean, also got to know all of the people in Design Studio, and did a fine job covering for Victor when he was on vacation. By the end of the pilot period, everyone at Design Studio had become very comfortable with the arrangement and decided that it should continue for the rest of the program.

When that new mid-sized vehicle reached the market several years later, it was a great-looking automobile that received the "Motor Trend Car of the Year" award. That was a real tribute to the entire systems engineering management team.

I was very proud to have been part of that program.

1. Be aware that polite, educated men in a white-collar male environment can be just as uncomfortable with a woman peer or boss as their blue-collar counterparts in a factory.

2. Focus on optimizing the final product and use a systems approach to understand how your work affects other parts.

3. Present a new way of doing things as a pilot program that can be reversed if the trial process doesn't work well.

Supporting Work-Life Balance

Getting to know the Vehicle Chief Engineer from the next generation mid-size car program ended up being very fortunate for me. One day he asked if I would be interested in another engineering group manager position—this one in Reliability and Test.

The Vehicle Launch Center project was winding down and the mid-size car program was ready to transition to mainstream engineering. I liked working in Die Engineering. However, the thought of doing work with full vehicle testing at the Proving Grounds was exciting, and this was the perfect time to make a transition.

I spoke with my boss and then went for the interview. I didn't know Vance, the Reliability and Test Director, but he had seen me around. "You know," he said, "I was surprised when you applied for this job; I always thought you were already a director, rather than a manager." That remark surprised me, but I figured it was a good sign—and I was pleased when the offer came.

I took the job.

~~~~~

I was assigned to manage an interesting group of reliability engineers at both the corporate and divisional engineering offices. My group was responsible for testing safety components and systems for the various models of automobiles, including doing exciting vehicle work at the company's proving grounds facility. The youngest reliability engineer was recently out of college. The oldest was in his 50s—the corporation's crash testing expert who, as a senior staff engineer at the top of his pay grade, made more money than I did as his manager.

I always tried to be supportive of the dreams, ambitions, and family situations of the people who worked for me. The corporation was finally starting to formalize, on a limited basis, the part-time work practice I had requested and been granted sixteen years earlier when joining the company. Many managers were leery of such a radical idea, but I strongly believed certain engineering assignments could be adapted to a 24-hour workweek.

One of the reliability engineers reporting to me was very interested in the legal aspects of product liability and was finishing law school at night. He wanted to work three days a week for six months, so he could study for his bar exam. With young children at home, he knew the reduced pay would be a sacrifice. However, passing the bar exam was important to him. We worked out a way to pare back his workload temporarily. He was able to work 24 hours a week, achieve his dream, and then return to a full-time schedule.

A female reliability engineer, named Marcy, asked to work three days a week after the birth of her second child and I agreed. She was an exceptional employee and wanted to retain responsibility for the testing of all of the seat belts she was currently assigned. Because of her shorter workweek, she requested to be excused from attending administrative meetings and some ancillary assignments. It was no problem to make those arrangements for her.

After six months, the Seat Belt Design Engineering Group Manager told me he had an opening for a design engineer and thought Marcy would be a good candidate; his only concern was her working three days a week. He wasn't sure he wanted such an unconventional work arrangement in his department.

"Let me take a look at the list of other engineers you have as candidates for the job," I said.

He handed me his short list. "Well, I know about half of these guys. In my opinion, Marcy is an excellent engineer, however, she resists any type of micromanaging. Personally, I would take three days of Marcy over five days of the guys I know on your list. Your best bet is to see if she is interested in interviewing for the job, then speak with her about your concerns."

The next day, Marcy came to see me to let me know the Seat Belt Design Engineering Group Manager had asked her to interview for an opening in his group. Marcy said, "I told him that I'm not interested; I'm happy right here, working for you."

"Well, I'm glad you're happy working for me. However, there will come a day when you will be ready for a new challenge. You should know that I will support you when that day comes."

About ten months later, that day came. I approved Marcy's move—to become the first part-time seat belt design engineer in the company.

Pearls from Pat

1. Know that sometimes subordinates with highly specialized skills make more money than their bosses.

2. Use your power as a boss to help people accomplish their dreams, achieve work-life balance, and still get the job done.

When a Younger Peer Becomes Your Boss

Less than a year after I joined the Reliability and Test Department, my boss Vance moved on to a new assignment. A newly promoted director came in to take his place. To my surprise the new boss was Helen, the female engineering group manager who had been my younger peer when I worked for Steven in Die Engineering. Hearing the announcement, I felt a pang of disappointment, wishing it could have been me. However, Helen had more years with the company, having started as a co-op student when she was eighteen. She had worked many years in various engineering groups and had the support of a number of engineering executives; I had only been in engineering for a few years. I adjusted my attitude and determined to learn as much as possible from Helen. She would be a fine engineering director.

Helen had a number of interesting practices, which made her very effective. One was her habit of scheduling a planning meeting with herself, often in a small conference room. When Helen worked alone away from her office with the door closed, everyone knew not to disturb her about anything short of World War III.

In order to enhance departmental team spirit, Helen organized an off-site meeting for the managers and engineers. For several days we met at a wooded location about 25 miles away. Outdoor climbing experts and facilitators showed people how to help one another develop trust and overcome fears. The trainers had everyone using harnesses and ropes to climb poles, walk on balance beams twenty feet off the ground, and swing from trees. It was fun, and the shared experience increased the cohesiveness of the department.

When it came to staff meetings, Helen was agenda driven, and did not allow time for the extensive discussion of issues. Instead, she would allocate five or ten minutes to bring up a new issue at the meeting, and only answer questions of a clarifying nature. Then she would tell us to think about the topic and talk about it among ourselves during the week. Helen would routinely put the item on the next week's meeting agenda for a decision. Everything was handled this way—simple items that appeared unworthy of being on two meeting agendas, as well as complicated issues that some thought needed more full group discussion time at staff meetings. No matter what, when the subject's allotted agenda time was over, the discussion was terminated until the next meeting.

Once all of us managers got accustomed to Helen's way of running staff meetings, we found that it worked quite well. Staff meetings never ran long. Sometimes we managers would informally get together during the week to discuss the pros and cons of more complicated issues, or run alternatives by each other in order to be clear and concise at the next staff meeting. Often items, that appeared to be "no-brainers" on the surface to some of us, had more significant ramifications for others. In the end, we all benefitted from the one-week delay in decision-making.

Helen was a good executive who had the right blend of caring for people and a no-nonsense approach, which kept people focused on doing what was important. She was a woman accustomed to trailblazing many positions throughout her entire career.

I feel fortunate to have had the opportunity to work for Helen—even though she was once my younger peer.

1. Remember that when a younger peer becomes your boss, you need to focus on the person's strengths, be supportive, and learn as much as possible.

2. Schedule a meeting with yourself at a location other than your office as a way to get important work done without interruption.

3. Consider running effective staff meetings by limiting each item's agenda time, encouraging informal discussions during the week, and scheduling the decision on the next meeting's agenda.

Corporate Snakes

In all my years working in the auto industry, I was never asked by a boss to do anything dishonest or illegal. From my experience, the company and the people in it were very ethical. However, I had a good friend named Kirk in another part of the auto industry, who said his corporation contained at least one isolated pocket of dishonesty.

After a corporate reorganization, a man named Lyle unexpectedly became Kirk's boss. Lyle had a reputation for misleading and using people to get what he wanted, and he was usually successful. People from other areas, who liked Kirk and knew Lyle well, advised Kirk to find an assignment under a different director as soon as possible.

Kirk was unaware that there existed people like Lyle, sometimes known as "snakes in suits" (Babiak & Hare, 2006, p. xiv). "Snakes" were corporate psychopaths without conscience, who used dishonesty, manipulation, control, and deception to stealthily work their way into executive positions of companies to serve their own purposes. Kirk naïvely viewed Lyle as simply a difficult boss. Because he had experienced difficult bosses in the past, Kirk believed things would be fine, as long as he did excellent work.

Kirk was the manager responsible for the maintenance programs on certain types of equipment that were at all of his company's plants. It soon became apparent that Lyle was making numerous presentations to various groups around the company, grossly oversimplifying and misrepresenting a new equipment installation program. He reported only the positive cost-saving aspects, but none of the negative operational impacts and additional installation and maintenance costs that would be incurred.

Kirk was convinced the real cost to the company was nearly double the amount that was being presented—and this did not include the technical obstacles, retraining, and cultural resistance of the operators who would be using the new equipment. By telling only part of the story, Lyle was able to obtain corporate approval and funds for the new program.

Lyle asked Kirk to put together an appropriations request for a pilot equipment installation at a large plant. When he did, Lyle reviewed it, and then told Kirk to cut the total amount of the job in half.

"But the work can't be done for half the amount," Kirk protested.

His boss responded, "I've already told upper management we are doing it for the lower amount, so write it up that way."

"I won't sign an appropriations request that's a lie," said Kirk firmly. "If you want it done that way, you'll have to sign it yourself." Instead, Lyle told another manager to write up and sign the appropriations request.

As the presentations and planning work continued, Kirk kept voicing his concerns verbally, and was constantly told that his concerns were not relevant. In good conscience, he could not participate in the deception required to push through the project that Lyle wanted the corporation to implement. Concerned he was being associated with a project he believed to be headed for disaster, Kirk wrote an email to Lyle and sent a copy to Lyle's boss—summarizing his concerns and the steps he thought were needed to go forward with the program. Kirk had intended the note to be viewed as a proactive action plan. Instead, Lyle came out of his office cursing and shouting, "This memo could kill the program!! Now I've got to do damage control and get all copies of that &^$$%# email deleted before my boss reads it!"

The next day, Kirk was told he was officially off of the project and someone else was taking over all of his maintenance management responsibilities. Lyle then put Kirk on "special assignment" handling routine clerical tasks.

Devastated by the reduction in responsibility, Kirk went to his Human Resources (HR) representative, showed her the documentation he had explaining what was happening, and expressed his concern about the hostile work environment that punished him for speaking the truth. The HR representative said she would look into the matter and get back to him. Kirk gave me permission to share the written response he received:

The actions taken to remove you from the job assignment are in line, in that your efforts to circumvent your manager's direction can be interpreted as insubordination. Your behavior sends the message that you have a disregard for authority and disrespect for Management. Although we may not agree with all of our Management's decisions or direction, that does not give us the right to try to do an "end run" around Management to put forth our own agenda. There is no organization in this company or other companies that supports or condones that type of behavior. Your Management's reaction to your behavior does not constitute a hostile work environment. It is evidence that Management does not trust your willingness or ability to work as part of the team. Therefore, it is deemed best at this time to place you in an assignment where you

would work as an individual, not a member of
a team.

It did not surprise me that HR was supporting those in power. I encouraged Kirk to pray for the strength to survive this trying time, go into work smiling and holding his head up high, and tear into his new clerical assignment with all the vigor and excellence that he had brought to his previous manager position. I also suggested he start talking with other directors for whom he had worked in the past and let them know he was looking for a new challenging assignment. He should say nothing negative about Lyle and what had happened. People in the department already knew the "snake" had put Kyle in "jail" and was just waiting for him to crack, quit, or request an early retirement.

A few months passed, and the manager of an area Kirk had supervised seven years earlier, decided to retire early and move out of state because of some family issues. He told his director that Kirk was the only person who could step into his job during this crucial time and keep things going without missing a beat. When that director offered Kirk the manager's job, Kirk was delighted.

His maintenance colleagues congratulated him for getting out of "jail" and away from Lyle. More importantly, they also told him how much they admired the positive attitude he had maintained throughout his whole ordeal.

Kirk took the job—with more gratitude and relief than he had ever felt for a new assignment.

~~~~~

One year later, Lyle's unethical behavior finally caught up with him. His reputation for being deceptive and mistreating employees was widespread. Lyle was forced into an early retirement and left his job and the company in disgrace without saying goodbye to anyone—not even his faithful secretary of many years.

1. Have the courage to revise an earlier recommendation when you get new data indicating a program you supported is no longer financially feasible.

2. Realize that if your boss tells you to do something dishonest, immoral, or illegal, you have to decide whether to obey your boss or remain true to your values—and hope in the long run you come out okay.

3. Keep good documentation and strategize carefully before speaking about an immoral supervisor with HR or an appropriate well-connected executive. You may experience negative short-term consequences until others come forward with similar reports.

4. Try to move to a different area when you work for a corporate snake, even if things are going well, because a snake can turn on you at any time.

5. Be proactive when you feel especially low at work—unappreciated, misunderstood, put down, or generally depressed. Instead, pray for strength, work energetically, cheerfully interact with people, and believe that your next big break is just around the corner—because it is, and you don't want to miss it!

Teach What You Want to Learn

In the 1990s, Stephen Covey's book *The Seven Habits of Highly Effective People* was a national best seller. One of the divisions in our company invited Dr. Covey to teach a seminar on his effectiveness principles, and was very pleased with the results. Corporate engineering executives attending the seminar decided it would be cost effective to have some interested engineering group managers become certified to teach "The Seven Habits" course material to the thousands of people in the company's engineering organization.

There were about twenty engineering group managers who signed up to take the first four-day course. We were all proponents of lifelong learning and found the effectiveness principles in the course to be common sense concepts—presented in an interesting, entertaining, and thought-provoking manner. The content was consistent with my own personal values, and articulated much of what I believed. The best way to learn this worthwhile material better was to teach it.

All but two engineering group managers in our starter class agreed to take additional training to become certified facilitators. We all committed to carve out time from our regular workload to facilitate a four-day class with a co-facilitator every quarter.

"The Seven Habits" were simple statements of consistent behavior exhibited by effective individuals and organizations:

1. *Be Proactive*
2. *Begin with the End in Mind*
3. *Put First Things First*
4. *Think Win/Win*
5. *Seek First to Understand, Then to Be Understood*
6. *Synergize*
7. *Sharpen the Saw* (Covey, 1989, p. 11)

Normally, a new "Seven Habits" facilitator got paired with an experienced one; however, we did not have this luxury. We were all inexperienced. I was paired with a man named Chris, whom I did not know well before the class. As we discussed how to split up presenting the course material, we found that Chris's preferred "Habits" were different from my favorites; we complemented each other perfectly.

Maybe it was because we were two engineers, both nervous about our first time teaching non-technical, motivational material. Maybe it was because we both used our own life stories to illustrate the principles. Maybe it was because our students responded positively. Most probably it was because we realized that together we had influenced our students for the better, and in doing so, we had also made a positive impact on our company. Whatever the reason, the result at the end of the class was an adrenaline rush and a feeling of euphoria—a truly memorable experience.

Over time, I mastered the motivational material, became more polished in my delivery, and continued to co-facilitate the course with a variety of engineering group managers. However, no class was as memorable as that first one.

~~~~~

Student participation was an important aspect of "The Seven Habits" course. Facilitators do their best to get everyone to contribute, since participants often learn as much from one another as they do from the facilitators. In one class there was a young woman who said almost nothing throughout the entire four days of the course. As she left on the last day, I felt a little disappointed, assuming from her lack of participation that she had not found the sessions very meaningful.

Unexpectedly, this young woman stopped to shake my hand. She said, "Pat, this class has been just what I needed. I'm at a crossroads in my life and have to make some changes. The past four days helped me to think about what was really important in my life. I've decided to quit my engineering job, move to a new city, and get my master's degree in the healthcare field. Thanks for all of your inspiring stories."

I was surprised. The non-participating student who appeared to get the least out of the course had probably gotten the *most* out of the class. Her boss might not be happy when she turned in her resignation, but I was glad she had the courage to make some well-thought-out changes in her life.

~~~~~

Facilitating this course reminded me of a pyramid chart I once developed, modeled after "Maslow's Hierarchy of Needs" (Maslow, 1962). I called it "A Teacher's Hierarchy of Student Response." Moving from the wide bottom to the narrow top, the pyramid shows the five-step progression of what a teacher wants a student to do.

Some teachers can't get their students to accomplish Step 1 (Stay Awake). Average teachers get students to Step 2 (Listen). Good teachers get most students to Step 3 (Understand) and occasionally to Step 4 (Modify Thinking). Great teachers get their students to Step 4 and sometimes to Step 5 (Change Behavior).

A Teacher's Hierarchy of Student Response

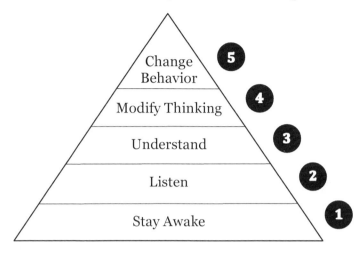

I had been a physics instructor before joining the corporate world and knew a teacher's special joy, which comes from observing the "ah-ha" expression that passes across a student's face. Something you have said makes sense, and he or she suddenly "gets it." However, there's a big difference between watching a student come to understand "Einstein's Theory of General Relativity," and watching a student come to understand what is really important in his or her life. Teaching the principles contained in "The Seven Habits" raised my sense of meaning and purpose to a whole new level. Without any mention of God or the Bible, those effectiveness habits actually aligned with many of the Biblical principles that were already foundational in my life.

~~~~~

When our son Joe graduated from college and became a high school math teacher, he taught me something special: great teachers of any subject matter understand the importance of teaching more than the material in the textbooks. Skillfully between theorems and mathematical proofs, Joe wove in memorable anecdotes that taught his students important life lessons.

Here is one of the stories Joe told his class that involved me:

As a kid, I always hated art class. Because I was never good at drawing, every art assignment stressed me out. While in seventh grade and living in Boston, I was so desperate for a good grade that I turned in one of my sister's old art projects as my own, changing the name "Jean Schuch" to "J. Schuch." Teachers are smart, so of course when my art teacher discovered the truth, he phoned my mom to come in for a meeting.

My mom's immediate response to my dishonesty was to say to my art teacher, "Joe's behavior is totally unacceptable. As part of the consequences for his cheating, I won't allow him to go on the New York City field trip."

Looking down at his watch, my art teacher said, "It's too late for that, Mrs. Schuch. The field trip bus left 40 minutes ago."

My mom replied, "Well, I'll just jump in my car, catch up to the bus, and have the driver pull over. Pulling Joe off the bus and keeping him from attending this field trip will be something that he will always remember. Maybe it'll help him choose to do the right thing, if he is tempted to be dishonest again."

My art teacher didn't think this was a very good idea. He somehow convinced my mom to wait and deal with my dishonesty and me after I returned home from the field trip.

Now, class, my math question for you is this: The bus was traveling at 55 miles per hour. If my mom left 45 minutes after the bus departed and traveled at 70 miles per hour, how long would it take her to catch up to the bus? Since the distance from Boston to New

York City is 200 miles, would my mom catch the bus before it arrived in New York?

When this cheating incident had occurred, I was at Harvard, and it had been difficult for me to believe that our wonderful son could do such a morally wrong thing. I had mixed feelings years later knowing Joe had taken a very troubling event and turned it into a math problem—one that the high school kids found to be hilarious. On the other hand, even though I had not chased after the field trip bus, Joe had never forgotten the incident. He was using it not only to teach math, but also to teach his students about the importance of honesty.

Joe, who received the 2011 Teacher Award for Excellence in Mathematics Education in Ohio, describes his job like this: "Some people think I teach mathematics, but I see myself as a person who uses math to teach kids about life."

Pearls from Pat

1. Do something new and difficult and meaningful—getting it right, especially the first time, is exhilarating.

2. Weave lessons about life, character, and ethical behavior into any subject matter you teach.

3. Have faith when you teach—the seeds of ideas that you sow may not come to fruition until months, or even years, later.

First Things First

As facilitators of *The Seven Habits of Highly Effective People* course, all of us engineering group managers believed it was a matter of personal integrity to practice the principles we were teaching. We frequently encouraged and reminded one another of principles that applied to our current work situations.

Habit 3, "Put First Things First," was the habit that stressed prioritization principles as part of effective time management. All tasks could be grouped into one of four quadrants:

Quadrant 1: Important and Urgent

Quadrant 2: Important and Not Urgent

Quadrant 3: Not Important and Urgent

Quadrant 4: Not Important and Not Urgent

(Covey, 1989, p. 151)

Effective people spend most of their time in the fire prevention state of Quadrant 2, working proactively on things that are important before they reach the firefighting state of Quadrant 1. When one of us saw a fellow facilitator performing engineering duties in a somewhat anxious state of mind, he or she silently held up first an index finger and then held up two digits—the index and middle fingers. This was our sign language for "Are you operating in Quadrant 1 or in Quadrant 2?" The fellow facilitator then usually smiled, nodded, and held up an index finger, admitting he or she was currently operating in the less effective fire-fighting mode of Quadrant 1.

One day I passed by the windowed office of a friend and colleague who had a good sense of humor. Seeing him bustling around his desk, I motioned through the glass the familiar hand signals for the question, "Are you operating in Quadrant 1 or in Quadrant 2?" He promptly conveyed just how urgent and important things were by smiling and raising one digit—his middle finger!

Another general rule of prioritization I found to be important was to put people ahead of tasks. In the corporate environment, it is very easy to be drawn unknowingly into a behavior pattern that prioritizes work ahead of people.

To counteract this, the acronym PFTS was posted above my desk at work. PFTS meant, "People First, Task Second." Sometimes when we are working, we become very engrossed in tasks. It is important to get the job done, we have to meet our deadlines, this report has to be revised, that assignment has to be completed, etc. Sometimes we even manipulate the people around us just to get the work finished. However, we have to stop and think, "People—colleagues, subordinates, bosses, friends, family—are always more important than the task that has to be done." We can do significant harm to our relationships when we put tasks first and people second.

This same idea is conveyed in this paraphrased Biblical story of Mary and Martha (Luke 10:38-42). Mary and Martha were friends of Jesus and they had invited Him over for dinner. I identified with Martha. She was out in the kitchen cooking dinner when her guest, Jesus, arrived. Martha's sister, Mary, went to the door and started chatting with Him. After a few minutes, Martha called from the kitchen, "Hey, Mary, I could use some help in here. Jesus, can you please tell Mary to come into the kitchen and help me?" To Martha's surprise, Jesus responded that it was more important for Mary to stay and converse with Him than it was for her to help Martha in the kitchen. Jesus was underscoring the point that people are more important than tasks. After really studying this story, I changed the way I entertained. Instead of making elaborate preparations when expecting visitors, I made simpler meals and did less work. I acted like Martha before the guests arrived, but once the doorbell rang, I turned into Mary. Talking with people is more important than serving an extravagant meal that keeps you from being with your guests.

1. Prioritize important things ahead of unimportant things and do them before they reach the crisis mode.

2. Remind yourself amid the work stress of the moment that people are more important than tasks.

Constructive Feedback

I don't like the concept of "constructive criticism." To me, it's an oxymoron—"constructive" means to build up, while "criticism" implies tearing down. I prefer the term "constructive feedback." Ken Blanchard captures this positive spirit when he quotes Rick Tate, saying, "Feedback is the breakfast of champions" (Blanchard, 2009, August 17).

Feedback, if given in a spirit of love and support, should be like a good breakfast, which builds you up and makes you stronger even when it is corrective in nature. It should always address the behavior, not the person. If we respond positively to all the feedback we get, people will be more likely to help us by providing more feedback in the future. It is far easier for people to ignore us, than to take the time to offer suggestions for our personal growth; we need to appreciate their efforts to help.

It is interesting to observe how presenters respond to constructive feedback after their talks when they are discretely informed about a typing error on their PowerPoint slides. "Your presentation was really informative. By the way, you might want to double check slide 10, bullet 1. I think there's a typo—it says 'fiction' instead of 'friction.' I look forward to hearing you present again in the future."

Some presenters (like me) are really grateful, and make a note of the change that is needed before the presentation is given to another audience. Other speakers comment on how they have given this presentation numerous times and no one has ever said anything. Still others just look annoyed that anyone would even mention such an insignificant error.

When it comes to behavioral issues, Ken Blanchard and Spencer Johnson suggest bosses use a "one minute reprimand" as an effective means of constructive feedback. The steps of this process—which also works well for teachers and parents—are:

1. *Tell people beforehand that you are going to let them know how they are doing and in no uncertain terms.*

The first half of the reprimand:

2. *Reprimand people immediately.*

3. *Tell people what they did wrong—be specific.*

4. *Tell people how you feel about what they did wrong—in no uncertain terms.*

5. *Stop for a few seconds of uncomfortable silence to let them feel how you feel.*

The second half of the reprimand:

6. *Shake hands, or touch them in a way that lets them know you are honestly on their side.*

7. *Remind them how much you value them.*

8. *Reaffirm that you think well of them but not of their performance in this situation.*

9. *Realize that when the reprimand is over, it's over.*

(Blanchard & Johnson, 1983, p. 59)

We are all accustomed to receiving feedback from our bosses. Relatively few organizations encourage people to *give* feedback *to* their bosses. Personally, I found it very useful to get feedback from the people who worked for me or were my students. Most of the time, my desire to improve my performance outweighed any potential disappointment about the negative aspects of the constructive feedback.

Here is a simple evaluation form based on one used decades ago by one of my professors. I have since used it to solicit anonymous feedback for my performance as a boss, facilitator, instructor, spouse, etc. It only takes about two minutes or less for most people to complete.

Quit-Keep-Start Evaluation Form

1. What should your boss *quit* doing?
2. What should your boss *keep* doing?
3. What should your boss *start* doing?
4. Any additional comments or suggestions?

The word "boss" could be replaced with "instructor," "mom," "husband," etc. The form focused purely on behavior; the tone of the form solicited constructive feedback on what needed to change (questions 1, 3, and 4), and also reinforced positive behavior on what needed to continue (questions 2 and 4). I left the room while the reviewers filled out the forms and usually provided a large plain envelope in which they placed all of their completed evaluation sheets.

Spending time seriously reflecting on the stack of responses, I was occasionally surprised by the feedback. Sometimes certain employees wanted me to quit a particular behavior that others wanted me to keep doing. Whether or not I agreed with their responses, it was good to know how people perceived me. I always thanked the group for their feedback, and sometimes shared actions I planned to take as a result. It was surprising when seemingly unimportant behaviors were items they wrote down for me to keep doing. Obviously those actions were important to them.

Sometimes I made a conscious decision not to change. That was okay. At least they knew their constructive feedback had been heard.

1. Try doing a "one-minute reprimand" as a way to address the behavioral issues of your employees—and your family.

2. Use a simple Quit-Keep-Start Evaluation Form to receive insights about what is important to the people who work for you.

3. Appreciate any constructive feedback you receive from others.

My Big Chance

I always expected one day to become a corporate executive. Progressing through my 40s, I still thought this would happen, although high-level openings were few and far between.

One day, a professional headhunter called me. After chatting for ten minutes, he determined I was a good candidate for an executive opening in a large, non-automotive, international corporation I had admired since high school. It was one of the few large companies outside of the auto industry, where I could really enjoy working. The headhunter asked me for a resume so he could set up an interview the following week at the division's out-of-state location.

Taking a few days of vacation, Jon and I traveled 270 miles, so he could check out housing prospects, while I was having interviews all day. The prospective corporation was located nearly two hours from the nearest automotive facility where Jon could apply for a transfer. If I happened to get an executive job offer, theoretically we could live in the middle—an hour commute for each of us.

Arriving at the executive offices, I was greeted by a manager from Human Resources who got me something to drink, gave me my schedule for the day, and led me to a conference room. She explained that I would remain in the conference room all day and that the various executive interviewers would come to me.

A different executive came in every hour on the hour, each conducting a 50-minute, one-on-one interview— including a lunch session where sandwiches were brought in for both of us. After speaking with eight executives, I had a very good understanding about the staff members, and they had a multi-faceted view of me. It was gratifying to realize how much of my auto industry experience was very applicable to another industry. Yet there were just enough differences to enable me to bring a fresh perspective to complement their knowledge and experience. The staff was all men and they specifically wanted a qualified woman to fill the opening, but it had to be a woman with whom they would all feel comfortable working.

The HR Manager called the following Friday afternoon saying that all of the interviewing executives wanted me to join their team. The job was mine, if I wanted it. A formal job offer would be put into writing and mailed on Monday. I was requested to review the letter upon receiving it and call her with any questions about the details on salary and benefits that would be enclosed. Jon and I were both excited. However, we decided not to celebrate until the formal letter with salary and benefits arrived.

When Monday came, the HR Manager called. This time the news was not good. She said their company's CEO had just announced a freeze on all outside hiring. According to the directive, the executive opening I had been offered had to be filled from within the company. I was disappointed, but at the same time, a part of me felt relieved. The executive interviewing process had been a positive, validating experience. I knew I had what it took to be an executive at a large corporation; the interviews and verbal job offer from outside of my company had reaffirmed that. However, a part of me didn't want to move away from our home overlooking the golf course and the lake. There was no housing like it where the new job was located.

~~~~~

Some months later, I was pleased when my boss, Nate—who was Helen's successor—told me that his boss had recommended me as an interview candidate for a quality executive opening in our company. I was already in my late forties, and there were very few people who had been promoted to an executive position in the company once they passed 50. This interview was important for my career.

Arriving at the interview, I was put into a room with two other candidates. We were all told that the interview would be done in a round robin fashion in three rooms. The three candidates would go into separate rooms, each containing three executive interviewers who would ask the respective candidate questions for half an hour. At the end of the 30 minutes, each candidate would rotate to the next room for another round of questions with a different group of three interviewers. After another 30 minutes, the candidates would again change rooms and answer more questions. Then the nine interviewers would take one hour to compile their findings, eat lunch, and prepare to interview three more candidates following the same process in the afternoon.

As the introductory session continued, we were told that the scoring of each candidate's answers would be based on a new interviewing system that the corporation was piloting. It was called the STAR system where S stood for Situation, T stood for Task, A stood for Action, and R stood for Results. The candidate would be asked a question such as, "Can you give an example of a time when you had to make a difficult leadership decision under pressure?" The candidate would then have to give a short explanation of a specific situation he was in or task he was given, what action he took, and what the results were. If the candidate did this correctly, each interviewer would give him a STAR and assign a quantitative value based on the quality of the answer.

Walking into my first session, I realized this would be different from any job interview in the past. All of my previous interviews at the company had been one-on-one sessions with HR or the prospective boss. Those sessions had always gone very well. Even when I had been asked by a headhunter to interview for an executive job outside the auto industry, that experience had been a long series of unstructured one-on-one interviews.

Now facing the first three-person executive interview team, I hoped to do as well in this structured interview format as in past unstructured one-on-ones. The first question came and I responded naturally, temporarily forgetting about the importance of the STAR (situation/task, action, result) format. My answer must have been incomplete because one of the interviewers reminded me of the importance of STARs. On the next question, my mind went blank; I could think of no situation to use as an example. I persevered through the rest of the session, and was relieved when it was over.

Making a restroom stop, I tried to compose myself before walking into the next session. I prayed God would help me to remember experiences appropriate to the questions that would be asked in the next two sessions. Then I took several deep breaths and felt myself relax.

The next two sessions went well. The questions seemed easier to answer. Sometimes a story told in Session 2 could be easily tweaked and used to answer a question in Session 3. Progressing through the process, I realized instead of just telling each story, I could make it easier for the interviewers by stating succinctly: "The situation or task was___; the action I took was___; the result was___. In that way, I increased the likelihood of a getting a STAR and a higher score.

Two days later I was called and told that someone else was selected for the executive position. I had known five out of the six managers who were candidates for the job and had already mentally chosen the person I considered my closest competitor.

That individual was the person the interview team ultimately selected. I was disappointed and knew my less-than-stellar performance during the first session had contributed to my loss. However, I had learned a lot, and hoped someday soon another opportunity to interview for an executive position using the STAR process would come up again; next time I would be ready.

Unfortunately, no executive job interviewing opportunity at the company ever came my way again.

~~~~~

Instead, a few months later, two other opportunities presented themselves within a week of each other. I felt appreciated, and grateful Nate was campaigning to boost my career. He was now recommending me for a three-month overseas assignment in Germany, which would start in six weeks. It would be good to have overseas work experience on my record. I was very interested and could put to good use the German language skills acquired during my days as a foreign exchange student.

The following week, Nate called me into his office with another opportunity. The Director of Strategic Planning was looking for a "hi-pot" (high potential) engineering manager. This person would work as the Technology Planning Manager for two years and then return to engineering with critical cross-functional planning experience. I decided to go for the interview with the Strategic Planning Director to learn more about the job.

The Director's name was Travis and he had moved from engineering into strategic planning a few years before. His current Technology Planning Manager had been offered a position in the Research and Development organization and Travis needed to fill the position within a month. He needed someone who was comfortable working with both vehicle program teams as well as engineering directors, executive directors and executive group directors. An important responsibility of the position was to run Future Product and Technology meetings twice a month, facilitating issues discussions among the top engineering and planning executives.

Engineering was a huge organization. I knew my director and his executive director, but never interacted with anyone higher than that. The idea that by taking a technology planning manager job, I could suddenly be running the Future Product and Technology meetings for my engineering boss's boss's boss seemed amazing to me. I could be in the room where key strategy discussions were happening, setting the direction for the company's future technology development!

I mentioned the three-month overseas assignment my current boss was planning for me, and asked Travis if he decided to choose me, whether I could start the job after returning from Germany. He said, "No. I need this job filled now." He thanked me for meeting with him and said I was one of six candidates he was considering. He planned to interview the other five individuals within a week.

I liked Travis a lot. He seemed professional, straightforward, and people-oriented. When I asked myself a key question, "Can I learn something important from this person?" my response was yes. That affirmative answer was confirmed by talking with his direct reports. Olivia, a woman who reported to Travis, explained that by permitting her to work three days a week, her boss had helped her to achieve the work-life balance she needed to be home more with her children. Travis cared about getting the job done. He did not care about "face time" in the office and trusted his team; working from home as needed was fine. I liked the people in this planning group as much as the people who were currently my peers in engineering. That was a good sign.

There was one obvious difference between the planning organization and all of the other organizations where I had worked—there were noticeably more women. About 35-40 percent of the people were women in planning compared to 5 percent or less in engineering and manufacturing.

It was a win-win situation. If I did not get the Technology Planning Manager job, I would go to Germany for three months. If I did get the job, I would see engineering from an entirely different perspective. Either way, I'd start a whole new adventure.

Travis made me an offer.

I took the job.

Pearls from Pat

1. Take vacation time to interview with other companies to see how outsiders value your skills,

2. Prepare for a corporate executive interview by listing personal examples of leadership, teamwork, problem solving, conflict resolution, creatively working with constrained resources, handling moral dilemmas, and asking the right questions.

3. Consider all pros and cons before making a lateral move to a different part of the organization. Realize that things could change in the future and promises to bring you back cannot always be kept.

Thoughts on Self-Esteem

Many people have issues with self-esteem, especially when they are not recognized or promoted as high or as quickly as they expect to be. Eleanor Roosevelt addressed the subject with her famous quote: "No one can make you feel inferior without your permission." Actor Michael J. Fox expressed it this way: "One's dignity may be assaulted, vandalized and cruelly mocked, but it can never be taken away unless it is surrendered." Both quotes convey the strong influence the put-downs of those around us can have on how we view ourselves—but only if we allow it.

Many people who work in large companies get easily swept up into the culture of externally generated self-esteem. Paradoxically, some of the most influential people in human history were humble, but principled individuals, who did not run huge conglomerates: Jesus, Gandhi, and Mother Teresa, just to name a few. As founder of the Missionaries of Charity, Mother Teresa said, "At the moment of our death, we will not be judged by the amount of work we have done, but by the weight of the love we have put into our work" (Mother Teresa, 2002, p. 140). She changed the world, one dying beggar at a time, driven by her deep love of God, and her ability to see Jesus in the face of every unfortunate person.

Thinking about the words of Mother Teresa, I realized that what we do and what we have are totally irrelevant in the big scheme of things. Ultimate success and value are measured by our answers to these questions taken from the greatest commandment (Mark 12:30-31):

1. Do I love God?
2. Do I love others?
3. Do I love myself?

My personal relationship with Jesus has always influenced me—and my sense of self-esteem. From the time I experienced the overwhelming loving and healing presence of Jesus as a child, I knew God loved me completely and had saved me for a special purpose. There would be people I needed to help and others who would help me. This knowledge gave me a deep sense of meaning and joy. God also loved every other human being infinitely and specifically, and had a unique purpose for each person's life.

~~~~~

One of the people I felt called upon to help was a talented young woman named Kara who struggled with self-esteem issues, both personally and professionally. While I normally didn't discuss things of a spiritual or religious nature at work, I made an exception and gave Kara a copy of a long prayer I had written while going through a difficult period in my own life. She said this was a significant source of encouragement for her, especially since she, like me, had gained weight over the past five years. Here is the excerpt from the prayer that she found most meaningful:

Lord,
Let me see myself as You see me...
Let me see my body as You see it—as my earth
suit, the temporary physical home of my
soul while I live in this world—a truly
amazing creation.

Let me choose to like my body – even with its imperfections—appreciate its great functionality, and maintain it well.

~~~~~

One book on self-esteem I highly recommend for both adults and children is the short story by Max Lucado called, *You Are Special.* It beautifully illustrates how each of us is so uniquely important. When we really understand this, we stop comparing ourselves to others. We no longer feel superior—or inferior—to anyone. We also are not significantly affected by the criticisms—or praises—of the people around us. Instead, we listen to the still, small voice inside of us, do the very best we can in every endeavor, learn from our mistakes, and genuinely love the people who touch our lives each day. Who we are and what we accomplish may be interesting. But knowing *Whose* we are is what's really important.

That's the beginning of genuine self-esteem.

Pearls from Pat

1. Love God, love others, and love yourself.

2. Don't be overly influenced by either the praise or the criticism of others.

3. Think about self-esteem as explained in this verse: "For we are God's masterpiece. He has created us anew in Christ Jesus, so we can do the good things he planned for us long ago" (Ephesians 2:10).

The Lessons of Golf

Someone once jokingly told me that when it comes to success in business, playing golf well is probably more important than having an MBA. Over the years I have found in some organizations, this is actually true. Some of the departments where I worked never mentioned the word golf, while others were really into it.

I had never been exposed to the game while growing up, and Jon had never mentioned the topic while we were dating. When we got married a few months after I graduated from college, I was quite surprised when Jon brought up the idea of playing a round of golf together on our honeymoon. I was excited to learn something new, and assumed that this perfect man, who was now my partner for life, would be an excellent instructor. I agreed to rent some clubs and a pull cart to play my first round with him.

When we arrived at the public course, we were told there were open tee times currently available, however, a ladies league would start in 40 minutes. Instead of taking me to the driving range for some preliminary instruction, Jon decided we should head right for the first hole of the golf course.

After showing me the proper stance, grip, and swing motion, Jon instructed me on the proper pull cart etiquette. "Always bring your pull cart to a spot even with the ball. If you leave it behind you, you will need to walk back to get it; that wastes time. If you pull it forward of the ball, you might hit it, if the ball goes off the toe of the club. Always pull the cart up even with the ball."

I hit the ball and it went ten yards. Again I hit the ball and again it went ten yards. The next shot was a short jab. As I stepped forward to hit the ball again, Jon reminded me, "Always pull the cart up even with the ball." Painstakingly, I worked my way down the fairway.

As we approached the end of the hole, Jon inadvertently chipped his ball over the green. He was getting a little uncomfortable because the first foursome of the ladies league had arrived at the first tee. He knew we had taken far too much time getting down the fairway; we had to get moving. Going down the hill behind the green, he chipped his ball onto the putting surface. He walked up the hill to see how close he was to the pin. Getting to the top he saw that my ball and I were already on the green—and so was my pull cart.

Every golfer knows that greens are hallowed ground. You never bring a pull cart onto the short, specially groomed grass intended for putting. However, being a new golfer, I didn't know that. I was simply following Jon's instructions, "Always pull your cart up even with the ball."

My pull cart on the green sparked a Dr. Jekyll/Mr. Hyde metamorphosis in Jon, the likes of which I had never witnessed before. His face turned red and he started shouting, "What the #^&* are you doing? Get that &^$$%# cart off of the green!" I was confused by his anger and shocked—it was the first time I had ever heard Jon curse. Grabbing the cart handle, I began to pull the cart off of the green. This angered Jon even more. He shouted, "&^$$%# it, don't pull it off! Pick it up and carry it off!"

Lifting up the pull cart, I carried it off the green, and saw all the ladies on the tee watching us. I didn't care about them and what they thought. Setting the cart back down on the fairway, I walked with it back to the club-house. I could not believe what had just happened. That monster on the green could not possibly be my new husband. The Jon I knew was a wonderful man who never swore. Had golf revealed this man's true nature in a way none of our other experiences together ever had? The dawning possibility that marrying Jon may have been the biggest mistake of my life horrified me.

Fortunately, within half an hour, peace was restored.

~~~~~

I didn't pick up a golf club again until more than a decade later at a community education golf class. Getting the basics from a stranger was a lot less stressful than learning golf from my husband. From the class I discovered that, while not everyone can play golf well, anyone could be welcomed as a golf partner if he or she learned the rules and etiquette, and kept up the pace of play. With this in mind, an opportunity presented itself, and I decided to participate in my first golf scramble.

In the energy industry where Jon worked, golf was a popular activity, especially at the natural gas conferences he attended annually. Jon had invited me to come with him to a conference in Colorado, where he was one of the speakers. I assisted him by proofreading his material, and then flipping the transparency slides on an overhead projector while he gave his presentation to the large audience. After his speech and the rest of the morning meeting sessions were over, we participated in a golf scramble, where the teams were determined by handicap. Each foursome was comprised of a very good golfer, a good golfer, an average golfer, and a poor golfer, called A, B, C and D players respectively.

Jon and I were assigned to different teams. Naturally I was my team's "D" player—and its only woman.

In a golf scramble, all four people hit their balls, select the ball landing in the best position, and then all hit their next shots from that preferred location. The play continues until the ball rolls into the cup. I was a bit nervous, but the men on my team were gracious and put me at ease. The first hole went well even though none of my shots was used. Then we came to the second hole and the ladies tee was about 150 yards ahead of the men's tee. I hit my ball only 70 yards, but because our best player had sliced his ball into the woods, my drive landed in the best spot. This bolstered my confidence and we continued to play, cheering each other on and enjoying the round. Besides that drive, I contributed three putts and two chip shots to the green—not great, but decent for a new golfer.

After the 18-hole round, my foursome sat down to dinner with Jon's foursome, and the scramble winners were announced. I was pleased to hear my team had come in first place. My teammates and I went up to receive our prizes. Returning to our table with our individual envelopes, we opened them. Each of our four envelopes contained $150. Jon sat beside me speechless, realizing I had just won more money playing golf than he ever had.

~~~~~

Golf scrambles tend to generate a real sense of spirit and camaraderie. For this reason, they can be very good team-building activities for people who work together professionally. I participated in a union-management golf scramble while working in the assembly plant Body Shop in Ohio. It was surprising how two union officials and two superintendents—who normally might be at odds with one another at work—could join forces and cheer each other on to achieve a good team golf score.

Having learned this valuable lesson, I became an advocate of annual work-related golf outings, especially once we bought the house in Michigan on the golf course. Most summers Jon would organize an outing for his department and I would organize one for mine.

Now I was working for Travis in the corporation's strategic planning organization. I had volunteered to organize a departmental golf outing at the golf course adjacent to our home, encouraging everyone—even the non-golfers in our group—to participate in the scramble format. I did the usual job of forming teams by ensuring that each team had an approximately equal blend of strong and weak players. My team consisted of the following A, B, C, and D players: an excellent golfer who had a single digit handicap; me, who had a maximum handicap, but knew the course and the rules well; Olivia, who played golf once a year and needed to borrow some golf clubs; and a college summer intern who had never golfed before, but had played a lot of putt-putt.

Our team was having a fun time during the scramble, having some good holes and some bad holes, counting a lot on our "A" player to keep our overall team score decent. Then it happened. We arrived at the 15th hole, a very challenging par 5. It had multiple hills on the right side, and a fairway slanting from right to left, directly into a large marsh along the entire left side of the fairway.

We all hit our tee shots. Fortunately, the ladies tee was 123 yards closer than the men's tee. I hit a very good drive, which landed well beyond the other balls. When we all took our second shots, the young summer intern had an outstanding hit that landed 25 yards to the right of the green. Never had I ever seen any player or team so close to the green on #15 after two shots. With a little luck, we might be able to chip on, one putt, and get a birdie on this tough hole.

Olivia was the first to line up her chip shot. The green was undulating and difficult to read, but she put forth her best effort. The ball took off and was headed towards a point about four feet to the right of the pin. It landed, bounced, and then took an unexpected sharp left turn. It started rolling toward the pin; then the ball suddenly disappeared—directly into the hole!

The four of us stood there in total disbelief. Our team of relative golfing misfits had just gotten an eagle—a score of 3 on a very challenging par 5 hole—without using a single stroke from our "A" player! We jumped around and shouted from the shared sense of euphoria.

Working together we had accomplished something that, for us, was next to impossible.

Years later, after we each moved on to work in other departments, we would occasionally cross paths and talk about the amazing eagle on #15. That moment, and the feeling that accompanied it, is something we will always cherish.

1. Learn the rules of golf, the game etiquette, and how to keep up the pace of play—you will be welcome on the golf course and have fun regardless of your skill or handicap.

2. Build departmental cohesiveness by organizing company-sponsored golf scrambles or other types of fun team activities.

3. Remember that even untalented individuals working well together can sometimes produce amazing results.

The Pendulum Swings

One thing you become aware of, after working several decades in the auto industry, is what could be called "the Pendulum Syndrome"—the swinging back and forth of reorganizations and directional strategies. Some examples of this include the following:

- **Parts supply.** Most automotive original equipment manufacturers (OEMs) have, at some point, moved from horizontal relationships with parts suppliers to an in-house vertical integration strategy of parts manufacturing. This often happens after parts suppliers have failed to make a timely delivery of within-specification parts. Causing costly automotive assembly plant shutdowns, this leaves the OEM feeling unable to determine its own destiny. Desiring control and autonomy, the automotive OEM then develops a vertical integration strategy, taking over the manufacture of its key components first, and then, over time, other components as well. New parts divisions are created and held accountable for their own profitability. When making a profit is difficult for some to achieve, the parts divisions are consolidated into one or more larger entities. As the OEM realizes that making components is not its core business and that such work can be done less expensively by outside suppliers, the pendulum swings back. The consolidated parts divisions are sold off and the corporation moves away from a vertical integration strategy only once again to be at the mercy of its outside parts suppliers.

• **Computer services**. For everything from payroll to inventory control to production control to engineering design, computer services are essential to automotive corporations. This indispensability makes computer services vulnerable to the pendulum syndrome as the issues of high costs and technical expertise wrestle with the issues of tight control and corporate confidentiality. Also, when a corporation contracts out computer services, the service company will tend to try to use another program it can pull off the shelf and modify a bit to fit most of the corporation's needs. The users soon find out (after two or three years of costly development and modification time) that this new whiz-bang program doesn't provide half of the useful information that the antiquated customized in-house system did—and productivity suffers. As soon as the top executive who ordered the computer outsourcing is gone, the pendulum swings again and a new guy comes in to rebuild the in-house information technology empire, adding thousands of techies to the payroll.

• **Organizational structure**. Originally automotive corporations adopted the hierarchical organizational structure of the military. Every employee had one boss. Chain of command was clear and inviolable. Then came the era of project management and matrix organizations where everyone had two or more bosses—one functional boss and the other bosses leading the specific cross-functional product team(s). A professional employee could have two or more bosses depending on how many products he worked on in his functional capacity. Though chain of command was a little muddy and conflicts did occur, most professionals enjoyed the interesting dynamics that cross-functional teams provided. The overhead cost, however, is significant, When companies face severe economic hardships, the pendulum swings again, headcount is cut, and there is a return to the streamlined efficiency of a hierarchical organization where every employee has one boss.

- *Centralized vs. decentralized management.* When a corporation has operations in a variety of locations, the question arises about how much operational decision-making authority should be held by the individual locations, and how much should be held at corporate headquarters. The pendulum swings, depending on the view of the people at the top of the company.

- *Innovative thinking vs. standard practices.* Large companies need to have standardized processes for many aspects of their businesses. However, there's always a better way to do things, and innovative thinking needs to be encouraged for organizations to improve. As rogue innovations are tried in one part of the company, standard practices break down, impacting the smoothness of operation. Instead of maintaining a healthy balance between these essential stresses of standardization and innovation like the Japanese do, many American companies handle this with pendulum swings in their management mandates.

Change is a part of life, and is essential for every company. Organizations must adapt to fluctuating economic environments. Evolutionary changes are generally beneficial, and even those that are quantum leaps are often good. However, not all change is worthwhile. Often it is costly, especially when the change turns out to be something that is different, but not really better.

Over the years, I have come to the conclusion that there is no one best way to run things. Every system and strategy has pluses and minuses; you have to maximize the pluses and minimize the minuses. Most systems and organizations can work reasonably well if the people involved understand what they are supposed to do, and do it consistently. People should be encouraged to improve the system constantly, in a well-communicated and controlled way—what the Japanese call "Kaizen."

When corporate history starts repeating itself—and the pendulum swings back to practices common a decade ago—people question if the organization is really maturing or just going around in circles. The "old-timers" in the workforce just shake their heads and quote the memorable Yogi Berra, "It's like déjà vu all over again!"

1. Understand that organizations usually go through pendulum swings every decade or so, especially when there is a change in top management.

2. Realize that some changes are healthy adaptations to a shifting external environment; others are costly, disruptive distractions that do not result in genuine improvement.

Support vs. No Support

Working as the Technology Planning Manager in Travis' group was a wonderful experience. He spoke highly of each member of his staff in front of the group. He also let us run with most of the innovative ideas we had on how to morph our responsibilities to add more value to the corporation.

Part of my job was facilitating the Future Product and Technology meetings. In this forum, the executive directors in engineering and planning set strategic direction—determining what types of technologies Advanced Engineering would develop to address future customer needs. I was also communicating with all of the car program development teams on the latest technology development work being done in Research and Development (R&D) and Advanced Engineering. Product teams needed to choose the technologies they wanted on their vehicles, and include the costs in their program budgets. Working closely with and observing these corporate executives fueled one of my life-long passions—leadership.

It was genuine serendipity when one day while on a business trip, I came across an ad in an airline magazine for a doctor of management degree program in organizational leadership. I remembered being incorrectly addressed as "Dr. Schuch" years before, while teaching college physics, and how the title had sparked a desire in my heart. Reading that ad, I knew instantly that pursuing a doctoral degree in organizational leadership was exactly what I wanted to do next.

The doctoral program required a few weeks each year to be spent taking courses at the university's central campus, which was 1700 miles away. However, the program was geared towards working professionals, and the bulk of the coursework was to be done on-line, an educational approach that was not in widespread usage in 1999.

My company had a tuition reimbursement program that would cover the cost, as long as the following conditions were met:

1. I was accepted into the program by the university.
2. My boss supported my working on the degree.
3. The company approved of the degree program.
4. I continued to work full time while taking classes.

It would be difficult to take on so much schoolwork and write a dissertation while working full time. I discussed the idea with Jon first. For at least three and a half years, I would be spending every minute of non-working time on studying; I would not be able to keep up my normal share of household responsibilities. Jon would have to pick up the slack—or overlook what home tasks did not get done. However, unlike my MBA, during this degree program there were no children to care for at home.

Jon agreed to support me in this challenging pursuit.

Next I went to speak with my boss Travis. He was surprised I wanted to tackle such a long and difficult endeavor, but was quick to offer support. I could work from home as needed, so time generally spent commuting could be used for studying. The few weeks spent in courses on campus could count as my annual professional development training. He would review the doctoral program with his executive director to be sure he supported it as well.

Travis and his boss both agreed to support me in pursuing this goal.

Everything proceeded well for the first year. The coursework was brutal. However, my job was going well, and my brain cells seemed to be multiplying exponentially. I brought lessons learned from the online classroom into my job, and insights from my job into the online classroom. I enjoyed the interactions of my diverse classmates and professors.

Jon and I adapted to our new family routine. Instead of being 600 miles apart like we were during the Harvard MBA years, we were now 25 feet apart, but often just as isolated. After work I holed up in my home office with the door closed for five to six hours every weekday, and twelve hours every Saturday and Sunday.

Then it happened—the corporate "R" word— Reorganization.

~~~~~

The company decided to merge its separate car and truck operations into one new entity, called North American Operations. The entire organization chart changed dramatically, and the downsizing meant no promotions. Things were chaotic for months, while people changed jobs or had their positions eliminated or redefined. Travis moved from strategic planning to engineering.

My new boss, Oscar, was an intelligent man whom I liked and respected. However, we soon discovered an area of friction—Oscar was not interested in having someone from his group responsible for coordinating the Future Product and Technology meetings for the top executives of strategic planning and engineering. He believed the meeting coordination to be more of an engineering function. He agreed to let me continue in that role, however, because that's what all of the affected strategic planning and engineering senior executives wanted. They also decided that the meeting needed to be expanded to include the executives from the newly merged truck organization.

When the car and truck groups merged, I believed I could take on coordinating the technology communications with the truck program teams as well as the car program teams. Most of the technology communications were handled smoothly via quarterly technology meetings, monthly emails, and periodic tech plan updates from the planners on the vehicle program execution teams. Simply increasing the distribution list was a non-issue for me.

Oscar had a different vision. He wanted to create another layer in the communications chain, and hold meetings twice a month with representatives from all of the vehicle line teams. These representatives would then communicate what they deemed appropriate to their various program execution team planners—the guys with whom I had previously communicated directly. I saw these vehicle line team representatives as a bureaucratic filter layer of non-decision-makers. They could impede the information flow to the individual program execution team planners—the people who needed to make program technology spending decisions and keep their technology plans up-to-date. Plus, I had no desire to chair two meetings a month that I considered unimportant.

After being unable to sway Oscar to just try things my way for a few months, I reluctantly agreed to support his reorganization of work and give it my best shot. Deep down inside I was concerned about a self-fulfilling prophecy—this new process might fail because I believed it wouldn't work. I didn't want that to happen.

While I was still adapting to Oscar's management style, the university term ended and my grades arrived. When I asked Oscar to sign my tuition reimbursement form, he refused! He said having a doctorate was unnecessary for anyone working in the company, except perhaps the Ph.D.'s working in Research and Development.

I was dumbfounded. There were a few people wanting to get advanced degrees in medicine, who were denied upper management support for tuition reimbursement before they started the program. (There was too high a likelihood they would leave the company to use their medical degree somewhere else.) I had never heard of anyone being denied tuition reimbursement *after* they had gone through multiple terms of advanced study in engineering, business or management. I tried to understand Oscar as he presented his point of view.

When Oscar was done explaining how, in his opinion, sponsoring doctoral degrees was not a good use of company money, I understood and respected the fact that he believed strongly in his position. Convinced of the importance of acting in a way consistent with one's personal convictions and values, I expected him to do no less. However, now there was a problem. I was part way through a doctoral program that I intended to finish. My former boss, Travis, and his boss had committed the company to provide tuition reimbursement for the duration of the program. I would now have to go back to Travis for advice on what to do since my new boss would not approve the reimbursement.

Hearing this, Oscar simply shrugged his shoulders, and I left his office.

Telling Travis about my predicament, I hoped that he would offer to continue signing my tuition reimbursement forms. Instead, he simply shook his head and sighed, "Don't worry, Pat. I'll take care of this."

Two days later, Oscar stopped by my desk with his signature on my tuition reimbursement form. "Well, it looks like Travis went to his former strategic planning executive director who initially approved your doctoral program last year. That executive director then spoke with my executive director, and convinced him to continue supporting you. The bottom line is my boss told me to sign your tuition reimbursement form. I still don't believe it's the right thing to do, but when my boss says, 'Do it,' I do it."

When he turned to walk away, I thanked him. Seeing

Oscar's face left me with the sinking feeling that I had just won the battle, but lost the war. It was a cardinal rule never to go around your boss to get to his boss. However, unintentionally in a convoluted way, that is exactly what had happened.

I had to find another job in a different department.

~~~~~

Originally I had come to the planning organization from a job as a "hi-pot" (high potential) engineering group manager responsible for sixteen engineers. My boss intended for me to work two years in a developmental assignment as a technology planning manager. Then I would to go back to engineering, hopefully to a position with more responsibility.

Unfortunately, during those next two years, the entire company environment changed. Reorganization had merged all truck and car engineering departments, and the company was significantly reducing the number of engineers and engineering group managers, so there was no job for me in engineering. Besides that, I enjoyed managing strategy development and technology planning, influencing high-level decision-making, and having enough flexibility to finish my doctorate. I wanted to do similar work under another director in an assignment leading to a promotion.

The answer to my prayers came in the form of an R&D executive who remained in the conference room after a Future Product and Technology meeting. Ed was a tall, thin, humorous man, with an outspoken passion for innovative technology. His outgoingness was not typical in the introverted Research and Development arena. Ed came up to me after the meeting and said with a smirk, "So, how's everything going with your new boss?"

"Oh, just fine. But you know me. I'm always ready for a new challenge. Why? Do you know of any openings in R&D needing a person with my special skills?" I joked.

"Actually, one of the other R&D directors might have an opening that would be a good fit for you. Let me check and get back to you."

"That would be great. Just be sure to let him know I still have a few years of work on my doctorate to finish."

Ed replied, "Hey, no problem. Most of the people in R&D have their doctorates. People like me, with only a master's degree, are the exception, not the rule."

The next day, an R&D director named Marie called. I knew who she was, but had never really worked with her. "Ed suggested I phone you to see if you would be interested in interviewing for a job in my group. If you want to find out more, just say the word, and I will call Oscar and get his okay to interview you."

"I'd love to come for an interview. Why don't you wait until tomorrow to call Oscar," I replied. "I would like to speak with him first."

An hour later, I went to see Oscar in his office. I told him how, even though we liked and respected each other as individuals, our management style approaches and differing views on key issues sometimes made working together difficult. "I was thinking we both might be happier if I looked around for positions that might be available in other parts of the company."

Oscar replied, "Well, Pat, if you found something else that really interested you, I wouldn't stand in your way."

"Thanks, Oscar. I appreciate that."

Two days later I was sitting in Marie's second floor office. It overlooked the large Research & Development reflecting pool, with its striking stainless steel water tower in the shape of a Van de Graaff generator—just like the ones from middle school science demonstrations on static electricity. The atmosphere in Marie's office, as well as in the entire R&D building, was one of intense quiet. The private offices and laboratories were a sharp contrast to the bustling energy found in the interactive cubicle arrays of the planning and engineering buildings.

Marie shared her vision of improving the relationships the researchers had with both engineering and the vehicle program teams. Not enough of the research projects were making it through the development pipeline all the way to the showroom floor. Improved communication with engineering and vehicle program teams was needed to commercialize more research breakthroughs. Conversely, better understanding of future customer needs and corporate technology strategies could lead to establishing more relevant research projects.

Marie also wanted to improve communications with our European division's Advanced Engineering group to understand their work, synergize with similar work efforts in North America, and reduce redundant spending. For this work, my ability to speak German was a plus.

Already responsible for coordinating the allocation and project prioritization for the corporation's R&D and Advanced Engineering budgets, Marie wanted to move control of the Future Product and Technology meeting to her group, especially when I told her Oscar was not interested in keeping the meeting under his jurisdiction.

Marie said R&D in general, and she in particular, supported employees doing doctoral work. She would speak with Oscar about offering me a job in her organization. Then she encouraged me to talk with some of the people in her group, as well as other people in the R&D organization, before making my final decision.

I left her office amazed at this blessing. I not only had the prospect of a new adventure working for someone who supported my educational goal, but also was probably going to take the favorite part of my old position with me. Plus, I would be working with our European office in Germany. Walking down the hall, I passed Ed's office. He gave me a knowing smile and a nod. I stopped at his doorway and said, "Thanks for telling Marie about me. I really appreciate it."

I took the job.

Pearls from Pat

1. Remember that promotional opportunities increase when a company is expanding and decrease dramatically once the organization starts downsizing.

2. Surround yourself at home and at work with people who will support and help you to achieve your goals—or at least will not be a roadblock.

3. Think carefully before going around your boss. It can be a political kiss of death, even if it's done inadvertently.

4. Say nothing bad about your boss to others, even if you are not getting along. Simply indicate you are open to new opportunities.

Executive Decision-Making

During my early years with the company, I assumed executives made decisions at meetings in a way that resembled a TV courtroom drama. All of the information was presented at the meeting; various points of view were argued; then, after weighing all of the evidence presented during the meeting, a group decision was made.

Much later I came to realize that executive decision-making was often done in a behind-the-scenes manner that more closely resembled the U.S. Congress. I was not aware that politically astute presenters would discretely spend time talking one-on-one to key people during the week preceding the decision-making meeting.

It was Ed who had perfected an efficient technique for getting executive boards to make decisions in his favor. He was kind enough to share his personal methodology with me.

Ed's approach was based on the Pareto principle, developed by Vilfredo Pareto in the late 1800s and popularized by Joseph Juran in the 1940s. This methodology underscored the importance of identifying "the vital few and the trivial many" (Juran, 1951, p. 2-16). I had seen this concept applied when prioritizing potential defect sources for quality control issues in the factory. Now I was intrigued by the way Ed applied the concept to the members of an executive committee. He explained that in every democratic-looking, decision-making body, there are actually one or two people (the vital few) who really make the decisions. There are also one or two people, called influencers, whose opinions carry weight in a discussion. The individuals who are influencers may change from meeting to meeting, based on their areas of expertise and the decision that needs to be made. The rest of the people on the committee (the trivial many) are basically along for the ride. They will unconsciously mimic the positions expressed by the vital few.

Ed had a strategy for getting an executive committee to make a favorable decision on an issue he was presenting. First, he made a list of the people on the committee. After attending one or more committee meetings, he identified each person on the committee as a decision maker, influencer, or someone who just needed to be informed. He then made sure he had a concise explanation prepared to brief each decision maker and influencer individually during the week preceding the meeting. Sometimes Ed was able to get on the executive's calendar for fifteen minutes to review a few key slides and answer questions or concerns. More often, Ed used an "elevator speech," intercepting an executive while he was going to another meeting and hitting key bullet points during a 60-second walk to the parking garage or during an elevator ride. Any concerns or questions raised by the executive could be quickly answered and the formal presentation modified accordingly.

If Ed could not reach a decision maker personally, he found out from the executive's administrative assistant what the executive's preferred communication mode was. Some executives were speed-readers and preferred information sent in an email. Others were auditory in style and preferred to listen to a short voicemail while driving to or from work. Using the individual's preferred communication mode was key. This targeted personalized approach supplemented any official committee pre-meeting communications and material distribution that was the norm for all meeting attendees.

By the time the executive committee meeting was actually held, the skids had been greased, so the desired outcome was generally achieved.

Does this work all the time? No, especially if someone identified as one of the trivial many turns out to be an influencer who has not been brought into the fold. However, the other informed key people can generally carry enough clout to sway the outlying influencer.

1. Identify and briefly update "the vital few" individuals on any decision-making committee before the meeting occurs.

2. Remember that when it comes to executive decisions, a concise, 60-second "elevator speech" can be as important as a detailed, 20-minute PowerPoint presentation.

9/11

On Tuesday, September 11, 2001, Jon was on a business trip in San Antonio, Texas, attending an energy conference where he had been a presenter the day before. I had taken some vacation days to join him, see the Alamo, and enjoy taking a leisurely stroll down the city's famous River Walk. The conference was scheduled to end at noon and our flight back to Detroit would leave several hours later.

Arriving for breakfast in the hotel a little before 8 a.m. Central Daylight Time, we noticed a group of people from the conference clustered around a big screen TV. Joining the crowd, we were shocked to see the image of New York City's North Twin Tower in flames having been struck by an airplane. Then the South Tower was hit. We watched in utter silence realizing with horror that this was no accident. Jon and I were grateful that we were together, even though we were far from home.

The conference session started at 8:30 a.m., but the auditorium was less than 25% full. The moderator acknowledged the drama that was unfolding in New York and assured everyone that he would provide news updates between the speaker presentations. The first speaker began, but the small audience had its attention elsewhere, and a few people started leaving. Someone pulled the moderator aside and he then interrupted the speaker. "We just got word that the FAA has grounded all flights in the country indefinitely. Knowing that you all need to make alternate arrangements to get home, we are ending the conference now."

Jon and I had a short discussion, and then made a series of brief calls to update our parents, our children, and our bosses about our plans. We then joined the small group of people from the Detroit area who were huddled together talking about what to do next.

Some had originally arranged to stay in San Antonio for a few days after the conference, so they decided to follow their itinerary and hope the flight ban was lifted by the time they were scheduled to fly home. We felt blessed to be in possession of a rental car and offered to give a ride to anyone else who needed to get to Michigan. One very grateful man asked to come with us.

I called the rental car company to explain the situation, and they vehemently insisted that we return the car to the San Antonio airport as scheduled. "We are not asking for your permission," I explained calmly. "We are informing you that we will be dropping off this car at Detroit Metro Airport within the next two days, period. So please let your records reflect that fact. We will pay the additional charges for the extra time and the remote drop-off. Thank you."

Checking out of the hotel, the three of us started the 1500-mile journey home with Jon driving the first leg of the trip. While we all felt an urgency to get home, Jon was the most concerned. "We have to get through Texas as soon as possible. Having worked with the extensive natural gas pipelines here, I know we have a really long trip ahead of us."

Even rotating drivers, it took us forever to get out of Texas. Looking at long expanses of flat land with tumbleweeds rolling around was boring and a stark contrast to hearing the ongoing disturbing news on the radio.

As we drove, we noted posted gas prices increasing dramatically—doubling and even tripling in some areas. When too exhausted to go any further, we stopped at a hotel to sleep for six hours. Other travelers we met all were headed home. Nothing mattered to anyone except being with family.

After 26 hours of driving, we finally arrived at Detroit Metro Airport Wednesday evening. It was eerily deserted with no cars dropping off or picking up anyone. A security guard appeared, informing us that the airport was closed and we could not go in. However, we could pick up our personal cars parked at remote lots and drop off the rental car at the car agency's remote lot as well.

The man at the rental car office was very kind as we turned in the car. When we asked how much the extra day and the drop-off fees were, he calmly replied, "After all that has happened to you and everyone else in this country, there will be no extra charges. We're just glad you and the car got here safe and sound."

I felt like Dorothy in the *Wizard of Oz* arriving in Kansas after her journey. There's no place like home.

Pearls from Pat

1. Be aware that a crisis clarifies priorities and can embolden people to break the rules.

2. Remember that business trips can be tiring, interesting, and sometimes fun, but coming home is usually the best part.

Sacrificing to Achieve a Goal

Working on a doctorate in organizational leadership—while keeping my day job—was just what I wanted to do, even though it meant some significant personal sacrifices. It was fascinating and fun to study a vast variety of courses including leadership styles and theories as well as organizational dynamics. Two years of continuous classes, even difficult coursework, is a process of putting one foot in front of the other on a predetermined path.

Doing a dissertation starts out that way; then it quickly turns into hacking your own path through a jungle. After a while you're not sure if you'll ever reach your imagined destination, and you even start to question whether you really wanted to go there in the first place! Long hours of reading, researching, organizing, composing, editing, and suffering were all part of the dissertation writing process.

I personally knew a number of individuals who ended their doctoral programs ABD, "all but dissertation." They finished the doctoral coursework and then stopped midway through their respective dissertations out of pure frustration. Some worked on a topic for several years and during that period, one or more members of their dissertation review committees changed. Every time a new professor joined the review committee, there were things he/she did not like or wanted added, requiring rewrites. Other students who took several years to write their dissertations got caught up in changing university dissertation requirements or format changes, which also caused time-consuming rewrites. One way to minimize these detours and graduate on time was to complete the dissertation in less than seventeen months. That was my goal.

To accomplish this, I would have to work on the dissertation every day. This was a real grind. In addition to daily prayer to help me, I had two motivating sheets of paper posted above my home workstation. One was a quote from Philippians 4:13, "I can do all things through Christ who strengthens me." The second was a picture of the Nike swoosh icon with the words "Just do it!"

The title of my dissertation was "Dual Supervision, Directional Alignment, and Job Satisfaction in a Matrix Organization." The topic caught my interest as I watched my company experience the growing pains of transitioning from a hierarchical organization to a matrix organization in the area of vehicle line development. The mechanism for creating a next generation vehicle had expanded beyond the use of "Core Teams" to the formation of "Vehicle Line Teams." Now each cross-functional team member officially had two bosses—his functional manager (the direct supervisor in his functional area of work like finance, manufacturing, engineering, marketing, etc.), and his project manager (usually the vehicle line executive responsible for developing a particular car or truck program). My study would examine what effect having multiple bosses had on people in an organization, especially when those bosses gave conflicting directions.

Doing the preliminary research was not too difficult. I became engrossed in numerous books, studies, and online articles related to leadership, organizational structures, teams, project management, etc.

Once the research portion of the dissertation was completed, the real difficulties began—trying to come up with a solid methodology for collecting and analyzing data to prove or disprove my hypotheses. Working closely with my dissertation committee, I developed draft after draft of the content for a survey instrument to collect the necessary data. The quantitative portion of the survey had to be easy for the study participants to use, yet constructed so the data could be readily juxtaposed to run and analyze potential correlations. Qualitative elements were also necessary for capturing verbatims—open-ended written comments from the participants, regarding some of the issues under study.

I needed help in using statistical software and doing website design. Fortunately two angels came forward to assist me.

The first angel was a woman named Noreen who worked in my R&D building in a different department. She had recently completed her own dissertation, and was an expert in statistics. She already had the expertise and software necessary to run the correlations and other statistical analyses. Noreen offered to run all of my statistics—provided I would get her the data in the format her software required.

The second angel was our daughter Jean, who, by this time, had a master's degree in software engineering, and was experienced in constructing websites. Jean put my data collection instrument into a user-friendly "radio button" format on a specially set-up website for my survey participants to use. She also wrote the code necessary to download the data in the format needed by Noreen for the statistical analyses.

Months before, I had casually mentioned the topic of my dissertation to Ned, a supportive, make-things-happen leader in charge of the vehicle line executives. Ned indicated his interest and agreed to support my project when the time came to request vehicle line team members to complete the data collection survey.

Now it was time to share the proposed survey with Ned and his staff, and address any concerns they might have before the team members saw it. Everyone was pleased with the proposed survey; they said it was obvious I had spent a lot of time with vehicle line teams. The content seemed to capture the key issues they faced. The executive team looked forward to the future presentation I would give explaining the study's results.

Due to Ned's endorsement, 46 percent of the population of 473 vehicle line team members completed the voluntary survey! This was far more than expected, and it significantly increased the credibility of the data.

I had initially requested Noreen to do a limited number of correlations to address my specific hypotheses. Speaking from her own recent dissertation experience, she suggested we run every variable against every other variable, in case some surprising relationships emerged. After all, the software would do all the work.

Noreen overwhelmed me the next day with a huge roll of statistical output. She was right. After I plowed through all of the numbers, there were some unexpected significant correlations.

The biggest dissertation problems occurred when I experienced writer's block. At those times, it sometimes helped to set my alarm clock to ring in 30 minutes, say a prayer asking God for inspiration, take a deep cleansing breath, and then try to nap for half an hour. When the alarm went off, I went to my computer while still half asleep and typed whatever came into my head. I hoped God would put some ideas into my mind while it was in a relaxed and receptive state. This process often helped to get me going again.

Writing a dissertation reminded me of assembling a 1000-piece jigsaw puzzle. You have a general idea of how the final product is going to look. You also have miscellaneous pieces of literature research, data collection, and analyses. They feel like a disjointed mess, but you start to juxtapose these pieces within the dissertation framework established by your university. Like a puzzle, the more pieces you put into place as you write, the easier it gets to position the rest. Your dissertation committee points out where you have holes and need to look for missing pieces. (They also indicate when you have some extraneous pieces that belong to another "puzzle," and need to be discarded.)

There were very few special days when I experienced "ah-ha" moments, got in "the zone" oblivious to time, and typed a portion of the paper that practically wrote itself. Rereading those sections the next day, I thought, "I can't believe I wrote this. It sounds pretty good!"

Finally, the dissertation and my oral defense were completed. The last approval signature was penned sixteen months, three weeks and two days after I started it. I presented the results to Ned and his staff, who were pleased with the study and wanted it shared with the vehicle line team members.

The bad news was I had gained fifteen pounds from stress-related snacking and zero exercise during the grueling process. The good news was I had done my day job well, managed to stay married, and now was ready to celebrate coming out of my home office cocoon.

Three weeks later, Jon and I flew 1700 miles to attend my graduation ceremony. Jon was the only person who was directly impacted every day by the sacrifices made for the past three and a half years. He was my greatest supporter, and I really appreciated him.

Seven of the original eighteen doctoral students in my cohort graduated that day. Because my surname was near the end of the alphabet, I was the last to walk across the stage to receive a diploma. A thunderous ovation filled the auditorium. The audience had been asked to hold all applause until the end, and the clapping was really for all of the many students who had received bachelor's, master's, and doctoral degrees. However, the sound rose from the auditorium right after I had been handed my diploma, and it felt in that instant like the whole world was applauding just for me. I raised both arms in victory.

I was now Dr. Pat Schuch.

Pearls from Pat

1. Have something motivational at your workplace to remind you to stay focused on a task that requires long-term perseverance and commitment.

2. Obtain help for time-consuming ancillary tasks outside your area of expertise.

3. Complete your dissertation quickly to minimize the chances of changes—either in your review committee members or in university requirements.

4. Celebrate your degree and the knowledge you gained. It's something no one can take away from you.

The Urge to Lead

Walk into my home office and you will find the shelves filled with dozens of books on leadership, reflecting my passion for the subject. I often ended my work emails with a "Leadership Quote of the Week." One memorable statement was attributed to Thomas Paine who said, "Lead, follow or get out of the way."

I laughed when first hearing this statement, realizing the biggest impediments in organizations were those individuals who not only didn't lead and didn't follow, but also definitely didn't get out of the way. These people were the complainers who sneakily chipped away at a group's morale; sometimes they were the lazy people whose unfinished workload constantly had to be picked up by other members of the group. If the office was a noticeably happier and more productive place when certain people were on vacation, then they generally fell into this category.

Jon had this thought on leadership: "Good leaders are not afraid to make decisions, make the right decision more than 50 percent of the time, and never make the same mistake twice."

When it comes to skillful leaders, I agree with Peter Drucker's quote: "The important and difficult job is never to find the right answer; it is to find the right question." The most productive meetings I attended were those where the leader first listened well to all the information that was presented; then he or she asked just the right question, evoking a new line of thinking from everyone, as they left the room to pursue the answer.

Additional leadership thoughts I enjoy pondering include:

- "Leadership: Balancing self-discipline with a nurturing spirit that encourages, challenges, inspires, and believes in excellence." - Author unknown
- "Without a vision, the people will perish." - Proverbs 29:18
- "Catalytic leadership skills are: thinking and acting strategically; facilitating productive working groups; leading from personal passion and strength of character." - Jeffrey Luke (Luke, 1998, p. 149-150)
- "Before you are a leader, success is all about growing yourself. When you become a leader, success is all about growing others." - Jack Welch (Author unknown, 2013)
- The *4E's of Leadership* include: "Energy, Energizers, Edge, Execute." - Jack Welch (Welch & Byrne, 2003, p. 190)
- "The best executive is the one who has sense enough to pick good men to do what he wants done, and self-restraint enough to keep from meddling with them while they do it." - Theodore Roosevelt
- "This is pre-eminently the leadership quality—the ability to organize all the forces there are in an enterprise and make them serve a common purpose. People with this ability create a group power, rather than express a personal power." - Mary Parker Follett (Follett, 1933/1995, p. 168)
- "Become a servant leader. Work for your people. Help people to accomplish the goals that emanate from the vision. Give them the tools they need, and then turn them loose." - Colin Powell (Harari, 2002, p. 140)

- "Leadership is the ability to get extraordinary achievement from ordinary people." - Brian Tracy
- "The Law of Explosive Growth states, to add growth, lead followers—to multiply growth, lead leaders." - John C. Maxwell (Maxwell, 1998, p. 205)
- "Leadership is action, not position." - Donald McGannon (Author unknown, 2013)

When asked to give short talks on the subject of leadership, I most often refer to Stephen Covey's "Four Roles of Leadership: Pathfinding (Envisioning), Aligning, Empowering, Modeling" (Covey, 1999, xvi-xvii). I even developed a sentence to help me remember the PAEM acronym for these four roles. "If you're going to lead 'em, you've got to PA(y) 'EM." To elaborate, leaders have to create and clearly communicate their vision of a future state; align the organization's resources to work together synergistically to support the vision; empower, inspire and trust the people to do what is best to accomplish the vision (without micromanaging them); and constantly model trustworthy character, values, and behavior while achieving the vision.

A leader needs to focus the organization on its mission. For companies that have no mission statement, Covey formulated this generic version—"Universal Mission Statement: to increase the economic well-being and quality of life of all stakeholders" (Covey, 1992, p. 296).

Shortly before passing away, Stephen Covey wrote this leadership definition in his forward to L. David Marquet's book, *Turn the Ship Around*: "Leadership is communicating to people their worth and potential so clearly that they are inspired to see it in themselves" (Marquet, 2012, p. xiii).

Viktor Frankl's work highlights the motivational aspect of leadership: "Man's search for meaning is the primary motivation in his life" (Frankl, 1984, p. 121). People follow leaders who help them find meaning in their work.

Decades ago, I heard someone state this abbreviated, but powerful, interpretation of Lao Tzu's 17th Tao: "When the leader is bad, the people despise him. When the leader is good, the people praise him. When the leader is great, the people say, 'We did it ourselves!'"

~~~~~

I have noticed that no leader leads all of the time. It would just be too exhausting. Instead, people who are considered to be leaders are happy to serve in the follower role—or even in the "get out of the way" role—in a variety of circumstances. However, when a specific situation or mission arises, which ignites passion or a sense of duty, a person will feel what I call a compelling *urge to lead*. These prompts can be external or internal.

One example of an external *urge to lead* occurred when Joe came home distraught after the second day of band camp before his junior year in high school. The Band Director had asked him to give up his position as leader of the lively 24-person clarinet section, and instead lead the struggling 8-person sousaphone (tuba) section.

Joe explained, "I told the Band Director I don't even know *how* to play a sousaphone, so how could I possibly be the leader of that section?"

"What did the Band Director say then?" I asked.

"He said, 'The sousaphone section needs a good leader.' Then he added, 'Joe, it would be easier for me to teach you to play the sousaphone, than it would be for me to teach one of the sousaphone players to be a leader.'"

I sat silent for a moment, impressed by the powerful insight of that statement. I was surprised that the Band Director would even think of having someone who couldn't play the instrument be the section leader. It was actually a pretty creative—and desperate—thing for him to consider doing. I responded that the Band Director had to have a lot of confidence in Joe's ability to learn and adapt quickly, as well as in his ability to inspire the sousaphone players to improve their marching, section spirit, and discipline.

The Band Director had given him an *external urge to lead*. Joe needed time to internalize it and build up some passion before he could commit.

The following morning, Joe took the job.

Joe devoted more time and physical energy to band that year than he ever had done before. All of his hard work paid off as the sousaphone section improved and at the end of the season was designated the "Outstanding Section of the Year." The following year, his peers further recognized Joe for embracing his *external urge to lead* by electing him Senior Co-Leader of the award-winning 150-student marching band.

~~~~~

A different kind of experience can result from an *internal urge to lead*. This occurs when no one is asking you to lead; instead, you feel internally moved by a situation or mission or opportunity to take on a leadership role.

One memorable example of an *internal urge to lead* involved a non-profit organization I joined in 1975 while being a stay-at-home mom. At my introductory meeting of this women's community volunteer group, the President reviewed a list of potential fundraising activities and community service projects. The last one she presented involved organizing and building a "Safety Town" to teach kids who were about to enter kindergarten how to be safe going to school. Work elements included building a kid-sized town with streets, buildings, traffic lights, pedal cars, and crosswalks. It also required developing a one-week curriculum, getting volunteers to teach, handling registrations, and having the whole program operational in less than four months. By the way, there was no money in the budget for the project, so Safety Town had to fund itself.

A collective groan sounded from the group. "No way!" "It sounds too hard." "There's not enough time."

"We've never done anything like this before." The comments reverberated across the room. I was brand new to the group, and it seemed smart to keep quiet. However, a sense of passion filled my spirit, and these words came out of my mouth: "I know this is my first meeting, but this Safety Town is the most exciting and meaningful thing that's been discussed all night. Is anyone else here interested in working on this project?"

Two of the ladies quickly said they were extremely interested, but they didn't want to be in charge. Two other ladies also said they would be willing to help. The President then turned to me and said, "Pat, we usually don't have new people lead projects, but you seem to have the most passion about Safety Town. Would you be willing to be the lead on this if the group approves it?"

I took the job.

The next few months were a whirlwind of activity for the five of us on the steering committee. We developed a strategy and invited key community stakeholders to an informational meeting held to solicit their assistance.

As obstacles arose, our steering committee came up with creative solutions. For example, we had to figure out a way to put in a 100' x 100' section of asphalt adjacent to the existing school playground. The estimate for the asphalt job was thousands of dollars. We creatively decided to break the job down into a number of smaller tasks and ask a variety of companies to each do one part.

One company agreed to dig out the dirt and haul it away. A stone company donated the crushed material for the base. We got another company with dump trucks to pick up the stone and deliver it, and then solicited volunteers (mainly our husbands) to spread it. An asphalt company donated the asphalt material. One local company trucked in the asphalt, while yet another company provided the rolling equipment and some guys to spread the asphalt. The city road maintenance department painted all the Safety Town crosswalk and street lines.

In the end, we got 10,000 square feet of asphalt installed on time without paying a penny. Safety Town opened in August as promised and was a big hit with the kids and their parents. The annual Safety Town classes continue to be held in that community *four decades* later! And it all started with a strong *internal urge to lead.*

This brings to mind another favorite leadership quote, a classic attributed to anthropologist Margaret Mead: "Never doubt that a small group of thoughtful committed citizens can change the world. Indeed it's the only thing that ever has" (Lutkehaus, 2008, p. 261).

1. Understand that you can be a good leader, even in an area where you have no experience—if you are fueled by passion.

2. Realize that the "urge to lead" can be externally generated by another person, or internally generated by your personal response to a situation, mission, or opportunity.

3. Experience the thrill of leading a dedicated group of individuals to accomplish something meaningful that others think is too difficult to do.

From International to Global

Our company had been an international corporation for decades. Like many large companies, we had acquired existing automotive operations overseas, with each facility having its own local processes and procedures. There were some redundancies in advanced technical work development—nearly the same type of research was being done concurrently at multiple international locations without sharing information or resources. In short, we had to transition from having an international scope with isolated, regional activities, to becoming a single, coordinated, global enterprise.

Working with our overseas divisions was something that I had done occasionally and enjoyed over the years. It had been a disappointment to give up the three-month overseas engineering assignment in order to take the technology planning manager job working for Travis. Now, working for Marie in R&D, I was pleased to get an assignment that required me to spend seventeen days in Germany. My job was to learn the German processes for prioritizing and developing new automotive technologies, and then align and "commonize" their practices with our systems in the U.S. My boss noted that this visit to Germany, my first since completing my doctorate, was special. To everyone in the U.S., I was still Pat; however, in the formal meetings in Germany, my name changed from Frau Schuch to Frau Doktor Schuch.

Jon mentioned my seventeen-day Germany trip to his boss and an unexpected thing happened two days later. His boss said the head of the corporation's facilities operations in Germany had requested some short-term U.S. facilities help to improve their fork-truck systems and operations. Fork-truck systems and energy were Jon's areas of expertise. His boss decided Jon would be the perfect person to go. If his trip could be co-ordinated with mine, there would be some corporate business trip money to be saved—my department could take care of our shared hotel expenses and Jon's department could take care of our shared car expenses for the time we were in Germany.

In all of our years with the company, we had never heard of a husband and wife from different parts of the corporation both going on overseas business trips to work at the same location at the same time. Jon and I were excited, knowing the work we each had to do would be challenging. It would be especially meaningful, because we could share our experiences with each other. Plus, we could take some great side trips together throughout Germany on the weekends.

While Jon prepared for the technical aspects of his assignment, I put together some German language reference sheets for him to use to smooth the way for him culturally. It would accelerate his acceptance by his German colleagues if he memorized and used some basic German greetings and phrases, including some typical openings and closings in his emails. Jon would also have to tread the fine line of being knowledgeable enough to be respected, but not come across as an arrogant know-it-all who intended to "fix" their way of doing things.

In the meantime, I had my own work to accomplish. Part of my assignment was to "sell" my German counterparts on corporate common processes for advanced technical work; this translated into "start using our U.S. systems." However, I was very open to the possibility that there might be aspects of their systems and processes that were better than our own. "Seek first to understand, and then to be understood" is the fifth of Covey's *The Seven Habits of Highly Effective People* (Covey, 1989, p. 235). If you listen to and fully understand others first, you have a foundation upon which to work to better explain your own ideas.

For the first week I listened.

Initially I was mentally comparing everything they said to the U.S. way of doing things. However, in order to really understand them, I needed to forget about U.S. systems, and fully understand the world in which the German advanced engineers lived. The more important questions were:

- Which regional executives make the decisions about the advanced technical work projects that get funded?
- What information do those decision makers need to make those decisions?
- How can the necessary information best be assimilated?
- Once the advanced technical work decisions are made and appropriate money and people resources allocated, who is held accountable, and how is the project progress tracked and reported until completion?

The German organization was much smaller than the U.S. organization. One guy using a spreadsheet could pull together the information German executives needed to make decisions on how best to prioritize their technology projects. There was significantly more work being done by a lot of different people in the U.S. Using a database made more sense there.

After all, a computer system for tracking advanced technical work projects is just a tool. The reason people use tools is to make their jobs easier, not harder. For the Germans, using our database was definitely going to be more work for them. However, by learning to use the database, they would have access to information on all of the technology projects the U.S. was developing.

The best thing to do was to start with the basics. Looking at the spreadsheet the Germans used to track information on their advanced technical work, I asked if they could include several additional columns of data that we needed. If so, an analyst in the U.S. could take the information on the German expanded spreadsheet and do the initial data entry of all the German technologies into the database. I also requested copies of the upper management reports their executives required on advanced technical work. Our database managers would create the ability for German engineers to generate similar reports from the database at the click of a button.

For the time being, the Germans continued to work from their spreadsheet as they learned to access, use, and update what was eventually becoming the global database for advanced technical work. I continued to grow the database after visiting other regional offices—adding the Swedish projects, the Australian projects, and finally the Asian projects.

The time came when the corporation no longer allocated advanced technical money regionally by leaving the prioritization and decision-making solely up to the executives in each country. Instead, all of the corporation's advanced engineering projects in the world were reviewed and prioritized globally before money was allocated to any region. Engineers working on similar projects across the world started communicating with their counterparts overseas, learning from one another. Projects were combined and redundancies eliminated. Occasionally frictions developed, but overall, the engineers and scientists really liked working with professionals from other parts of the world. Standards and accountability for reporting project progress and completion were discussed with all of the regions providing input into designing a common process.

No longer just international, we were truly becoming a global corporation. And with each bit of progress, the synergy and excitement grew.

1. Travel together as a couple on business, especially when it can benefit the company. You'll experience work-life balance in a whole new context.

2. Seek first to understand by listening with an open mind, especially when there are cultural differences.

3. Realize that a significant amount of work and culture change is required to transition from being an international company with regional activities to becoming a global corporation working as a coordinated worldwide enterprise.

Being a Mentor and Role Model

One of my favorite quotes comes from journalist Peggy Noonan, who states, "There is a great unseen circularity in life, and we are all interacting with the people we are supposed to help and be helped by" (Noonan, 2005, p. 209). While this statement applies to all aspects of life, it especially applies to mentoring.

Career mentoring is a time-consuming and very meaningful activity. It can be formal or informal, short-term or long-term, regular or sporadic. Mentoring is all about building a relationship between the mentor and the mentee that provides support, encouragement, and idea exchange.

When first asked to give a short talk on how to be a good mentor, the following bullet points were on my list:

- Be true to yourself—be the best YOU that you can be. This is the first step to becoming a good role model and mentor.

- Follow the "Golden Rule"—treat others, as you want others to treat you.

- Listen twice as much as you talk. It's why God gave mentors (and everyone else) two ears and only one mouth!

- Be an encourager. This is a critical aspect of mentoring. I hope that long after I'm gone, people will remember me as an encourager—someone who motivated them to be better than they thought they could be.

- Share your knowledge and wisdom, using as much as possible the Socratic method of leading a mentee to truth by asking key questions. Keep in mind that many people remember their mentors' lessons and pass them on to future generations.

- Be known for your good character as well as for your competence. Whether they realize it or not, mentors convey values first and career advice second.

- Walk your talk—it is the real meaning of integrity, a key ingredient of good mentoring. (Too many people of influence convey, "Do as I say, not as I do.")

The following anecdote illustrates this last mentoring point very well:

> There is a story of a woman in India who was upset that her son was eating too much sugar. No matter how much she chided him, he continued to satisfy his sweet tooth. Totally frustrated, she decided to take her son to see his great hero, Mahatma Gandhi.
>
> She approached the great leader respectfully and said, "Sir, my son eats too much sugar. It is not good for his health. Would you please advise him to stop eating it?"
>
> Gandhi listened to the woman carefully, turned and spoke to her son, "Go home and come back in two weeks."
>
> The woman looked perplexed and wondered why he had not asked the boy to stop eating sugar. She took the boy by the hand and went home.
>
> Two weeks later she returned, boy in hand.

Gandhi motioned for them to come forward. He looked directly at the boy and said, "Boy, you should stop eating sugar. It is not good for your health."

The boy nodded and promised he would not continue this habit any longer.

The boy's mother turned to Gandhi and asked, "Why didn't you tell him that two weeks ago when I brought him here to see you?"

Gandhi smiled, "Mother, two weeks ago I was still eating sugar myself" (Author unknown, 2008).

Here was a man with real integrity. Gandhi chose not to give advice, unless he was living by it himself. We should all do likewise.

~~~~~

Each of the mentoring relationships I've had over the years has been unique and taught me something special. We tend to underappreciate the wisdom that comes from our own life lessons. Things that seem to us like simple common sense, not even worth mentioning, can often provide important value and direction for someone with less experience.

Speaking less is often very effective. Instead of talking a lot, I encouraged mentees to brainstorm a myriad of possible solutions to address a particular issue, writing down options as they spoke. Then, the mentees talked through the possible consequences of each alternative. This process can be empowering to individuals who otherwise feel stuck.

One of my mentees, named Katherine, worked as a superintendent in a powertrain plant and was assigned to me through the company's formal mentoring program. Katherine had never been outside of the plant environment so I spent a full day introducing her to a wide range of people working elsewhere in the company. The areas included studios where future car designs were sculpted from clay, high tech engineering offices and testing facilities, a vehicle team meeting where the cost per car of vehicle options was heatedly debated between representatives from marketing and finance, and lastly, the fuel cell lab of a research scientist.

The scientist was very excited about his work. He recently had a breakthrough in his study and quickly pointed to some formulas and tables of results. His job was just one small aspect of the company's overall fuel cell research program. However, he understood very well the significance of his work, and the part it played in the company's future success.

Coming back to my office to debrief the day, Katherine commented on how she had no idea the company she worked for had so many varied and interesting activities going on. She was impressed that the people she had met were all happy about and very engaged in their work. "Especially that research scientist," Katherine remarked. "I have no clue what he was talking about, and I wouldn't want to have his job. But one day, I want to feel as passionate about my work as he does about his!"

~~~~~

One young woman I mentored had been a math major in college. As we talked about her work and interests, I shared with her my "Life Formula."

In mathematical terms, if L stands for Life and C stands for Choice, then:

$$L = C_1 + C_2 + C_3 + \ldots + C_\infty$$

$$\text{or} \quad L = \sum_{n=1}^{\infty} C_n$$

"We don't always have control over the things that happen to us," I explained. "However, we always have the ability to *choose our response* to what happens. My life is the sum of all the choices I make from birth to death. That is what the "Life Formula" conveys. If you want to change your life, change your choices.

~~~~~

In addition to my one-on-one mentoring activities, Jon and I did mentoring as a couple. At one point we were asked to host a college co-op student from Germany who was going to work for the summer at our company's proving ground facility twenty minutes from our home. Our own children were married, so it was wonderful to have a young person in the house again with us for three months. Martin helped me to sharpen my German, and I helped him improve his English.

We took him on several excursions, including visiting two things Martin wanted to see most—Niagara Falls and the Woodward Avenue Dream Cruise (Suburban Detroit's annual celebration of viewing and driving vintage automobiles). We also had long discussions about the differences between life in the U.S. and Germany. The U.S. was ahead of Europe in health concerns about smoking. Enjoying cigarettes as he did, Martin had to adjust to the growing number of "smoke free" zones he encountered in the U.S. We placed an ashtray on our deck and explained to Martin that he could not smoke inside our home; we received a special rate on our home insurance premiums for having no smokers in our household. A few days later Martin found it very disconcerting when he passed a large billboard on the highway that proclaimed, "Kissing a smoker is like licking an ashtray." He said you would never see something like that in Germany.

We appreciated our time with Martin—and years later enjoyed visiting him at his home in Germany.

~~~~~

As part of addressing the emotional void of our empty nest, Jon and I also felt moved to become licensed foster parents. We wanted to nurture and share our home and, in some small way, continue to impact the lives of children in our community. We focused mainly on emergency care and temporary short-term placements of less than two weeks. The two of us juggled our work schedules and took vacation days as needed in order to care for more than twenty of these children in crisis over the years—including shuttling them to and from their court appointments and school, as needed. The children were amazing individuals in difficult situations, usually caused by the irresponsible adults in their lives.

As part of mentoring these foster children, we developed our "Schuch Family Mission Statement." This put into words the family values that were the foundation for raising our own children and caring for the wonderful foster children who were only with us for a short time. The plaque in our kitchen reads as follows:

The Schuch Family Mission Statement

Our home is a safe, comfortable place where family members love, listen to, and encourage one another:

- To serve God and others
- To learn constantly
- To develop one's talents
- To live a happy, healthy life.

Having the mission statement prominently posted in our kitchen serves as a good reminder about what is most important, especially during the hectic moments of our daily lives.

Mentoring—like parenting, coaching, and teaching—is time-consuming and sometimes frustrating, but in the end, very meaningful. It involves nurturing relationships, and encouraging people to understand their own self-worth and reach their full potential. While mentoring usually provides no extra monetary compensation, it is heartwarming to be energetically greeted by someone you have not spoken with in years, and told that your mentoring made a difference in his or her life.

~~~~~

I've discovered that while mentoring is usually a specific decision one makes to coach or guide another person, role modeling is not always done by conscious choice. We can become role models—either positive or negative—without ever intending to, because people are always observing our actions.

Jon and I had the opportunity to reconnect with a wonderful woman with a successful career in Washington, D.C. She had lived next door to us in Ohio as a college student, and had been the babysitter for our children during several summers when they were nine to eleven years old, before we moved to Boston. After not hearing from her for decades, we received an unexpected Christmas letter in which she wrote:

> *I've described Pat to many throughout my adult life as the first career woman I ever met who successfully balanced it all. You, as a couple, were unique for my small town upbringing, and gave a welcome broader perspective. Together, you were a great example of a couple who managed it all—family, kids, faith, everything! I still remember Jon making supportive comments when Pat was accepted into the MBA program at Harvard. The temporary move to Boston must have meant sacrifices for you both. Times have changed now, but in my eyes, you were brave and admirable "pioneers." God has granted me exceptional blessings—many quite possibly undeserved. Having known the Schuchs, especially Joe and Jean, is among them.*

I was stunned. Jon and I had no idea we were influencing the teenage babysitter who lived next door to us for two years. Her letter served as an important reminder that, without our knowledge, people are observing and considering us as role models even decades later.

That's a pretty sobering thought.

1. Understand that mentoring is a time-consuming, meaningful, activity that is a great way to make a positive difference in the world by listening and encouraging others to reach their full potential.

2. Realize that you are already a role model—either positive or negative—whether you want to be or not, so act accordingly.

The Business Side of Technology

Research and Development in the automotive industry was similar to that of other industries; the work was considered top secret and great pains were taken to keep information from being leaked to competitors. The labs and research facilities were in a separate section of the corporate campus. While the rest of the company transitioned from working in offices to laboring in cubicles, the scientists and researchers kept their private offices. For them, an atmosphere conducive to solitary thought was preferred to one promoting communication.

This isolation created one big issue—not enough R&D projects ended up on manufactured vehicles.

Some R&D projects were created because of a "pull" mechanism—a vehicle program team asked for a new technology to be developed to meet a customer need or want. Other R&D projects resulted from a "push" mechanism—the scientists came up with ideas they wanted to develop first, before trying to find a vehicle program team that would actually offer the technology as a feature on its new vehicle.

Vehicle program teams grouped technologies into three general buckets:

1. *Required*: those developed to meet government mandates like safety or fuel economy.

2. *Desired*: those that fulfilled the wishes of the customer in a specific market segment. For example, soccer moms driving mini-vans wanted different features than single, career-driven men driving sports cars.

3. *Customer WOWs*: those unexpected and sometimes game-changing technologies that surprised and captivated the customer.

R&D often didn't think about the customer or these three buckets. There was a communication gap between the scientists or advanced engineers who developed the technologies, and the vehicle program teams who developed the vehicles. How could we get these groups to talk with each other in a mutually meaningful way?

I had been to various public technology displays like the Consumer Electronics Show held each January in Las Vegas. That gave me an idea to discuss with Marie. Why not host a company technology show targeting key program decision makers within our corporation? We could set up a two-day forum for the technology developers to explain their technologies to the vehicle program teams. They would also have to present the *business* aspects of their technologies and a clear statement of why the customer would want this on his or her car. We could set up displays with simple, standardized, one-page posters that concisely explained what was important to the vehicle development teams. It would include a photo or drawing of the technology, the technology description, the customer benefit, the estimated capital expense and piece cost, and the projected date when development was expected to be completed and ready for vehicle program implementation. Tables could be set up to support demonstration hardware as needed. We could schedule the program teams to come through at appointed times and visit technology stations manned by the scientists and advanced engineers. Naturally, we would need security to ensure that only appropriate individuals viewed the displays.

Marie thought the idea was a little wild, but she liked it and promised to discuss it with the Executive Director of Engineering, the Executive Director of Vehicle Development, and her boss, the Executive Director of R&D.

Several days later, Marie invited me to her office. "The executive directors liked the idea of an internal technology show. However, they have several conditions. First, the advanced engineers cannot spend an excessive amount of time working on this and preparing displays. Even spending two days staffing their stations has to be cut in half, so you must manage the logistics to get all of the vehicle program teams through the displays in one day. Second, you have to lead this effort and make it happen in addition to staying on top of your current workload. Third, you have to do this with no budget. Fourth, they want it called a Technology Symposium."

Undaunted by the conditions, my response was simple. "Great. I'll get started right away!"

I formed a small Symposium planning team with representatives from the various advanced engineering and research groups. We developed a list of poorly understood but promising technologies that we wanted showcased in the Symposium. Team members pitched in to draw up a floor plan for the displays and handle the myriad of details. We developed a one-hour training session for the participating engineers and scientists. I showed a standardized one-page PowerPoint technology poster and explain the business mindset of the vehicle program teams who would be viewing the displays. Besides financial estimates, the presenters needed to have short explanations of the technologies, in language that a high school student could understand. I asked each scientist to imagine and describe a future TV commercial showing a vehicle equipped with his technology—so he could see his project work through the eyes of the customer. Though this request was outside of their scientific comfort zone, I felt confident they would meet the challenge.

After the meeting, one young scientist came up to me and said, "You know, Pat, when I was in college, many of the A students went into science or engineering, many of the B students studied finance, and many of the C students majored in marketing. Now that I'm working, it seems like the B and C students are making most of the company's significant decisions."

My response was a guarded one: "I believe that is too much of a generalization, but if what you say is true, then it shouldn't be too hard for a former A student like yourself to learn some business lingo and influence the program team decisions. I look forward to seeing your one-pager and hearing your summary."

The next challenge was the zero budget constraint. I could print the one-pagers myself on 2' x 3' sheets on a printer readily available in R&D. After scheduling the symposium in a large room with portable fabric walls, I applied Velcro (found in an abandoned storage closet) to the 2' x 3' sheets and discovered it worked fine; the paper sheets lay nice and flat when attached to the fabric walls, even though they were not mounted on any costly, stiff poster board.

Measuring the effectiveness of the Symposium was important to me. We developed a simple survey sheet to quantify every program team's interest in each of the technologies before and after the Symposium. Detailed follow-up meetings between program team members and appropriate scientists and engineers were arranged. We also gave the program teams secured access to a virtual Technology Symposium on an internal company website, so they could revisit all of the information and displays they had seen in person.

The Technology Symposium was a genuine success. The engineers and scientists grew in self-confidence and expanded their understanding of the customer needs and wants. The program teams were excited to learn about the little known technologies currently under development. Some of the technologies generated no interest by the program teams and could be considered as candidates for funding cuts. Others generated a little—or a lot—of program team interest. In future years, the Technology Symposium would include overseas technologies, and U.S. vehicle program teams would reap even more benefits of globalization.

A year later, Marie moved laterally back to engineering. Another engineering director named Darcy took her place as Director of Global Technology Management. Darcy was an engineer with an MBA who understood the importance of integrating R&D activities into the company mainstream business. She and some other directors from R&D, planning, and finance, developed and taught a "Business 101" curriculum to train all of R&D in the financial and marketing aspects of the company.

Most importantly, the scientists were finally understanding the big picture of the auto industry and how they fit into it. What a concept!

1. Appreciate a boss who lets you run with an idea that ignites your passion.

2. Be aware that it is easy for a company's R&D activities to become isolated from the customers they are ultimately intended to serve.

3. Understand how your work fits into accomplishing the financial goals of the entire organization.

Am I a Failure?

Always enjoying an opportunity to deliver a message of encouragement and inspiration, I was pleased to receive an email request to be a guest speaker at a "Women in Engineering" luncheon. Calling to accept the invitation, I asked what the specific presentation topic was.

The coordinator's response was, "We'd like you to speak with the women about keeping a positive attitude when you're not getting promoted as fast as you think you should be. There is a growing sense of career frustration among our bright young female engineers, exacerbated by our organizational downsizing. The Board of 'Women in Engineering' believes you are a great role model—someone who has kept a positive attitude, despite not being promoted for more than a decade."

I took a deep breath and tried not to show how taken aback I was by this statement of painful reality, packaged in a sincerely spoken compliment. "Sure," I stammered. "I'll be happy to address that topic. Since this is over lunch, do you want the presentation to include PowerPoint slides and last around twenty minutes?" She agreed, and we said our goodbyes. I put down the receiver, and then just stared at the phone.

My mind was suddenly deluged with questions: Have I really reached a plateau in my career? Is it possible that I will never get another promotion? What if I don't achieve my goal of becoming a corporate executive?

An image from elementary school came to mind as I recalled the face of a slacker classmate of mine who had to repeat the fourth grade. Suddenly feeling like I was in the same category as that kid who did not get promoted to fifth grade, I shuddered at the thought.

My company, like most large corporations, had job levels arranged in a pyramid. The executives (directors, executive directors, vice-presidents, CEO, etc.) were the top point of the pyramid, usually comprising the highest paid 2-4 percent of the employees. I was at the top of the second portion of the pyramid—a high-level manager— ready, willing, and able, but not yet invited, to cross over to the executive ranks.

While preparing my presentation, I pondered my career to date and plotted out the job level of every assignment over time: The first ten years of assignments had a rising slope with four steadily increasing data points. Each level increase brought with it a double-digit percentage raise and more responsibility. The next thirteen years of job assignments were represented by seven data points in a horizontal line—at the pinnacle of middle management and the non-executive ranks. The manager level assignments had all been diverse and challenging. However, except for the small promotion I received when leaving my Ohio plant job to move back to Michigan, the assignments had all been lateral moves. That last in-level promotion had occurred when we moved to the house on the lake and our children had left home for college. With no kids at home and more focus on work, I had expected the career phase in Michigan to be the time for moving in the fast lane and for *more* advancement, not less. Ironically, that didn't happen. The graph clearly showed a picture of a career that had completely decelerated.

Totally depressed by this glaring visualization of my career plateau, I decided that the job assignments listed below the line only told half of my story. I needed to add above the line all the concurrent non-job milestones that had happened in my life—houses, kids' achiev advanced degrees, world travels with my husbana, pro-fessional certifications, charity board leadership posi-tions, etc. Slowly a totally different image emerged. In-stead of my career dominating the picture, it became on-ly a part—albeit a very notable part—of my life.

During the presentation, I advised the audience to "listen to the still, small voice in matters of both your career and your life." Also emphasized was the im-portance of balance, always doing your best, controlling the things you can, and not worrying about the things you can't. It was relevant to show the Women in Engi-neering group my personal mission statement (The 6 L's: Live, Love, Laugh, Learn, Lead, and Leave a Lega-cy), and the graph of my career overlaid with other life accomplishments. I also made the following adaption of a poem called *That Man is a Success*, written by Ralph Waldo Emerson:

THAT WOMAN IS A SUCCESS...

Who has lived well, laughed often and loved
   much;
Who has gained the respect of intelligent
   people and the love of children;
Who has filled her niche and accomplished
   her task;
Who leaves the world better than she found
   it, whether by an improved poppy, a per-fect poem, or a rescued soul;
Who never lacked an appreciation of earth's
   beauty or failed to express it;
Who looked for the best in others, and gave
   the best she had.

My final comment was this: "No matter what happens in your life or your career, choose to be happy, and be grateful for everything. Believe that the lessons you learn, no matter how painful, will serve you well in the future."

The audience applauded. Some even came up to tell me they were inspired. Little did they know the pep talk I had given to them, was one *I* needed to hear.

A few months later, when it was announced that a 40-something manager was being promoted to director, I found myself again thinking about the long-buried question:

Am I a failure?

To answer that question, I would have to determine once and for all what it meant to be a failure. Did it mean being less than what one was capable of being? If so, then I certainly was that. I had the education and experience and work ethic and drive to be a corporate executive. I was now over 50 and it still had not happened. Younger men and women had been slowly showing up on the company's organization chart as directors. Was it possible that the window of opportunity for me to be promoted and achieve my goal had closed without my even realizing it? If it wasn't meant to be, why was the desire to be an executive still so strong in my heart?

I suddenly envisioned what Moses must have felt like—spending 40 years wandering in the desert (detailed in Exodus 12-40, Leviticus, Numbers, and Deuteronomy). His journey to the Promised Land should have taken eleven days. (Talk about a lot of lateral moves!) Then I imagined Moses as an old man standing on Mount Nebo, in what is now modern day Jordan, looking westward out at the Jordan River and the land beyond, clearly seeing the Promised Land, but not being able to enter it. Was Moses a failure? Perhaps. Under somewhat different circumstances, he certainly could have achieved his goal.

However, maybe Moses didn't fail. Maybe Moses achieved exactly what God had wanted him to accomplish. By putting the dream of reaching the Promised Land in his heart, God guided Moses and the people he led, on a path of adventure and necessary learning and faith that was essential to their growth. Like me, Moses may not have *achieved* the goal God placed in his heart; however, by *pursuing* that goal, he accomplished God's *real purpose* for his life.

You can't be more successful than that.

1. Don't equate the lack of a promotion with failure.

2. Realize the saying, "Life is a journey, not a destination," can mean that what you experience while pursuing a goal is sometimes more important than actually achieving it.

3. Define success as accomplishing God's real purpose for your life.

Who's Your Sponsor?

The most significant mistake I made during my career was underestimating the importance of having a sponsor. Looking back, it's clear that the years when my career was accelerating in the fast lane were the same years when someone two levels above me was interested in my professional development. Those individuals didn't interact with me much, yet they invisibly orchestrated opportunities for me to grow and demonstrate my abilities. I didn't realize that my own hard work and talent were necessary—but certainly not sufficient—for advancement. I subconsciously and incorrectly believed the corporation was like school—do excellent work and you automatically get promoted.

Choosing career moves, especially lateral ones into different parts of the organization, I broadened my experience—but sometimes inadvertently distanced myself from an upper level of support that I was unaware of at the time. Although it isn't talked about, people who advance high in an organization generally have one or more sponsors. To think you can achieve success without someone pulling for you in a Human Resources promotions meeting is naïve and unrealistic.

Becoming disconnected from an upper level of support sometimes happens during reassignments, reorganizations, retirements, or when executives fall from power and influence. Those who lose their behind-the-scenes, high-level sponsor, end up moving from the fast lane to the middle lane—or sometimes even to the slow lane—often without realizing it for a year or two.

A sponsor is the high-level person who is like an agent working on your behalf to make sure your name is on all of the important lists: the "high pot" or high potential list; the short list of people for specific promotional opportunities; the list of candidates for overseas developmental assignments; the list of presenters for high exposure meetings; and, the list of those getting the largest annual merit raises and bonuses.

Sometimes where you went to college makes a difference in whether or not you have a sponsor. Many of our company's top executives attended one specific fine—but relatively obscure—university. Graduates from that particular university were found at every executive level. Many talented individuals who graduated from that school seemed to have a built-in sponsor network making it easier to get executive promotions.

When you have a sponsor, you are free to focus all of your energy on doing excellent work. You find yourself speeding along in the fast lane with all sorts of good things happening like magic behind the scenes. When you don't have a sponsor, you still do the same excellent work, and you derive great satisfaction from the work itself—but you may not be able to move out of the middle lane, and the promotions do not come.

It is hard to say what moves an individual to go to bat for another person. Sometimes the sponsor glimpses a spark of potential—or sees something that provokes personal memories—and feels moved to help. The Biblical quote, "Many are called but few are chosen" (Matthew 22:14), aptly explains how even the most caring of executives chooses to sponsor only a select few in the organization at any one time.

Looking back at the second half of my career, I don't know what I could have done to encourage someone to sponsor me without becoming manipulative. In general, you do not choose the sponsor; the sponsor chooses you.

I do know, however, that while moving around, I could have done more to keep in touch with the people who did sponsor me early in my career. I could have sent each one an annual Christmas card and maybe invited them individually to lunch every year or two, even if we worked in different cities. By keeping in touch, my former sponsor might even have felt moved to speak with someone in my current chain of command about my career development.

Unfortunately, I mistakenly thought my success was due primarily to my own fine work; and, I did not thank God enough for putting sponsors in my life to help me.

Working in the auto industry today, there are some people who were promoted because of *my* sponsorship. Some of them may naïvely believe their promotions happened solely because of their own excellent work.

As a sponsor I did what I believed to be right for the company. I am proud of the people I helped to get promoted—whether they were aware of my help or not.

1. Know that great work is necessary—but not sufficient—for promotion. You need a sponsor.

2. Be aware of who is working on your behalf when a promotion comes your way—and say thank you.

3. Continue to nurture relationships with your sponsors, even after career circumstances change and they no longer appear to have an influence on your future.

One Door Opens

My assignments in Global Technology Management kept evolving while I worked for Darcy. I was still facilitating Future Product and Technology meetings for the Executive Directors of R&D and Engineering, who started to envision the portfolio of global advanced technical work to be more than a collection of technologies. An idea began take shape—establish focus areas and assign director level executives, called Strategic Leads, to oversee the development of global advanced technical work strategies for each focus area.

I felt passionate about my new assignment—develop a process and coach the eight newly named Strategic Lead executives to do the following:

- Formulate the global advanced technical work strategy for their focus areas.
- Align the technologies currently under development that supported the strategies.
- Identify where additional development projects were needed.

The strategic plans included driving the implementation of key technologies in targeted vehicle programs. As each strategy document was completed, it was reviewed with upper management and revised as necessary. The entire process took nearly a year to complete; the result was a solid integrated global technology roadmap. The executive directors were pleased with the results. I was relieved when the grueling assignment was finally finished and the high-security, individually watermarked hard copies of the strategies were ready to be personally delivered to the company's top executives.

~~~~~

In mid-December 2006, Ben, the Executive Director of R&D who was my boss's boss, asked to meet with me immediately. Once I was seated in his office, Ben said my boss Darcy had given him notice that she was leaving the company. She would not be returning after the Christmas break. He had tried for a week to dissuade her, but Darcy was firm in her decision. He asked me if I would temporarily take over her executive departmental responsibilities and be the acting Director of Global Technology Management—until another executive was named as her replacement, in two to six months.

My immediate feelings were mixed. I was surprised to hear Darcy was leaving; I was also grateful for and excited about being offered the opportunity to realize my dream of having executive responsibilities, even though it was only temporary.

Ben reminded me that the latest restructuring and downsizing in the Engineering organization had resulted in an excess of technical directors, one of whom would be laterally transferred to R&D. He looked me straight in the eye and stressed that there was absolutely no chance I would get promoted or hold Darcy's job on a permanent basis. He already had several executive candidates in mind. Ben also emphasized that my department's work would have to be done with no additional headcount to replace myself as manager temporarily or to replace another manager who was retiring at the end of the month.

Two issues came to mind and I felt it best to put them on the table right away. "Ben, you should know I have outpatient LASIK eye surgery scheduled the first Friday of January that may keep me out of the office for a day or two. I also have a vacation to South America and Antarctica planned for several weeks in March. Will either of those be a problem with this new assignment?"

Ben replied, "No problem."

I took the job.

~ ~ ~ ~ ~

Walking back down the hall, I passed Darcy's office. She motioned for me to come in and speak with her. With a sparkling smile she said, "Well, I can see from your face that Ben has told you the big news. Congratulations on your new assignment! I always tried without success to get you promoted. Maybe now you will at least have the chance to experience what it's like to be an executive, even if it is for just a few months. And who knows what may happen in the future?"

I was full of questions about why Darcy was leaving. She explained that after more than twenty years with the company, she felt moved to make a career change while she was still in her forties—take a risk, do consulting or something different outside of the automotive industry, and relocate to a southern city where she could live closer to her aging parents.

Darcy went on to say she was in the process of downloading to a flash drive all of the files needed in my new assignment. I was already familiar with many—but not all—of her departmental responsibilities, since I was the person who had gotten Darcy up to speed when she came on board as our director several years before.

~ ~ ~ ~ ~

Sitting in her office, I suddenly remembered one business trip Darcy and I had taken together. The purpose of the trip was to coordinate the Global Technology Management activities of the company's advanced technical operations in Australia, China, and Korea. Darcy was a very sharp dresser with a large wardrobe and I had seen her take large checked bags, plus carry-on luggage, on a recent group business trip to California. When I found out that she and I would be traveling together to

Australia and Asia, I tried tactfully to encourage her to take only carry-on luggage—one briefcase for work materials and one carry-on roller suitcase for clothes. I explained that this would eliminate the chance of lost luggage on our many flights, dispense with the long waits at baggage claim, and make it easier to change flights if ours was cancelled at the last minute. I even gave her my own packing checklist. She strongly disagreed with my suggestion.

Just imagine my surprise when she arrived at the airport with only one briefcase for work materials and one carry-on roller suitcase for clothes!

Our two-week business trip to Australia, China, and Korea went very smoothly and Darcy was well received by our global counterparts.

~~~~~

Now Darcy was leaving the company. As we continued to talk in her office, she warned that my biggest challenge would be working directly with Ben and his staff. The R&D directors received high-level assignments that involved strategy, finances, politics, and human resources.

The following day, I asked Ben if there would be a farewell party for Darcy. He quickly said that when executives leave the company before retirement, there is generally not any fanfare. I firmly believed no one who worked twenty years for the company should leave without some kind of recognition for their years of service. I decided to host an impromptu combination Christmas party/farewell party at my house for the Global Technology Management department, the Strategic Leads, and anyone else who wanted to say goodbye to Darcy.

The people who came to the farewell party told funny stories about their experiences with Darcy. Ben did not attend, but called my house at a prearranged time during the party to say a few words about Darcy over the speakerphone to the people present.

The party ended on a happy note. Darcy left energized, appreciated, full of faith, and ready to start the next chapter of her life. The exact details of her future were uncertain. She expected a challenging period of transition, since she did not have a specific new job defined yet.

The only words of wisdom I could think to give her were these: "Remember: when one door closes, another one opens...but the hallway is always a bear!"

1. Try to take only carry-on luggage when traveling.

2. Be ready and willing to fill in temporarily for your boss. It can provide developmental experience, widen your exposure, and increase your chances for more opportunities in the future.

3. Show appreciation and recognition to people who leave an organization after years of service.

4. Have the courage and faith to leave your company when the still, small voice within guides you to do so. Be prepared to weather some transitional storms.

The Temporary Executive

The beginning of the year arrived, and it was time for my first department meeting as the acting Director of Global Technology Management. After reviewing the goals of the organization, I asked everyone to think about any changes that needed to be made. We had two to six months before the department would get a new director. During that time, I wanted to know what I could do to help each person accomplish an individual developmental priority. We also had to figure out how to get the department's important work done with less headcount. The former we discussed in individual one-on-one sessions. The latter we accomplished with an all-day assignment consolidation workshop.

My plan for the workshop was simple: before the meeting, each person listed his/her responsibilities and rank-ordered them by their importance to the organization. I did the same for my own manager responsibilities and those of the manager who had just retired. Everyone—managers and non-managers alike—then had a chance to discuss which of the available high priority assignments he/she was interested in and which of his/her own current responsibilities could be dropped or changed in scope without adversely affecting the organization. If someone was interested in a stretch assignment outside of his/her usual type of work tasks, I was open to considering it. I wanted this departmental transition to be viewed as an opportunity for professional growth, exposure, and new skill development.

The results exceeded my expectations. Everyone chose to take on additional unfamiliar work. Each person struggled initially and then felt the satisfaction that comes from learning and accomplishing more than he or she ever thought possible. There was a positive rhythm, a synergy that was amazing to behold. Emphasizing the department's goal, spending some time coaching and encouraging, and then stepping out of everyone's way was the leadership formula that worked best for these dedicated, self-motivated individuals. In our time of crisis, a good team became a great team. I was very proud of every one of them.

In the meantime, I had my own challenges dealing with my new boss and his staff. Realizing now how much Darcy had shielded our group from the Executive Director, I found myself doing the same thing, not wanting my department to be distracted from the work they were doing.

I quickly learned that Ben was a speed-reader and an impatient listener. He disliked voice mail and communicated best via email. Being the exact opposite, I had to adjust my communication style when dealing with him. If I tried to speak with him about something, he cut me off before I reached the main point, jumping incorrectly to where he thought I was going. I disliked leaving an email about some things, but often it was the only viable course of action. At least he would speed-read my written thoughts to the end, as long as they were arranged in bullets.

There were some minor victories I won along the way. One battle I did not win was convincing Ben to hire a man who had been working for years in our group as a professional contract engineer hired through an agency. This contract engineer did an outstanding job with every assignment he was given, and was long overdue for a permanent placement in our department. However, just as there were no executive promotions being made in Ben's organization, there were also no contract conversions being made, no matter how deserving the individual might be. In fact, I was told the few remaining contract employees in the entire company were likely to be gone within a few months. Even as an acting Director, I did not have the power to change this. Life is not always fair—especially corporate life.

Ben was intelligent and clever and politically astute. I learned a lot working for him. He was always figuring out a way to get what he wanted from his peers and superiors. After working together for a while, he said he had never met anyone like me. I was someone who genuinely had as a top priority the good of the whole organization and fought persistently for the welfare of my subordinates, peers, and boss. My own career advancement was a number three priority instead of number one. This, he thought, combined with an insufficient amount of political savvy and killer instinct, explained why I had not climbed higher up the corporate ladder.

Ben didn't see the bigger picture. Deep inside, I knew the real reason: though I had all of the necessary qualifications and experience, my becoming an auto executive for more than a few months was not part of God's plan for my life.

When Ben told me Stella was the Engineering Director who would be moved laterally to take over as Global Technology Management Director, I assured him I would bring her up to speed. The transition timing was good because I could brief her well, and move out of her new office before going on our scheduled overseas cruise vacation. I was proud of my team and knew they would adjust to the new boss. Stella would decide by the time I came back what responsibilities she wanted me to assume.

~~~~~

While on our cruise, I had time to think about my life and my job and what challenges I wanted next. I liked experiencing corporate executive life as the acting Director of Global Technology Management, and experienced a sense of satisfaction from doing the job well. I thanked God for giving me the opportunity to accomplish the longing in my heart to work as an auto executive even though it was just for a few months.

Thinking about it, aside from better compensation, being a corporate executive was not too different from parenting, teaching, managing more than 350 people in a manufacturing plant, being president of the Board of Directors for a charity, and every other leadership position I held over the years. The common elements were straightforward, but the execution was never easy. Parenting, teaching, and being a boss at any organizational level all amounted to creating a clear vision for people to work towards; helping them to discover and develop their talents and reach their full potential for themselves and the organization; and encouraging them to have fun learning and working with others to achieve the organizational vision.

Soon I would have 30 years of company service and be eligible to retire. I had never planned to retire at the young age of 57. Yet the same small voice that called to me to apply for part-time work at the corporation decades earlier, seemed to be saying it was time to leave the company.

I came back from vacation energized and ready to work. Stella had made a few changes in my absence and was ready to give me some of my former manager responsibilities, plus some new work. I was upbeat and positive and supportive of Stella and her leadership role. She had strength and ambition and was Ben's choice to be a permanent member of his staff.

Deep inside there were things I now missed. It was a little disappointing to no longer be in the executive office with the administrative assistant nearby in her outer office. It had been nice to have an executive parking spot for a few months. What I missed most of all was the new level of empowerment and possibility and fun. During this transition, I exercised basically my same style of leadership. The difference was that this time I was promoted within the same group in the company, instead of being moved to lead a new group. It was the first time I could closely observe the same people's behavior before, during, and after my period of leadership. I had always wanted to be a company executive—and for a few months I had achieved my goal.

Returning to my manager's job now simply felt like, "Been there, done that." I was ready for something new.

Pearls from Pat

1. Realize that successful executive leaders have many elements in common with successful teachers, parents, and other types of organizational leaders.

2. Plan vacations far away from the office to think about your life, your job and what challenges you want to tackle next.

3. Take care of the people who work for you and they will take care of you.

Deciding to Retire

Memories came to mind about an older acquaintance, who several years before had been a financial manager at another "Big Three" automotive company. Year after year, Celia was passed over for promotion. Then one day her company was forced to offer retirement packages across the board to every salaried employee over a certain age. Celia's boss and boss's boss came to her and told her not to accept the retirement package they were forced to offer her—they needed her to stay. When Celia said she planned to take the retirement package, they offered to promote her to director. When she still said no, they offered her a two-step promotion to a higher-level director position. Again she said no. She had experienced enough stress and was tired of being passed over for promotion by people less competent than she. Their offer was too little, too late.

Celia retired as a manager—and was glad she did.

~~~~~

My situation was somewhat different from Celia's. I was not being offered a special incentivized retirement package, and I still wanted a permanent promotion. However, deep in my spirit, there was a voice saying it was time for me to retire soon. Not knowing what to do and wanting to be sure, I prayed, "Lord, if you want me to keep working here, give me a sign by providing me with a promotion, even in another department. If you want me to retire, then let there be no promotion."

Working harder than ever, I introduced Stella to key people from all over the world, so she could build the alliances necessary for our department and our company to keep moving forward.

Deep inside I kept hoping that either a miraculous promotion would come or the desire to retire would leave my heart. Neither happened. Instead, Jon, who would soon turn 63 with nearly 40 years of company service, also began to talk about retiring. He even suggested maybe we could retire on the same day. After all, we had spent decades working well as a team handling our home and individual work responsibilities. It seemed that one of us retiring while the other kept working would somehow upset the work and home life balance we had successfully maintained for decades.

Jon expressed our options very well: "Pat, if you retire and I keep working, you'll start spending more time golfing and maybe start beating me at the game. If I retire and you keep working, you'll expect me to have dinner on the table when you get home from work. I don't like either of those scenarios."

Unlike many people in the auto industry, Jon and I both worked in departments that had not offered any special early retirement packages to their employees in many years. We each applied for standard retirement proposals, reviewed the numbers, and carefully studied our finances. I started to imagine life without two hours or more each day in the car commuting to the office, without 6 a.m. teleconference meetings with Germany, and without 10 p.m. phone calls to Australia. We discussed all the things we wanted to do outside of the auto industry while we were still young and healthy. We looked at best-case and worst-case financial scenarios thirty years out into the future. Then we prayed for divine guidance. The answer came deep inside of us with a profound feeling of peace.

We decided to both retire on August 1, 2007.

~~~~~

Since Jon and I were retiring on the same day, my colleagues suggested that it might be fun to have a joint retirement party, even though our workplaces were eighteen miles apart. Elaine, who was one of the managers in my department, organized the party with the help of the administrative assistants from my department and Jon's department. She even recruited her husband to make a video recording of the evening.

We were deeply touched by the people who came, including one of my former colleagues who surprised me by traveling 200 miles to attend the party. We appreciated the funny stories that were told, the gifts that were presented, and the kind words that were spoken by co-workers and bosses.

After summarizing Jon's 40-year career, his colleagues and bosses praised him for his extraordinary achievements in reducing the company's energy costs and adding to corporate profit through his innovative natural gas brokering programs.

My new boss, Stella, summarized my 30-year career and my significant contributions to the Global Technology Management Department. She then said the following:

> *The team recognizes Pat as the go-to person. She has really been the cornerstone of the department and people rely on her and call her from all over the place. She is a very special person not only to me, but also to our team. Pat is extremely knowledgeable, very passionate, very committed to everything that she does and she will be missed very much.*

Later in the program, Stella came up to the microphone and read a letter from Ben, the Executive Director who was my boss while I was the acting Director of Global Technology Management. Ben wrote:

> *Pat ... You are one of the few players who have contributed from the start on the global convergence of our advanced technical work activities. You have had a major role in the transformation from isolated, regional activities within silos to a single, coordinated, global enterprise operating to strategic objectives. I especially appreciate the extra effort you put in to get us through our Tech Management leadership transition. Your passion for making our corporation a better company is contagious. I will miss your smile, which I could always count on, even during times of stress...*

Our children, Joe and Jean, also attended the retirement party. They were given podium time to speak of the adventures they experienced having two parents who worked for the company for as long as they could remember. Joe told some funny stories about our dual-career household illustrating some of our core family values, including: having a relationship with God, the importance of family, the value of hard work and the wisdom of good money management. Now that he was the father of four, Joe appreciated these lessons even more. He ended by saying that while he knew his parents were looking forward to retiring from their company jobs, he personally was "very glad Mom and Dad can never retire from the job of being our parents."

Jean then took the microphone and spoke about how she and her brother benefitted from her parents working for the company. Besides the financial benefits, there were the medical and dental benefits, new company cars, and educational support—including Harvard and the family's adventures living in Boston. I was especially touched when Jean said, "My parents were constantly busy working. However, they both always made time to be with us kids, to coach our sports, and to involve us in their do-it-yourself projects."

When it came time for me to speak, I comm. how the words spoken by the presenters and our chil dren deeply moved me. Looking around the room, I thanked the various groups of people from my past who were there—technology managers, strategic leads, engineering directors and managers, "Seven Habits" facilitators, reliability and test managers and engineers, and a former shift superintendent from the Ohio car assembly plant where we had worked together twenty years earlier.

Inwardly I realized that no one in the room except Jon, Joe, and Jean had known me during the early trailblazing years of my career. For this reason, I felt moved to comment on how far the company had come in its treatment of women during the past 30 years.

I contrasted the early days when there were no women's restrooms, to the present day when the number of women in executive positions was steadily increasing. It was noteworthy to witness the company's transition to diversity of gender, race, and ethnicity at nearly every level.

Then I closed with the very last leadership lesson I would share with my colleagues, "The Story of the Cracked Pot." It was an ancient tale found on numerous websites, whose original source is unknown:

> An elderly Chinese woman had two large pots. Each hung on the ends of a pole, which she carried across her back. One of the pots had a crack in it, while the other pot was perfect and always delivered a full portion of water. At the end of the long walk from the stream to the house, the cracked pot arrived only half full.
>
> For a full two years this went on daily, with the woman bringing home only one and a half pots of water. Of course, the perfect pot was proud of its accomplishments, but the poor

cracked pot was ashamed of its own imperfection, and miserable that it was able to accomplish only half of what it had been made to do. After two years of what it perceived to be bitter failure, it spoke to the woman one day by the stream: "I am ashamed of myself because this crack in my side causes water to leak out all the way back to your house."

The old woman said, "Did you notice that there are flowers only on your side of your path, but not on the other pot's side? That's because I have always known about your flaw and I took advantage of it. I planted flower seeds on your side of the path and every day while we walk back from the stream, you've watered them. For two years I have been able to pick these beautiful flowers to decorate my table. Without you being just the way you are, there would not be this beauty to grace the house."

The moral is that each of us has our own unique flaws. We're all cracked pots. But it's the cracks and flaws we each have that make our lives together so very interesting and rewarding. You've just got to take each person for what they are, and look for the good in them.

Then I continued: "So as we come to the end of this retirement party, I challenge each of you, not just to utilize each other's strengths, but to be as smart as the old Chinese woman and utilize your co-worker's, your boss's, and your spouse's flaws and bring some kind of good from them. Ultimately, that's what great leadership and what great families are really all about."

As the people in the room applauded, Jon joined me, we held hands, and said thank you and goodbye to all our guests. I was so grateful to Elaine and the others who helped her organize our retirement party. Jon and I had worked very hard for the company and we were glad to have such wonderful closure. We knew the company would go on just fine without us. And we would go on just fine without the company. The sense of two-way appreciation was very gratifying.

I glanced down at the message stenciled on the golf ball table favors, "The best is yet to come." The still, small voice within me let me know I would receive another purposeful assignment soon. I imperceptibly nodded my head in agreement.

As always—I'll take the job.

Pearls from Pat

1. Follow the still, small voice when you face a retirement decision: if you don't feel moved to retire, don't. If you are financially comfortable, have a post-retirement activity plan, and feel very strongly moved to retire, then do so.

2. Be genuinely grateful if a colleague plans a retirement party for you, providing wonderful closure to a long career of service.

3. Realize that you never retire from being a parent and from being on call for God's special assignments.

EPILOGUE

Within a few months of retiring in 2007, Jon and I adjusted to living on our company pension checks. We wanted to preserve the retirement savings we had accumulated, and took everything out of our company sponsored retirement accounts. We felt moved to convert everything to IRAs in the form of conservative investments that did not involve the stock market.

Little did we know then that during the next eighteen months, the stock market and the auto industry would be in crisis, company sponsored retirement accounts would be plunging, and automotive companies would be going through massive layoffs and forced retirements. In the fall of 2008, Jon's former department had a single group retirement party for 90 people who were leaving. Throughout the company, morale was low and those still employed were burdened with exhausting workloads. As the organization shrank, a number of directors were demoted to managers.

It took years, but the "Big Three" American auto companies did come back out of the crisis—leaner and poised for success in an even more competitive global marketplace.

I can look back at my career and ask the typical question, "What if?" What if I had encouraged Jon to turn down the Ohio gas field operations manager job, allowing me to stay in Michigan at the Truck Division—would my strong, invisible executive mentor have guided me through a few key manager assignments to an early executive position? What if I had stayed at the Ohio fabrication plant a few years longer—would the young Plant Manager who replaced Chuck after I left have made me the complex's first female executive—instead of the younger, less experienced woman he selected? What if I had stayed longer in engineering and accepted the three-month assignment in Germany—would the Executive Director who recommended me earlier for an executive opportunity have done it again and succeeded in the short time before the massive engineering headcount cuts hit?

Not knowing the answers to these questions, I don't dwell on them. Listening to the still, small voice inside me, I trusted and obeyed the will of God for my life and was exactly where He guided me to be. I have chosen, and continue to choose, to be happy regardless of my circumstances.

I believe His will for me was to spend the second half of my automotive career driving in the middle lane instead of the fast lane of corporate career advancement. After all, when the Creator of the universe chose to spend His life on earth as a simple carpenter, it's hard to complain to Him about not being a top-level executive. Instead, I am grateful for experiencing so many facets of the auto industry in reverse order from the end of the process for making vehicles and components to the beginning—from quality inspection to assembly, to reliability and test, to engineering, to product development, to strategic planning, and finally to research and development.

There are more than 200 "Pearls" that I have compiled—lessons learned about business and life from my years in the auto industry. If I had to distill them down to a few short lines, they would read:

- Handle both the good things and the bad things that happen to you with grace and gratitude.
- Love God, love other people, and love yourself.
- Trust and obey the still, small voice within you.
- Choose to be happy in your work and in your life.

May God bless the auto industry and the many thousands of fine men and women who work there, serving one another, their customers, and the world.

Each person—regardless of department, or level, or job title—has a purpose and makes a real difference. Perhaps that, above all, is the most important lesson learned.

REFERENCES

Author unknown. (2008). *http://preilly.wordpress.com /2008/07/19/gandhi-story/*

Author unknown. (2013). *http://www.forbes.com/sites /ekaterinawalter/2013/09/30/50-heavyweight-leadership-quotes*

Babiak, P. & Hare, R. D. (2006). *Snakes in Suits: When Psychopaths Go to Work.* New York: Harper Collins.

Bass, B. (1990). *Handbook of Leadership: Theory, Research, & Managerial Applications* (Third ed.). New York: The Free Press.

Blanchard, K. & Johnson, S (1983). *The One Minute Manager: The Quickest Way to Increase Your Own Prosperity.* New York: Berkley Books.

Blanchard, K. (2009, August 17). *http://howwelead. org/2009/08/17/feedback-is-the-breakfast-of-champions/*

Carroll, M. A. (1972, February). "Women in Administration in Higher Education." *Contemporary Education.* XLIII.

Covey, S. R. (1989). *The Seven Habits of Highly Effective People.* New York: Simon & Schuster.

Covey, S. R. (1999). *The Four Roles of Leadership Facilitator Manual.* Provo, UT: FranklinCovey.

Deming, W. E. (1986). *Out of the Crisis.* Cambridge, MA: M.I.T. Center for Advanced Engineering Study.

Drucker, P. F., et al. (2008). *The Five Most Important Questions You Will Ever Ask Your Organization.* San Francisco: Josey-Bass.

Follett, M. P. (1933/1995). "The Essentials of Leadership." In P. Graham (Ed.), *Mary Parker Follett—Prophet of Management: A Celebration of Writings from the 1920s* (pp. 163-177). Boston: Harvard Business School Press.

Frankl, V. E. (1984). *Man's Search for Meaning.* New York: Washington Square Press.

Harari, O. (2002). *The Leadership Secrets of Colin Powell.* New York: McGraw-Hill.

International Bible Society (1988). *The Holy Bible, New International Version.* Grand Rapids, MI: Zondervan.

Johnson, D. (1971). "What Is the Future of Women in School Administration?" *Women: A Significant National Resource.* Washington, D.C.: National Council of Administrative Women in Education.

Juran, J. M. (1951). *Quality Control Handbook* (Third ed.). New York: McGraw-Hill.

Kübler-Ross, E. & Kessler, D. (2005). *On Grief and Grieving: Finding the Meaning of Grief Through the Five Stages of Loss.* New York: Simon and Schuster.

Lucado, M. (1997). *You Are Special.* Wheaton, IL: Crossway Books.

Luke, J. (1998). *Catalytic Leadership: Strategies for an Interconnected World.* San Francisco: Jossey-Bass.

Lutekehaus, N. C. (2008) *Margaret Mead: The Making of an American Icon.* Princeton, New Jersey: Princeton University Press.

Marquet, L. D. (2012). *Turn the Ship Around.* Austin, TX: Greenleaf Book Group Press.

Maslow, A. H. (1962). *Toward a Psychology of Being* (2nd ed.) New York: Van Nostrand.

Maxwell, J. C. (1998). *The 21 Irrefutable Laws of Leadership: Follow Them and People Will Follow You.* Nashville: Thomas Nelson, Inc.

Mother Teresa. (2002). *No Greater Love.* Novato, CA: New World Library.

Noonan, P. (2005). *John Paul the Great: Remembering a Spiritual Father.* New York: Viking.

O'Toole, J. (1995). *Leading Change: The Argument for Values-based Leadership.* New York: Ballantine Books.

Schoonover, Jean Way. (1974, February 28). "Why Corporate America Fears Women." *Vital Speeches of the Day.*

Smalley, G. & E. (2008). *http://www.smalleymarriage .com/resources/qa.php?catID=28&resID=14.* "Fostering Spiritual Intimacy with My Spouse."

Welch J. & Byrne, J. A. (2003). *Jack: Straight from the Gut.* New York: Warner Books, Inc.

For additional copies of this book, visit:

createspace.com/5382421

For discussion questions and more about the author, visit:

integraresources.org

Made in the USA
Charleston, SC
27 October 2015